Bigger
pockets

30-DAY STAY

30-DAY STAY

A Real Estate Investor's Guide to Mastering the

MEDIUM-TERM RENTAL

BY ZEONA MCINTYRE
AND SARAH WEAVER

BiggerPockets®
PUBLISHING
Denver, Colorado

30-Day Stay: A Real Estate Investor's Guide to Mastering the Medium-Term Rental
Zeona McIntyre and Sarah Weaver

Published by BiggerPockets Publishing LLC, Denver, CO
Copyright © 2022 by Zeona McIntyre and Sarah Weaver
All rights reserved.

Publisher's Cataloging-in-Publication Data
Names: McIntyre, Zeona, author. | Weaver, Sarah, author.
Title: 30-day stay : a real estate investor's guide to mastering the medium-term rental / Zeona
McIntyre and Sarah Weaver.
Description: Denver, CO : BiggerPockets Publishing LLC; 2022.
Identifiers: LCCN: 2022940033 | ISBN: 9781947200821 (paperback) | 9781947200838 (ebook)
Subjects: LCSH Real estate investment--United States. | Rental housing--United States--
Management. | Real estate management--United States. | BISAC BUSINESS & ECONOMICS / Real
Estate / General | BUSINESS & ECONOMICS / Investments & Securities / Real Estate | BUSINESS &
ECONOMICS / Personal Finance / Investing | BUSINESS & ECONOMICS / Real Estate / Buying &
Selling Homes
Classification: LCC HD1394.5.U6 .M35 2022 | DDC 643/.2--dc23

Published in the United States of America
Printed in Canada on recycled paper
MBP 10 9 8 7 6 5 4 3 2 1

Dedication

By Zeona to Zaira Blasini. Look, Mom, we did it!

By Sarah to every investor who dreams of having a bigger life along with a bigger portfolio.

Our success would not be possible without those who supported us along the way. This book is for those who invest in hopes of increasing cash flow. Our hope is that you not only do that but also book the flight, take the trip, and live a bigger life because of it all.

TABLE OF CONTENTS

PART 1
Understanding the MTR Strategy

PART 2
Acquisition

FOREWORD

Twenty years ago, my husband was diagnosed with melanoma. After a host of tests, the doctor found that things were worse than we thought. Rich had four growths on his liver; the doctor told Rich that because the deadly skin cancer had spread to his organs, he probably had about six months to live.

We were shocked. My husband was a big, strong athlete who skied cliffs, surfed hurricane waves, and even bungee jumped in the first-ever X Games.

I refused to believe the doctor and instead put all my energy into learning how to take over the finances so that Rich could take some time off to get better. I had been in the news business before, but I became a stay-at-home mom when we had kids. After years of not being in the workforce, I had no idea how to get back in. I also didn't want to leave my kids all day, or my husband…if the doctor was right.

I knew I needed to find a way to make money and still be home with my family. While I'd heard of this thing called "passive income," I didn't know anyone who had achieved it.

To keep me somewhat connected to the news industry—and for fun—I was hosting a weekend radio show in San Francisco. I decided to use that platform to learn how certain people were able to create passive income.

I also needed money immediately, because medical bills can eat up saving accounts very quickly, so I started looking for a big sponsor for my radio show to bring in some instant cash.

It was the mid 2000s, when radio waves were filled with mortgage brokers promoting their low rates. I pulled out my phone book, flipped to a list of mortgage brokers, and proceeded to call every one of them. I was subsequently rejected by every one of them.

Feeling defeated but not deflated, I wondered how I could make an offer no one could refuse. I picked up the phone and tried again. This time, I said, "Hi,

I'm looking for a mortgage broker to be my cohost. Are you interested?"

The answer was an enthusiastic "Yes!" The broker agreed to my price without hesitation. And while this sponsorship would bring in much-needed cash flow, I was suddenly the cohost of a mortgage show.

When I told Rich what I'd done, his first reaction was to laugh.

"YOU are going to have a mortgage show?" he said.

Rich knew I had very little interest in finance, though I was newly eager to learn. So he suggested, "Instead of talking about rates like everyone else, why don't you interview his clients and see what they're doing with all those mortgages?"

I loved the idea and shared it with my new cohost. He agreed and was quickly able to line up a bunch of clients. As the interviews began, I couldn't believe the stories of how his clients were building tremendous wealth and creating passive income through real estate.

There were people borrowing funds to buy old properties, fix them up, and resell them for huge profits. Some were buying fixer-uppers, living in them while making improvements, and then selling after two years, which allowed them to keep up to $500,000 in tax-free gains. Young people were buying fourplexes with just 3 percent down, living in one unit, and renting the rest out to live for free.

There were so many ways to make money that I'd never heard of. There was something for everyone! You just had to find strategy that worked for you and your lifestyle.

For me, that strategy was buy-and-hold rentals. At the time, you could get an unlimited number of no-money-down investor loans. If you could find a property where the rent was higher than your expense, the remaining cash flow could go in your pocket.

This is exactly the thing I was looking for: cash flow.

I couldn't believe you could borrow the money to buy an asset while keeping all the upside. You could have a renter pay off the loan for you, all the while getting income and letting the government give you tax breaks for doing it. Once I learned that creating passive income was a possibility, I dove in to learn absolutely everything I could about the topic.

The more I discovered and gave away the secrets of investing for passive income, the bigger my radio audience grew. I was clearly not the only person who wanted to hear this information. The problem is my show was in San Francisco, and there's only one kind of cash flow there—the negative kind!

In 2005, I had the opportunity to interview Robert Kiyosaki, the author of *Rich Dad Poor Dad*. He explained that all those stated-income, no-money-down loans would not end well. I knew this personally because by then, I had joined my cohost in becoming a mortgage broker.

I saw what was happening. Lending standards had become so lax that people could fill out mortgage applications with absolutely no verification required. Even people with low credit scores could get stated-income loans—they just had to pay a higher interest rate.

Kiyosaki said he was selling all his properties that had shot up in value in the "sand states" (California, Nevada, Arizona, and Florida) and was going to 1031 exchange them for high–cash flow properties in Dallas, Texas. Dallas property values were 26 percent undervalued at the time, yet it had the strongest job and population growth in the country. It just made sense.

Rich and I jumped on a plane to Dallas and ended up buying nine properties near Plano, a fast-growing area. When I came home and talked about it on the *Real Wealth Show*, our phones started ringing off the hook with people wanting to do the same.

One lady heard me on the radio and called in. She said she loved the concept but hated being a landlord. She owned and self-managed three old homes in a high-crime area of Stockton, California. The homes were old and always in need of repair. Sometimes the tenants wouldn't pay at all, leaving her with the bill.

It turned out she could sell those three properties for $420,000 each. She was able to do a 1031 exchange, and I helped her buy nine new homes in the Dallas area that rented for $1,200 each. That was more than she had been getting on her three Stockton properties. Practically overnight, she went from nearly zero cash flow to $6,000 per month in net passive income. This was enough to supplement her retirement. She quit her job the next month!

Building a portfolio of cash flow properties is not just a game-changer, *it's a life changer.*

As my show grew, I started to get asked to speak at various real estate investment groups around the Bay Area. I remember going to these events and being surprised to continually see only a couple of women in the audience. I often wondered why more women weren't interested in the topic.

I'm so glad to see that has changed today.

Twenty years later, in 2022, I was speaking at the Best Ever Conference in Denver. I sat in awe of all the young, brilliant investors in the room. They are doing things today that we didn't even know about two decades ago when I started.

One of those women was Sarah Weaver. I sat with her at lunch and got to hear how she was living on the road and traveling to the most exotic places. I was intrigued. How was she funding it?

"Do you work in tech?" I asked.

"No, I own MTRs," she replied.

I didn't want to sound stupid, but I asked anyway. "What's that?"

She laughed and said, "Medium-term rentals."

Sarah went on to explain that it was like a short-term rental in that people would pay more to rent a furnished unit. But an MTR is taxed more advantageously, like a long-term rental.

I had to hear more.

She explained that today, there are more "digital nomads" who can work from anywhere and like to stay in one-to-three-month rentals. Traveling nurses are also in need of month-to-month furnished rentals, as are many others we don't think about—professionals needing housing during short-term projects, homeowners or renters displaced from renovations, and the list continues.

Medium-term rentals are self-manageable, offer flexibility in location, and can produce higher cash flow. Plus, you can buy properties that may not appeal to the average homebuyer, such as one-bed, one-bath homes. I was particularly interested in the point that since many cities are trying to reduce or eliminate short-term rentals, medium-term properties are acceptable in those metros, as they are regulated more closely to long-term leases.

Sarah told me medium-term rentals have allowed her and others like her to travel the world and live in exotic places while self-managing her properties from afar.

I told her, "You really need to write a book on this so that others can learn how to dramatically increase cash flow to fund their dream lives."

She replied, "I am, with Zeona McIntyre!"

I was in such awe when she told me about Zeona, another young real estate rockstar. She started with short-term rentals back in 2012 when the app was in its infancy, and she reached her financial goal in just two years. A true industrious investor, Zeona smartly pivoted to medium-term rentals during the pandemic and came out ahead.

Zeona created so much personal success that she got her real estate license and has been helping others acquire and manage short- and medium-term rentals. She lives in Boulder, Colorado, half the year and travels the world the other half, having visited forty-seven countries thus far. It was such an amazing thing to hear about these brilliant, impressive women dominating the real estate space. And considering the fact that I'm writing this foreword from deep within the Norwegian fjords, their lifestyle obviously resonates with me!

If you dream of a life with more flexibility that honors your personal values and goals, Sarah and Zeona have paved the way. Their secrets are captured within the pages of this book.

Life shouldn't be spent working to collect more money. Let money work for you so that you can collect more fabulous memories.

Oh, and by the way, the doctor was wrong. Rich is alive and well today. Dreams do indeed come true.

Wishing you the best life you can imagine,

Kathy Fettke
CEO and Cofounder of the Real Wealth Network, author of *Retire Rich with Rentals*, host of *The Real Wealth Show*, and cohost of BiggerPockets' *On the Market* podcast.

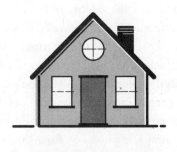

PREFACE

Never get so busy living that you forget to make a life.
—DOLLY PARTON

SARAH

On the first of the month, a few days after my mortgage payments left my bank account, rent checks were deposited into my account—all the while, I was 9,400 miles away.

Riding through the mountains of Northern Vietnam on a motorcycle, I stopped for coffee and checked my emails. Notifications that rent checks had been deposited into my bank account sat there unread, and I couldn't help but think, "I've made it."

A few weeks later, I was snorkeling in Palawan, in the Philippines, when my tenants texted me letting me know the neighbor kid had shoveled the driveway. I came up for air, lay on the beach, and used Venmo, a payment app, to pay the kid for the work. Knowing there was snow shoveled at my rental while I was lying in the sun, I thought, "This is the life."

In these moments, I knew I was onto something. Confident that owning rental properties was my path to financial independence, I committed to growing my portfolio massively over the next five years. I wrote in my journal that I wanted to earn $8,000 in cash flow by 2025. Little did I know that with the medium-term rental strategy I would cut that timeline in half. Later that year, I'd be a guest on a real estate podcast and vocalize that very same goal. That podcast host and I would end up writing this book together.

When Zeona and I met, we became fast friends. We quickly learned that we had a lot in common. First, our shared love of travel was undeniable. She had traveled to forty-seven countries. Having traveled to forty-four countries at the time, I was a few behind. During my time abroad, I had met dozens—if not hundreds—of other backpackers and avid travelers; meeting someone who loved to travel was not particularly noteworthy. But Zeona was different.

Like me, she was using rental income to fund her best life. A mere six months after meeting online, we were sharing Ubers to conferences, swapping travel stories over hot tea, and comparing notes on furnished rentals.

In the short car ride to a financial conference in Austin, Texas, it became clear to us that we needed to bring this book to life. We needed to share the power of the medium-term rental strategy with others. This book is in your hands, on your phone, or in your ears because we believe we found the sweet spot in real estate investing: maximizing cash flow with our rental properties by renting out furnished units to tenants for thirty days or longer. And we want to show you how you can too.

In this book, you will see how furnished rentals built our wealth and granted us the freedom of time to pursue our passions. I will show you how I furnished a rental in Nebraska from New Zealand and how I closed on a property in Missouri from Mexico. The following pages will be a guide on your real estate journey. Whether you own three units, thirty units, or none, this book is tailored for you. We will cover everything from how we find investor-friendly agents to how to manage and even furnish a rental from afar. Above all, we want to share this information in an easy-to-implement way because we believe you, too, can add passive income using the medium-term rental strategy.

ZEONA

Like Sarah, travel is a big part of my life. During college, I spent a semester living on an 800-person cruise ship through a program called Semester at Sea. After that experience, the desire to see the world was an integral part of my being; I had been bitten by the travel bug.

At the time, being location independent or working from anywhere with a Wi-Fi connection felt like a far-off dream. This flexibility felt reserved for programmers or graphic designers—not for someone who struggles with technology, like me. Then, in 2011, my lucky break came through in the form of a very persistent friend. He told me that, after a year of testing out this new Airbnb concept, he had made $50,000 off his New York City apartment—that he didn't even own! That light bulb moment would change the course of my life. This was the pivot point. I began to build a real estate business that would allow me to live anywhere I wanted while collecting rent checks.

For my first two years of hosting furnished rentals, I didn't even own any of the properties. They were one- and two-bedroom apartments that I rented from a landlord, meaning my name was on the long-term lease. With the permission granted from a sublet clause, I would list the individual bedrooms or the entire apartments on Airbnb. The additional income was a gift that allowed me to quit my job, but it wasn't enough to purchase a home yet.

I remember when one day, months after I'd started running a successful Airbnb rental business out of my apartment, it dawned on me: I was already living the dream that had once felt so out of reach. With the power of a smartphone, I could accept reservations from anywhere in the world. I knew I was onto something. And I was right. Three years after first hearing about the power of furnished rentals, I was financially independent.

My dream of being location independent came true because of furnished rentals. While traveling the world may not be your goal like it was for Sarah and me, the freedom to do what you want likely is. That's why this book is here. In this book, we will show you how to identify a market, create crystal clear deal criteria, build a dream team, secure tenants, and build a portfolio using the medium-term rental strategy.

While I was subletting out to Airbnb, my mother was battling cancer. When I stepped into the role of her primary caregiver, I was eager to finally purchase a home for us to live in. Before my mother moved to Colorado, I had been shuffling between two apartments, living out of a suitcase, and staying in whichever place wasn't rented. In 2014, two years after her diagnosis, I went under contract.

My mother never did walk the property or celebrate with me at the closing table. She lost her battle with cancer just twenty-three days before I closed on my first rental property.

This book is dedicated to her.

—Zeona McIntyre and Sarah Weaver

INTRODUCTION

A river cuts through rock, not because of its power,
but because of its persistence.
—JAMES N. WATKINS

SARAH—A Journey of a Thousand Miles

"I want to be location independent," I wrote in my journal.

Eight days later, I accepted a remote position with a recruiting company in the real estate industry, and my dream of being a digital nomad came true. This was in 2015.

It is notable that I didn't write this in my "magic" journal and then take a nap. No. I wrote this down and then started to apply for jobs online (eighty-three positions, to be exact). I applied for so many jobs that I had to use a spreadsheet to track all the positions I had applied for in the span of a week.

To understand how I got here, however, we need to take a step back even further. My first job after graduating from the University of Kansas was with a travel company based in Spain. My job as the head receptionist was to check in more than 1,000 backpackers as they poured into a temporary tent village in Munich for Oktoberfest. More or less, my job was to babysit drunk backpackers, and I had to sleep in a tent when it was thirty degrees outside (Fahrenheit, not Celsius!). I quickly accepted another internship, this time back in the States with a popular publication. That also didn't last, and before long, I was on a plane to South Korea to teach English for a year.

Sounds like a great résumé for a real estate investor, right?

After a year of teaching 14-year-olds reading comprehension, and then sing-ing karaoke in private rooms until the wee hours of the morning, I closed my workbook, set down my bottle of soju, and moved to Austin, Texas. Armed with a journalism degree, the gift of gab, and a few thousand dollars in my pocket, I earned my real estate license, thinking that it was a good idea to sell real estate in a new city where I knew no one.

My weekdays were spent cold-calling for-sale-by-owner and expired listings and knocking on doors in the ninety-degree heat and humidity of Texas in the summer. Every weekend, I held open houses all over town.

My first listing was a rental property in Killeen, Texas. Seventy miles north of Austin, Killeen is home to Fort Hood, the second-largest military base in the U.S. The house was worth less than $25,000 and renting for $500 each month. I knew little to nothing about real estate investing, but because it was currently being rented, I knew that I could sell this house to an investor. I searched online for a nearby real estate meetup. (Keep in mind that I knew fewer than three people in the entire city of Austin, which forced me to be creative.) Armed with what I thought was a good deal, I walked into the sports bar hosting the meetup, stood there, and pitched the deal. Four days later, the house sold with an all-cash offer.

First, I thought, "This is way better than driving buyers around!"

Next, I thought, "I made, like, no money on that deal."

My commission after broker splits was less than $400.

During this time, I met an agent who owned a handful of investment properties. I didn't understand real estate investing strategies back in 2015, but I understood good and well when she told me she was receiving what she called "mailbox money." I know now that she was using the house hacking and live-in flip strategies to build her rental portfolio, both of which we will describe later on in this book.

I was a good agent, and I went on to make more than $400 in commissions. But the traveler inside of me had other plans. I joke that I was a real estate agent for about five minutes, but not because I wasn't good at being an agent. I had several listings within months of being licensed. But I started being honest with myself about my desire to live abroad again. I missed the adventure of living in a country with people from all over the world. I missed the challenge that came along with navigating public transportation when you don't speak the language. I wanted that back, and I quickly realized I couldn't do that as a real estate agent in Austin.

I interviewed for a job at a recruiting company in the real estate industry, and just like that, my dream of being location independent came true.

When I gained the freedom and flexibility of being a digital nomad, I moved from Texas to Colorado. I spent three months in Crested Butte, six months in

Denver, and then three months in South America, in Colombia. I was thrilled to be living my dream of traveling the world and earning a living in a career I loved, but something was missing. Living back in Denver, I wanted to build a rental portfolio like that agent I admired. At the time, I thought home prices were too high in Colorado to make the numbers work.

I started to look into buying a house in Kansas City, where my parents live. The prices there were lower, yet the rents seemed high enough.

At the time, I had no calculator, no deal criteria, and little to no clue what anything meant. I was simply looking at rent minus the monthly mortgage payment, and if there was money left over, I thought, "Cool. That's a deal." Lucky for me, this naivety worked. To be fair, I was a licensed real estate agent, so I did know a thing or two about comparable home prices and how mortgages worked.

I asked an agent in Kansas City to help me find a rental property in the suburbs on the Kansas side. She set up an automatic search, which pushed dozens of properties into my email inbox. I would text her, "What can this rent for?"

"I don't know. Sorry," her texts read.

"How much rehab does that house need?"

"Not sure," she said.

This agent was not going to find me deals, nor was she as investor-savvy as I needed her to be. (In Chapter Nine, we will show you how to find investor-friendly agents.) I realized I needed to take matters into my own hands.

As an agent in Austin, I had spent more than two hundred hours door-knocking. So I drove my Prius from Denver to Kansas City and started knocking on doors. This is what investors call "driving for dollars," although I didn't know the phrase for it then. I drove to what I thought was a "nice" neighborhood where houses were still under $300,000, and I knocked for nearly seven hours.

My day ended with me standing on the lawn of a 1940 Cape Cod–style house in an A-class neighborhood in Prairie Village, ten miles south of Kansas City. In the yard was a red-and-white "For Sale by Owner" sign.

I first knocked on the door.

No answer.

Next, I stood in their driveway and called the number on the sign.

No answer.

I spotted a neighbor across the street, so I approached her to inquire about the house. To my surprise, she was not only helpful but also a neighborhood gossip. She had all the goods; she told me the middle-aged couple across the street was looking to sell because they were sick of the maintenance of the home.

"I'd love to help them with that problem," I thought.

"They want $215,000," the neighbor said.

"Sorry. Two fifty? Or two fifteen?" I asked for clarification.

"$215,000," she repeated.

At the time, comps (comparable properties) in the neighborhood were $245,000–$275,000, depending on upgrades. I was internally jumping for joy.

"Stay cool," I told myself.

Within the hour, I was walking the property with the seller. The neighbor was correct. They no longer wanted to maintain the property, and they didn't want an agent. What they did want was $215,000.

The next afternoon, my dad and I walked the property with the kind couple. My dad worked for a home construction company in Kansas City and taught me everything I know about home building. His job that day was simply to play bad cop and point out everything wrong with the house while I played good cop saying things like, "I can see myself living here." As we toured the house, I had a purchase agreement inside my purse. I had printed it off the internet and filled it out by hand. While I was licensed in Texas, I did not have a real estate license in Kansas.

Sitting at their kitchen table, I walked the couple through each section of the purchase agreement, paragraph by paragraph. They hadn't bought or sold a house in over four decades. To my surprise, they signed it right then and there.

I gave them more than they were asking for. I offered them $217,000 but asked that they pay my closing costs. This was at a time when it wasn't unheard of for sellers to pay closing costs.

My dad and I walked out of the house and got into my Prius. Too stunned to speak, I started the car. My dad looked over at me with a cheeky grin and said, "That was really fun. Let's do it again!"

At the time, I didn't have an unlimited amount of funds, and while my dad has extensive construction experience, he had never bought an investment property.

I simply laughed and said, "That was fun, Dad."

A month later, I closed on my first property. With tears in my eyes, I drove a U-Haul across I-70 from Denver to Kansas City. I renovated the house, taking the entire upstairs down to the studs. I added a full bathroom, a fourth bedroom, and a master closet that was the envy of the neighborhood. I took this Cape Cod from a three-bedroom, 1.5-bath to a four-bedroom, two-bathroom house. I placed two roommates in two of the four rooms, and we made the fourth bedroom a guest room. Then, I hit the road.

My PITI (principal, interest, taxes, and insurance) monthly payment was $1,478, and my roommates paid $750 and $800. After paying my third of utilities, I was often paying $30 or less to live there. I furnished the common areas and rented out the bedrooms unfurnished. It was my first taste of furnishing a rental, and found that I not only love it, I'm also good at it. Little did I know that I would start a company, Arya Design Services, helping investors furnish their investment properties, too. (In Chapter Eleven, we will teach you how to furnish your medium-term rentals.) In early 2019, a little over a year after purchasing this house, I started living fully nomadically and have been doing so ever since.

That year, I spent most of my time in South America. I was still working forty hours a week for the real estate recruiting company, flying to real estate conferences with just my carry-on forty-six-liter Osprey backpack. Eventually, I officially moved out, replacing myself with a third tenant who paid $725. My rental income was $2,275 and my PITI was still $1,478. That was all from a less-than-$7,000 down payment and $10,000 in renovation costs.

The best part was that while living in South America, I kept my monthly expenses around $1,100 each month, sometimes even less. Between my salary and the $700 cash flow from my rental, my bank account gradually grew. I thought, "Whoa! I can do this again."

And that's exactly what I did.

I bought a duplex in Kansas City—this time on the Missouri side—for $180,500 in November 2019 while living in Mexico. Each unit had three bedrooms and one bathroom. I intended to rent out the bottom unit and live in the top unit with a roommate. At the time, I rented out the bottom unit for $975 and my roommate paid $650—a total of $1,625 against a monthly payment of $1,079. Between my two rental properties, I covered my living expenses with rental income and was able to save 75 to 90 percent of my salary. Like my first property, I only needed 3 percent down, equating to less than $6,000. This 3 percent conventional loan was a part of the HomeReady program offered at the time.

What is the HomeReady program?

A few things on HomeReady.

You do not need to be a first-time home buyer.

The big hurdle is you need to make LESS than 80 percent of the county's median income. This will vary from county to county. For example, Johnson County, where I bought, has a median income of $86,300. Thus, 80 percent of that is $69,040. To qualify for HomeReady, I needed to make $69,000 or less. If one can do that, the rest is pretty easy.

You do need a 660 or higher credit score.

More on financing the deal in Chapter Four.

So, the day after I closed on my second property, I quit my job.

"Buy a house; leave a job" would later become a theme for me.

After living in Mexico and South America, I accepted a new position that was still 100 percent remote and in the real estate industry but less restrictive on time zones, allowing me to move to Bali, Indonesia. I really believe in the earn-while-you-learn strategy, so if you are reading this book and want to learn how to grow a real estate portfolio or master a new investing strategy, I highly recommend taking a position in the real estate industry—especially one with an investing focus. Extra bonus if they let you move to Bali and work from there!

As a side note, it's now years later and my boss from that first job, Vanessa, will call me for real estate investing advice, which is a fun dynamic shift. It feels good to be the one with the answers for someone I admired for years—she led a female-owned-and-operated company in the U.S. while living in Spain. I've tended to work at female-owned companies, and all of my bosses have been avid travelers too. I am thankful for bosses like Vanessa and everything they taught me over the years.

After closing on my duplex in Kansas City, I negotiated nine weeks off between jobs, something I recommend to anyone who will listen. During that time, I traveled to China, Hong Kong, Macau, the Philippines, Vietnam, and Singapore. I then made my way to Bali, intending to move back to Kansas City at some point. I was primarily traveling to inexpensive countries and earning a salary from my full-time work at U.S.-based companies. This is known as geoarbitrage. In Chapter Seven, we will talk about this concept more. It is something both Zeona and I have used to increase our savings rate.

I had been living in Bali for three months when COVID-19 swept the world. Less than twenty-four hours after the U.S. president announced that the United States would shut its borders to Europe, I decided to board a flight to New Zealand. I arrived in Auckland in March 2020, just four days before they, too, shut their borders. Continually extending my ninety-day visa, I lived out my dream of owning a van. Yes, #VanLife.

From that van, I analyzed more than one hundred deals all over the U.S. Addicted to the cash flow, you could say, I was determined to buy my third rental property.

During my time in Indonesia and New Zealand, I had built relationships with a handful of what I call investor-friendly real estate agents in towns like Omaha, Nebraska; Des Moines, Iowa; San Antonio, Texas; Kansas City, Missouri; Columbus, Ohio; Phoenix, Arizona; and Clarksville and Chattanooga, Tennessee.

I wrote eighteen offers that year and went under contract five times. But I terminated each one for various reasons. I was unbelievably frustrated and utterly exhausted. I was stretching myself way too thin, looking in too many markets, analyzing too many deals, and focusing on too many strategies. It wasn't until I became crystal clear on my criteria that things started to improve. In Chapter Six, we will show you how to determine your deal criteria.

I decided I wanted to do one of two things. I wanted to own a furnished rental or use the BRRRR strategy.

DEFINITION BRRRR

Buy, rehab, rent, refinance, repeat, or BRRRR, is a term coined by Brandon Turner that allows investors to recoup most if not all of their money back after refinancing. More on this in Chapter Four.

I was confident I would be able to do both of these strategies from afar—even 8,000 miles away.

And I did.

In May 2021, I bought a fourplex in Omaha, Nebraska. That's a duplex in Missouri bought from Mexico and a fourplex in Nebraska bought from New Zealand. Alliteration is not the name of the game, but the coolness factor of this is not lost on me.

Within weeks of closing on my fourplex, I boarded a plane from New Zealand to Nebraska. Just like three and a half years earlier, I moved hundreds—this time thousands—of miles to house hack.

After closing on that fourplex in Nebraska, I bought two duplexes in Des Moines, Iowa, that I would end up using the BRRRR strategy on. Then I bought *another* fourplex and used the medium-term rental strategy to maximize profits. In a matter of ninety-three days, I went from owning three units in two states to owning fifteen units in four states.

In 2022, the year of this book's writing, I purchased two more duplexes in the Des Moines area and plan to rent some of the units out to traveling nurses for $1,800–$2,000 each. The increased cash flow makes this strategy so attractive, and I am excited to show you how you, too, can do it.

As I have built my portfolio over the years, I relied on my intuition and learned on the fly. I took what I already knew how to do—the house hacking strategy—and paired it with a new strategy—the medium-term rental—which would quintuple my cash flow. By reading this book, you won't have to do like I did and learn everything on your own. We will show you how you, too, can use the medium-term rental strategy—in your own house, in your market, or hundreds or even thousands of miles away.

SARAH'S PORTFOLIO

As of July 2022, I own nineteen units in four states and run nine of the units as medium-term rentals.

Kansas

I purchased this in November 2017 from the second owner, a couple who were determined to sell their house as a For Sale by Owner because they did not want real estate agents to get a commission. If they had listed with an agent, a professional would have told them to list for $250,000, giving the agent a 3 percent commission of $7,500. Instead, the couple listed for themselves at $215,000. I offered them $217,000 but asked that they pay $5,000 in closing costs, upgrade the electrical panel for $1,500, and give me a new furnace at $4,000. But good thing they didn't give a real estate agent a commission?

My down payment was less than $7,000, and the seller covered nearly all of my closing costs. In addition, tenants were paying my mortgage in full within 100 days of buying the property.

I bought this three-bedroom, 1.5-bath house knowing I could do two things to increase the value wildly.

1. Add a shower in the closet attached to the half bathroom upstairs, turning it into a full bathroom.
2. Turn the unfinished attic into a fourth bedroom.

After repairs, the property's value increased at least $40,000, and considering the couple sold it to me under value, I had about $75,000 in equity from the beginning. Don't be fooled, though. I knew nothing about leveraging my equity, HELOC (home equity line of credit), or cash-out refinance, so things were slow going for me as an investor.

Missouri

Two years later, in November 2019, I purchased a duplex in Kansas City, Missouri.

I received a text message from an investor-friendly agent that read:

"You need to buy this."

The agent had my deal criteria and knew I was looking for an owner-occupied duplex in a B-class neighborhood with value-add potential. It was listed on the Multiple Listing Service (MLS), yet my agent knew to text me directly when they found something.

I quickly analyzed the deal, wrote the offer, and went under contract the next day. I lived in Mexico City at the time, but happened to be in Nashville,

Tennessee, for a real estate event. A few days later, I drove to Kansas City to attend the inspection, which was the first and last time I saw the duplex before closing remotely from Mexico.

I purchased it for $180,500, and my PITI was $1,079 per month. My real estate agent offered property management, which I kindly declined because I was occupying the top unit and am unfathomably frugal. However, he offered to do tenant placement, which I gladly accepted. To my surprise, he found a tenant willing to pay $985, leaving me with $94 left on my monthly payment. I shared the top unit with a roommate who paid $660.

To say I was hooked on the house hacking strategy is an understatement. To add, as of July 2022, I rent the bottom unit for $1,100 and the top unit for $900. The ability to give yourself a raise over time is incredible.

Nebraska

I was determined to house hack one more time before leaving my W-2 job. I had used owner-occupied conventional loans on the first two properties but had yet to use the Federal Housing Administration (FHA) loan, which allows owner-occupied loans of only 3.5 percent down. More on FHA loans in Chapter Four. Finally, my investor-friendly real estate agent in Omaha, Nebraska, found me an off-market fourplex that was perfect for a house hack.

I will talk about this deal in more depth later in the book. In short, I bought this property with $11,200 down. My PITI is $2,017, and I make $4,580 in rental income from three of the four units. The cash flow is $3,000 each month, even with me living in one of the units.

Within months of closing on the first fourplex, I bought the fourplex next door and rented three of the four units to traveling nurses, who each pay $1,875 to rent a one-bedroom, one-bathroom unit. Now, all four units in that building are medium-term rentals, and it brings in $7,500 of rental income each month as a medium-term rental. That's what this book is about, after all.

Iowa

In July of 2021, I purchased two duplexes next door to each other. My investor-friendly agent found a duplex listed on the MLS and ran the numbers only to find out it could be a near-perfect BRRRR.

I bought that duplex and the duplex next door for $385,000 using hard money and private money. (More on hard money and private money in Chapter Four.) With only $22,000 in repairs, they appraised for $525,000 ($260,000 and $265,000). Each unit rents long-term for $1,325, except for one unit with an inherited tenant, who will move out early next year. When they do, I will furnish their unit and rent it to a traveling nurse for at least $1,900.

In 2022, I purchased two more duplexes in the Des Moines area. I bought one for $207,000 and the other for $185,000. Traveling nurses rent a unit for $1,850–$2,000.

As I continue to grow my portfolio, I will focus on maximizing cash flow using the medium-term rental strategy. I am thrilled to dive into the specifics of why I love using this strategy in the hopes that you will use it too.

ZEONA—Financially Free in Two Years with Airbnb

Growing up, my parents were always broke. "We can't afford that" was a common phrase heard in our household as I watched my parents struggle and suffer to make ends meet. When I looked around at my peers, it didn't seem like everyone else had it this hard. I thought, "There must be a better way."

As someone who only ever fleetingly experienced having money, I was curious about it and daydreamed about what a life with it must be like. Finally, when I was 18 years old, my mother decided to improve her financial situation. We bonded over watching *The Suze Orman Show* and reading personal finance books (and yes, I was a bit of a nerd).

Since neither of my parents had graduated college, I thought higher education might provide me the opportunity to have an easier financial life. I was wrong. After my stint in design school, I had $50,000 in debt and only a faint idea that I didn't want to work in interior design, marketing, or—god forbid—a cubicle.

I needed to clear my head. Travel and nature were my direct lines to spirituality, so I took a job as a cross-country tour guide. By the time I circled back to college in 2011, this time in the massage therapy trade, I was armed with something powerful: the idea of financial independence. It was a few months before my move to Boulder, Colorado, for massage school that I found the *Mr. Money Mustache* blog.

Some refer to *Mr. Money Mustache* as the godfather of the financial independence (FI) movement, also known as the financial independence, retire early (FIRE) community. When I first discovered the FI movement, I didn't have a plan. I thought I would copy the blog author, who saved up $600,000 by age 30 and invested in index funds to produce $2,500 per month in dividends. He could then live off of the dividends in perpetuity, and I wanted to do the same.

The only problem? For me, $600,000 felt like an impossible sum to save up; it might as well have been $1 million! It took Mr. Money Mustache ten years to accomplish FI by age 30, and I was already 26 years old and only making $15 per hour. Airbnb opened my eyes to another path—a faster path—to achieving financial independence. It was that path, starting with Airbnb arbitrage and leading to my current portfolio, that has given me the independence and flexibility to live where I want, do what I want, when I want.

ZEONA'S PORTFOLIO

As of 2022, I own twelve units in four states, diversified across the short-, medium-, and long-term rental strategies.

Colorado

I own two one-bedroom condos a couple doors down from each other in Boulder, Colorado, the beautiful college town in the mountains where I currently live. This includes the original condo I bought for my mom and then lived in and rented on Airbnb for the next four years. Both are furnished medium-term rentals. Boulder's short-term rental laws require that, to rent a home short-term or fewer than thirty days, it must be one's primary residence. Boulder does, however, allow you to Airbnb out your rental property for thirty days or more. Boulder is a popular destination for incoming scientists and technology professionals with large salaries who don't bat an eye at rental rates comparable to top-tier cities. It is also a common choice for digital nomads and athletes, as there is easy access to nature and skiing.

The newest addition to my collection is a two-bedroom medium-term rental in Denver, Colorado. When I received a tip about a property in Washington State that would make an excellent short-term rental, I cleverly lined up selling one of my places in St. Louis to close two days before the purchase, allowing for a seamless 1031 exchange.

> **DEFINITION** 1031 Exchange
>
> A 1031 exchange gets its name from Section 1031 of the U.S. Internal Revenue Code. This exchange allows you to defer paying capital gains taxes when you sell an investment property and reinvest the proceeds from the sale within certain time limits. The property or properties you exchange into must be of like kind and equal or greater value.

Then, in the last week before closing, we realized that my business partner qualified to buy the Washington property as a primary residence, since he was location-independent at his job. We decided to pivot our strategy to take advantage of the lower interest rate. This left me scrambling to find a new investment to purchase in forty-five days. It was right at the beginning of 2022, when prices were already high and interest rates seemed to double overnight. Everything was selling over asking price with multiple offers, pinching homeowners at both ends and making it incredibly challenging for investors to cash flow.

I called everyone I knew, including Sarah, wanting to learn about their favorite markets. As my deadline crept nearer, I explored closer to home, thinking it would make furnishing easier (it wasn't until I was drafting the contract that I realized I would be in Europe for closing and furnishing week). From managing my MTRs in Boulder, I knew there was high demand for nurses near a specific hospital complex in Denver. Lastly, I chose Denver because I am a big believer in Colorado's appreciation potential. By a stroke of luck, I went under contract the day before my identification window expired.

I also own a one-bedroom single-family home with a finished basement in Colorado Springs, which operates as a furnished short-term rental. I purchased this rental in 2018 with a money partner, whom I know from the Boulder circus community (you can find partners anywhere!). We were fortunate enough to acquire this in the early days before the city regulated short-term rentals. In 2019, Colorado Springs brought in regulations limiting the number of possible short-term rental licenses. Luckily, our license was grandfathered in, meaning we enjoy little competition and ever-increasing rental rates.

Missouri

Over the years, I have owned four single-family homes in St. Louis, Missouri. As my strategy and portfolio have matured, I have sold three of the four homes, capitalizing on the equity, and in turn using leverage and the 1031 exchange to purchase more expensive properties.

I originally purchased the low-dollar-amount homes with cash; later, I used the proceeds from their sales as a down payment on more expensive properties while taking on a mortgage.

The remaining home I own is a highly successful medium-term rental. St. Louis is a wildly affordable market, where many properties right off the MLS can make a 10 percent cash-on-cash return as a long-term rental. You can often double that profit when you add in the power of furnished rentals! Medium-term rentals are in high demand in St. Louis because numerous nearby hospitals attract traveling nurses in droves. I believe this market has a strong need for furnished inventory and offers an opportunity for someone excited to dive in.

Florida

I own six units in Ocala and Panama City Beach, Florida: a quadplex, a single-family home, and a townhome vacation rental. In 2021, I ventured into my first experiment with long-term rentals. When I started investing, the only homes I could afford were over 100 years old and required a lot of maintenance to keep them up to short-term rental standards. After five years and a constant flow of repairs, I longed to transition into something easier to maintain. New construction fit the bill and sounded like a dream. At the idea of five to ten years without anyone calling me for a repair, I thought, "Sign me up!" I found these opportunities through a turnkey provider, who offered the use of their vetted property managers.

DEFINITION Turnkey Provider

A turnkey provider takes a property that needs renovations (or works with a developer to offer new construction homes), invests their own money in renovating or building the property, connects you with a property manager, and places a quality tenant before handing it over to an investor. The investor then reaps the benefit of a lifetime of passive income. Turnkey providers have gotten a bad rap since there have been some newsworthy scam artists in recent years, but there are still fantastic providers out there. Looking for a recommendation for a vetted provider? Ask your peers for firsthand experience in the forums at www.biggerpockets.com.

After nearly ten years as my own property manager, I was feeling burned out. I loved the idea of letting someone else take the reins. While I agree with the adage that "no one will ever care about your property as much as you do," overall, I'm pretty happy with the service I've received. Never before had I experienced the concept of "mailbox money," where rent is deposited into my account every month and my properties hum along without my involvement. Still, I highly recommend self-managing for those just getting started or hoping to maximize cash flow. With the tips you'll receive in this book, we hope you will find self-managing a breeze, and by the time you are ten years in (or sooner!), you hopefully will have built up enough cash flow to also retire yourself from that role. Many investors consider property management the worst part of owning real estate, and for a good reason! Over time, my goal is to create more passive income; to be truly passive, I need to stop self-managing my properties.

In 2021, I added another unit to my portfolio, a short-term rental townhome in Panama City Beach, Florida. I know you must be thinking, "What about all that talk about being passive? Short-term rentals are *not* hands-off." And you are right. For this property, I brought in a hustle partner who will be managing the property for us. Unlike a property manager, he will be invested in maximizing our returns for the duration of our unit ownership. As someone who grew up on an island, owning property near the beach has been a lifelong dream. But even a year ago, it felt like a pipe dream. At $650,000, it is my most expensive property by and large. However, the power of real estate investing is such that I was able to go from being a massage school student $50,000 in debt to owning an income-producing property two blocks from the beach. The best part? I won't pay my mortgage on that beach property; my tenants will!

Washington

One of my favorite things about consulting investors is how much I learn from them! Occasionally, an investor will propose a deal in a little-known, hidden gem of a market and want me to help them analyze it. This is exactly what happened for this cabin in Union, Washington. (Never heard of it? Yeah, neither had I.) Situated ninety minutes from Seattle and forty from Olympia, hugging the scenic coast of the Puget Sound, this is where I suspected the high-income tech employees came to retreat. Looking over the numbers, it looked like a solid investment. When my client got cold feet and pivoted to the Phoenix market instead, I decided to take a chance on this lesser-known hamlet.

Our Passions

We believe in the power of the medium-term rental strategy for a number of reasons. But the first one is cash flow. Real estate investing has changed the course of our lives—forever.

Zeona became financially independent in just two years at the age of 28 simply from renting out furnished units. Upon becoming financially independent, she had to redefine her "why." Zeona didn't have family members nearby to spend more time with and she was already traveling the world.

What was going to motivate her to keep going? Why would she keep building her knowledge and empire? The answer is YOU! We are incredibly passionate about teaching others to create furnished rental businesses as we have—businesses that have allowed us to live life on our terms. That is the purpose of this book.

A leading value in our lives is freedom. We want to wake up when we want, create what we want, and travel where we want. We want you to have this flexibility too. Our firsthand knowledge of personal finance combined with the power of real estate investing allows us to help others supercharge their portfolios to find their freedom. Sharing our stories to help others is a gift, and for that we say *thank you*.

We cannot wait to hear where your journey takes you.

HOW TO USE THIS BOOK

It's the little details that are vital.
Little things make big things happen.
—JOHN WOODEN

As you will notice throughout the book, we both value freedom and travel. We often have this in common with the types of guests and tenants our units house! But we know that for some of you, travel is not a part of your "why." When we share travel stories, think of yourself living out *your* dreams. For you, it might be pursuing a passion project, spending more quality time with your loved ones, or quitting a job you no longer want to show up for. Whatever that "why" is, we are here to show you how the medium-term rental (MTR) strategy can get you closer to the life you are meant to be living. Our love of travel made us fast friends, but our understanding of how to maximize the MTR strategy is what we are most proud of and why *30-Day Stay* is here for you.

Throughout this book, you will see why we both love the MTR strategy and what it has afforded us both in such a short amount of time.

Inside the following pages, we will show you:

- How the MTR strategy will help you increase cash flow rapidly and achieve financial independence (Chapter Two).
- The best way to finance these deals and set yourself up to get unlimited loans (Chapter Four).
- The importance of the market and how picking the right location isn't as difficult as you might think (Chapter Five).

- Six tips for finding investor-friendly agents and how they can save you hours when acquiring moneymaking properties (Chapter Nine).
- Why furniture and decor matters and how to furnish a unit from afar (Chapter Eleven).
- The importance of marketing and how to get as many eyes on your furnished units as possible (Chapter Thirteen).
- How to manage multiple properties in your local market, or even from thousands of miles away (Chapter Sixteen).
- And so much more!

We wrote this book as a step-by-step guide for investors to rent their units furnished for thirty days or more and to master the medium-term rental strategy. This book will cover the basics, and once you have mastered them, you'll be amazed at the simplicity of the strategy.

We broke the book into five sections, allowing you to skip ahead if you need or follow along step-by-step so you do not miss a beat.

1. Understanding the MTR Strategy
2. Acquisition
3. Your Team and Why They Matter
4. Listing Strategy
5. Responsible Landlording

This book will give you the tools to find, analyze, finance, and manage MTRs. We will weave in our stories and emphasize the impact this strategy has had on both of our lives. Our hope is that this book gives you the strength and the tools you need to master this strategy.

While this book will act as a step-by-step guide, our hope for you is that these pages teach you how to do real estate investing differently too. We will cover everything from finding a cleaner to finding the right bedding for your rental. But as important as sheets are, it's also important to us that you walk away from this book feeling confident in your ability to analyze a deal and a market, and ultimately make the right decision for you and your portfolio.

The MTR strategy has the potential to change your life—and faster than you'd think! It is for us. You may never know where in the world either of us are—we're often hopping on a last-minute flight—but one thing is for sure: We could not do it without our medium-term rentals.

PART 1
Understanding the MTR Strategy

CHAPTER ONE

WHAT IS A MEDIUM-TERM RENTAL?

To begin, BEGIN.
—WILLIAM WORDSWORTH

What is the Medium-Term Rental Strategy?

The medium-term rental (MTR) strategy is a form of real estate investment where an investor furnishes a condo or home, usually in an urban market, to rent by the month to traveling professionals. This strategy is quickly gaining steam in cities where short-term rentals (STRs) are outlawed. In addition, this strategy works well in densely populated areas near universities, hospitals, and office parks, which may seem less desirable to longer-term tenants. There has also been an uptick in demand in rural locations for experiences in cabins, glamping, or farm stays.

DEFINITION What is a Medium-Term Rental?

A medium-term rental, also known as a month-to-month rental, executive rental, or a traveling nurse rental, is a furnished unit rented out thirty or more days at a time.

Short-Term vs. Medium-Term vs. Long-Term

A short-term rental is a furnished unit, rented for fewer than thirty days (in some markets under twenty-eight days), that caters to guests on vacation. The average length of stay is three to four nights. While there have been many cities and counties outlawing this rental strategy in the past five years, due to complaints around diminishing affordable housing and lobbying from the hotels who are losing their desirability, there are still many traditional vacation rental markets (generally near national parks and beaches) that have continued to allow these and likely will for years to come.

The medium-term strategy has swept in to save the day for those operators who have had to pivot after the laws in their cities changed. Instead of transitioning into long-term rentals, which may not earn enough income to cover the mortgage, investors can continue to utilize their furnished spaces in a strategy that they may enjoy even more. This strategy is especially powerful near hospitals, as the trend of traveling nurses is on the rise—as of this writing, there are more than 30,000 open, high-paying traveling nurse positions available. A medium-term rental can be as short as one month, but it is usually three to six months, centered around traveling nurse assignments.

A long-term rental is a concept most of us are familiar with. It is often applied to an unfurnished unit with a twelve-month lease. Since tenants stay longer and move in their furniture, landlords frequently must perform maintenance each time a tenant moves out, such as repainting the home or replacing carpets. Turnover expenses like this can be costly and can absorb an investor's annual profit if their tenants stay for only a year. Unfortunately, while any necessary or cosmetic work is being completed, the home also sits vacant. Long-term rentals have become less sexy for investors because they often come with low cash flow returns, requiring an investor to collect a large number of properties to replace their W-2 income. In our recent crazy market, where home prices are rising, it has become increasingly challenging to find long-term rentals that can earn enough to cover high monthly mortgage payments.

Who Do We Rent To?

People often want to know who our tenants are. In our history as landlords and property managers, we have realized that tenants can make the job of a landlord a headache or blissfully easy, depending on who you choose. While hosting Airbnb guests in a C-class neighborhood in St. Louis, Zeona noted the vast differences between the short- and long-term tenant pools. Many of the long-term rentals and occupied homes in the neighborhood were in rough shape. In contrast, the Airbnb guests were traveling professors, international students, or people passing through on road trips. They were happy to pay $100 per night and were barely there, and the regular cleaning and maintenance an STR necessitates meant the properties stayed in top condition. Compared to the $850 per month one could get long-term, it was a no-brainer! Tenants can make or break your strategy, so be sure to pick the plan to help you align with the tenants you want to attract.

With MTRs, we get some great tenants of a wide variety. Let's dive into the most common guest types.

TRAVELING NURSES AND DOCTORS

Have we said how much we love traveling nurses? They are gainfully employed, highly background checked by their employer, and barely ever home. Unfortunately, just because they are medical professionals, that doesn't mean they will make fantastic tenants, so it is still essential to go through the screening process in Chapter Fourteen. Traveling nurses tend to have thirteen-week assignments and often ask to extend for another thirteen weeks, which is perfect for filling in the slow season. There are high- and low-demand times for tenants, so being price-aware is a critical skill, which we will go over in Chapter Twelve.

Markets are not created equal. Zeona has medium-term rentals in St. Louis, Missouri; Boulder, Colorado; and Colorado Springs, Colorado. St. Louis is the clear winner between the three for traveling nurses. Eight to ten new prospects can be found on a given day on the lead-generating website Furnished Finder. With a cluster of hospitals all within walking distance of one another near the Central West End, a robust medical program at Washington University, and a university hospital, the demand is high. Do your research to find active, thriving hospital complexes; it could be your ticket to money-making rentals.

EXECUTIVES

Executive rentals: Remember this aging term from circa 1990? These are the original MTRs, yet they never really caught fire—at least not as they have now. Historically, these operators needed to create relationships with placement agencies and the human resources departments at several large employers in the area. Thank goodness Airbnb made all this a heck of a lot easier. Now a lot of these placement agencies *reach out to us* on Airbnb.

Even though traditional business travel has slowed since COVID-19, people are still traveling. It now just means for longer stays. For example, three to four months is a common length of stay for professors in town for a semester, scientists working on a project at the leading research center, and business professionals in their initial ninety-day probationary period before they have locked in the job and can commit to relocating.

DIGITAL NOMADS

COVID-19 changed the game by making most professions location independent overnight. According to the Future Workforce Pulse Report, the number of Americans who will be working remotely is expected to more than double from pre-pandemic levels by the year 2025, from 16.8 million to 36.2 million.[1] The first brave souls pushed this to the limits, and we have seen our fair share of digital nomads (travelers who can work from anywhere) pop in for a month on their journey. Why not take the opportunity to explore the U.S. for a lot less than it costs to rent in the big cities? (While we collect those high city-comparable rents!)

What's the difference between the executives and the digital nomads? Those executives often come to town to go into a local office, while the digital nomads will be turning your furnished rental *into* their office. In 2021, Airbnb added the ability to upload a speed test of your Wi-Fi to your listing to accommodate this. Another trend is furnishing your rental with a desk monitor. It is so convenient, especially for someone working in tech, to plug their laptop into a larger screen during their stay.

FULL-TIME AIRBNB RESIDENTS

A new trend is emerging: living out of Airbnbs full-time. Airbnb reported that the share of long-term-stay bookers who used their stays to lead a nomadic lifestyle grew from 9 percent in 2020 to 12 percent in 2021. Unlike digital nomads, many of these folks are retired or taking a leave of absence to travel.

Contrary to popular belief, living out of an Airbnb full-time can work out cheaper than a traditional lease. Plus, there are lots of perks that come with it. For example, if you get into travel hacking through credit cards, you can earn thousands of points and miles from your "rent" each month, possibly getting you a flight to your next destination for free.

Debbie and Michael Campbell are full-time Airbnb residents. In 2013, after retiring from their jobs in Seattle, Debbie hoped they'd have "one more adventure."[2]

---

1 https://www.businesswire.com/news/home/20201215005287/en/Upwork-Study-Finds-22-of-American-Workforce-Will-Be-Remote-by-2025

2 Erica Browne Grivas, "This Retired Couple Sold Their House and Have Traveled the World Living in Airbnbs," *Seattle Times*, August 17, 2021, updated August 17, 2021, https://www.seattletimes.com/life/travel/this-retired-seattle-couple-sold-their-house-and-have-traveled-the-world-living-in-airbnbs/.

"The hypothesis was: Could we retire, live in other people's houses, and spend the same amount of money we'd spend if we'd stayed in Seattle?" Debbie said.

The Campbells rented out their house and hit the road. Two years into the experiment, they decided to sell their home and have never looked back. As of 2021, the Campbells have lived in 270 Airbnbs in 85 countries. They only plan their lives about six months in advance. You can follow their adventures on their blog at www.seniornomads.com.

"What [Airbnb] learned during COVID-19 is they had a very significant uptick in people booking long-term stays. Instead of working in your basement in Ballard you can work on the beach in the Bahamas, so people were doing that," Debbie said.

CASE STUDY

"The Nomadic Investor" by Michael Castaño

As a 27-year-old, first-generation college student and investor, I invest in real estate because it is a vehicle that indirectly provides the most scarce asset in the entire world: time. My parents, immigrants from Cuba, fled the grasp of communism, one in 1967 and the other in 1984, to establish a better life in the United States with only the clothes they had on when they arrived. My father left behind his wife at the time and three children in an effort to preemptively find work in Florida and ensure their well-being when they arrived. My mother had barely finished high school in Cuba when her mother and grandmother tore her away from the community she grew up in to go live in a different country. Tasked with the burden of working endlessly in Miami to make ends meet, neither of my parents knew what investing was or how investing could help them achieve what they wanted—a better life for the entire family. It was only years later, in 2010, when my entrepreneurial father began dabbling in real estate and purchased a rental property, that I learned how real estate could put money to work for you.

Today I own eight rental units across Florida, Michigan, and Arizona. I have lived in all these places for work, which has allowed me to purchase most of my rentals by way of owner-occupied, primary-residence bank loans. My main investing strategy revolves around "buy and hold." I own several small multifamily homes, which I occupied for a minimum of one year and then rented out once I was eligible to purchase a new home. The best part is, while I occupied one of the units, I was still able to rent out the others, which helped cover the monthly mortgage payment and allowed me to save much faster. A good example of this is a duplex I purchased in Michigan for $349,000 in 2020. Since it was an FHA, owner-occupied loan, I was able to do a 3.5 percent down payment option. Combined with a 3 percent seller concession, I was able to close the deal with $12,815 at the closing table and a monthly PITI of $2,016. One month after closing, I found a tenant who rented out the unit nextdoor to the one I would be living in for $2,300/month. I was living for free in my own home!

The Numbers
- Purchase price: $349,000
- 3.5% FHA down payment: $12,815
- Monthly PITI: $2,016
- Rental income from one of the two units: $2,300

Through investing in real estate over the last few years, I have managed to achieve a level of financial independence, which allows me to afford a lifestyle where I decide what I want to do with my time. I have decided to travel full-time to experience a nomadic lifestyle and see if it's the right fit for me. My real estate portfolio is able to sustain my current cost of living, which is minimal because I have yet to establish a family and can enjoy the benefits of having few responsibilities outside my real estate business.

At the time I am writing this, I am traveling across Mexico, meeting locals, investors, and other individuals who have also achieved financial independence. This is only cementing what I already believe—this lifestyle is attainable and brings with it so many new opportunities and a different perspective on life that is priceless. I will be traveling to Southeast Asia next, followed by Europe and eventually South America, growing my network and net worth along the way.

Achieving this feat has come with its share of adversity and roadblocks along the way: family health complications, job changes, maintenance repairs, and managing contractors and tenants from afar. But nothing deterred me from focusing on my goals. Each obstacle became a learning experience and another tool in my toolbox that I will apply in the future to avoid the same mistakes. For instance, being an out-of-state investor requires you to manage a team of individuals who are local to your properties and can address any issues that may come up. I learned the hard way that having a good team is key to running a successful and profitable portfolio with little to no stress, and if I had to do things over again, I would place a lot more emphasis and time on building a strong, trustworthy team that will know how to operate the business even if I'm not present. Despite my setbacks, I look to apply my learning going forward and continue my real estate investing journey. I am actively exploring creative financing, syndications, and the short-term rental market—new ways of investing and building a robust, diverse portfolio that will help me be ready for new opportunities. I never shy away from challenges and use my newfound time to make the most of the life my parents sacrificed everything for me to have.

Find out more about Michael @firstgeninvestor on Instagram.

SEASONAL TRAVELERS

For the majority of the decade that Zeona has lived in Colorado, she has made a valiant effort to avoid the winter season. Instead, she hops around in warmer places like Spain, Hawaii, the U.S. Virgin Islands, Puerto Rico, and Florida. Now, many renters do the same. In 2021, Zeona picked up a Florida short-term rental, and she hopes to find some lovely Canadians who will want to "winter" there medium-term during the slow season. But, of course, this category doesn't have to be just snowbirds; in Boulder, Zeona has seen the opposite in folks who are excited to work somewhere they can quickly access the ski slopes for a half-day run.

RENOVATORS OR THOSE WAITING FOR A HOME

This is one of our favorite categories! Why? Because renovations and construction always take a little longer than people anticipate. Cha-ching! These guests are great. They often live locally and spend a lot of their time in the community, not in the home. They are grateful to have a quiet, construction-free zone to live in and will keep you up to date on their progress. The only con is that they may try to move a lot of their belongings in. Be sure to inquire if they are getting a storage unit and make sure they are not planning to carry over any furniture.

New construction has been on the rise, and many families need to sell before they can afford to buy their new home; this usually leaves a gap of a month (or a few months) when they need to rent furnished in between move-out and move-in. As a real estate agent, Zeona has even been able to get a few clients from her Airbnbs: people moving to the area from out of town and renting a furnished space while they start their search for a home to purchase.

Sarah's Renovation Refuge

In November 2021, Sarah had a one-bedroom unit in Omaha listed on Facebook Marketplace and in a handful of Omaha housing Facebook groups.

She received a message from a young couple who were native to Omaha. Their kitchen was being renovated, making working from home too tricky with the noise. Thus, they were looking to rent a furnished apartment with reliable Wi-Fi and, ideally, a functioning kitchen so both husband and wife could work remotely. Plus, they also had two dogs.

They rented Sarah's unit for $1,375 and signed a one-month lease. But Sarah knew they would want to extend. In Sarah's experience, renovations never take as long as the contractors say they will; they almost always take twice as long! Thinking proactively, Sarah blocked off her unit for the month following the end of their stay. Sure enough, the guests called Sarah in a panic, explaining that their contractors were not finished with the kitchen renovations, and Sarah was able to put them at ease, telling them that she had already anticipated this scenario.

Not all medium-term tenants will be traveling nurses!

NATURAL DISASTER VICTIMS

During the height of the COVID-19 pandemic, Zeona had relief workers from medical practitioners to military personnel renting her homes. This demand also extends to hurricanes, fires, floods, and other natural disasters. For example, on December 30, 2021, a raging fire swept through towns surrounding Boulder, Colorado, engulfing 1,000 homes. This tragic event left many families needing long-term furnished rentals while waiting to rebuild or find a more permanent place to stay. Zeona has even seen requests come through from people needing to vacate their homes for restoration work from the smoke damage. A majority of homeowners have insurance that covers most of these costs, and these insurance companies pay higher rates for housing.

Another investor in Boulder was able to pack up her belongings so she could offer her house to those in need. She booked a last-minute flight to Mexico, where she usually spends half of the year, and was able to rent out her three-bedroom South Boulder home for $9,000 per month, paid for by an insurance company. Only able to host one family at a time, she even had the difficult task of choosing between a few families. Her high-demand rates, only seen in the height of summer, had never gone above $7,000 in a given month (short-term). This influx of cash was a blessing for her. She was in the midst of a home-build project in Mexico that was tighter than expected with the increase of supply costs since the start of the COVID-19 pandemic.

One benefit of being a host is the ability to help those in need. If you feel generous, Airbnb allows you to offer your home for free to victims for disaster relief.

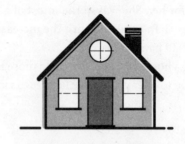

CHAPTER TWO
WHY MTRS?

Courage is not the absence of fear,
but rather the assessment that something else is
more important than fear.
—FRANKLIN D. ROOSEVELT

Why Would You Want to Do the MTR Strategy?

A change is coming. For many of us who have been short-term rental operators for some time, we have seen it approaching slowly over the horizon. It's happening in waves: tightening restrictions and municipalities outlawing nightly rentals. For the past few years, everywhere you look in Airbnb-related news there is another small hamlet or widely unknown lakeside community shutting STR hosts out. These communities cannot say "no rentals," so somewhere along the way a short-term rental got defined as a stay under one month, allowing the new gray area of the thirty-day rental to become the next Wild West.

ZEONA

On March 8, 2020, COVID-19 was all over the news. We had been hearing about the measures taken in Italy and China to lock people into their homes, and collective fear was high. I had just gotten off a podcast interview where the host asked me what was happening to my rentals, and so far, things were good. We were ramping up to what looked like another profitable summer season. I was already seeing a smattering of bookings into May. Sure, I had seen one or two canceled travel plans due to COVID-19, but it seemed like news channels might have been overhyping what was actually happening. Ever the optimist, I wasn't worried.

Seemingly overnight, all the reservations for the fifteen rentals that I owned or managed at the time fell off the calendar. People were canceling in droves, and as hosts, our hands were tied. We were blindly issuing refunds. It looked pretty bleak. And then an interesting thing began happening: Within a day or two of the wave of what I like to call "the great cancellation," I started to receive requests. People were returning from trips abroad and needed to quarantine for two weeks before returning to their families. Emergency aid workers and military personnel were assigned to cities to help, and they needed housing. Even though many asked for discounts, we kept our properties occupied; we just transitioned to longer stays. Shortly after that, families began to realize that they needed more space if they were going to work and educate their kids from home. Once quarantines were lifted, the digital nomads started to make requests, realizing that they could "work from home" in fantastic locales near the mountains or by the beach instead of in their claustrophobic home city.

I saw the trend and pivoted fast. I began to list my properties on sites like Furnished Finder, marketing to medical professionals (primarily nurses), and in Facebook groups for nurses. I remember being unsure whether I could manage this strategy from afar like I had the short-term rentals. Still, I picked it up quickly, realizing that, like STRs, many of these renters are choosing their rental sight unseen. All the necessary communication—messages, leases, and payments—could be handled virtually. I put together leases for the different states and hit the ground running.

This strategy has only grown in demand in the past two years, forcing Airbnb to adjust its platform to attract longer-term stays. In fact, in the final quarter in 2021, Airbnb reported one out of every five nights booked on the platform were for stays of twenty-eight days or longer.[3] The medium-term rental strategy is here to stay.

Data shared by Airbnb supports Zeona's hunch. In the last two weeks of March 2020, the company saw the number of guests booking longer-term stays within their same cities *nearly double*.[4] Airbnb's CEO, Brian Chesky, acknowledged in an interview that while the desire to connect and travel had been reinforced during the time of quarantine, the "way it manifests will evolve as the world

---

3 https://news.airbnb.com/brian-chesky-to-live-on-airbnb-as-the-travel-revolution-becomes-reality/

4 https://news.airbnb.com/longertermlocalstays/

changes."[5] As a result, Airbnb quickly introduced several new tools to make their listings more widely available to long-term guests and new visibility settings for displaying local listings in the search results.

Of Airbnb's 5.6 million–listing portfolio, more than 1 million listings offer monthly stays. The company said it's seeing more people—such as students, doctors and nurses in residency, and others in long-term work assignments—turning to Airbnb to find housing for six- to nine-month stays. In 2020, Airbnb said it had seen bookings for more than 600 days; the longest booking made so far was more than 700 days.

By summer 2020, while people remained cautious, the pent-up desire to travel was palpable and turned into increasing demand. In April 2021, Chesky made a public call for hosts: "To meet the demand over the coming years, we're going to need millions more hosts," he said. "We think there's going to be a travel rebound coming that's unlike anything we've ever seen."[6] And he was right. During the summer of 2021, nightly rates were at record levels with sky-high demand. "People are discovering that they don't have to be tethered to one location to live and work," Chesky said. "They are getting in cars, and they're traveling to small towns and rural communities, many of which don't even have a hotel. People are traveling anytime, anywhere, and they're staying longer."[7] As guests cautiously reenter the world after bouts of outbreaks, we suspect travel demand only to increase. We think this leaves a perfect opportunity for you to become the next host and help fill this need!

In Airbnb's 2021 Q1 earnings call, Chesky told investors, "Our business rebounded faster than anyone expected, [and] our business improved without the recovery of two of our strongest historical segments: urban travel and cross-border travel."[8] Medium-term rentals are often in urban markets, meaning that as fear of COVID-19 dwindles, we believe these markets stand to see a surge in demand. Airbnb posted a year-over-year average daily rate increase of 35 percent for 2021. Airbnb is betting that how and where people work will evolve; in the company's view, it's heading toward longer-term stays.

As the world undergoes a revolution in how we live and work, more people are blending life with travel, and furnished rentals make that possible. At the

---

5 https://techcrunch.com/2020/04/08/airbnb-rolls-out-new-features-aimed-at-its-next-big-bet-longer-term-stays/

6 https://www.cnbc.com/2021/04/16/airbnb-ceo-says-company-is-going-to-need-millions-more-hosts-to-meet-demand.html

7 https://www.travelweekly.com/Travel-News/Hotel-News/Airbnb-said-quarter-of-guests-booked-long-stays

8 https://www.travelweekly.com/Travel-News/Hotel-News/Airbnb-said-quarter-of-guests-booked-long-stays

beginning of 2022, Chesky announced his plan to join the community of Airbnb guests living and working remotely full-time using the platform.[9]

This "live anywhere" trend is a decentralization of living, and it's changing the identity of travel. Among the trends Airbnb has announced that they expect to see are:

- People will continue to spread out to thousands of towns and cities, staying for weeks, months, or even longer. In 2021, demand for rural stays grew 85 percent.[10]
- More people will start living abroad, others will travel for the entire summer, and some will even give up their leases and become digital nomads.
- Cities and countries will compete to attract these remote workers, leading to a redistribution of where people travel and live. More countries are changing their visa and tax rules, and more than three dozen countries currently offer some form of digital nomad visa.

11 Reasons We Love the MTR Strategy (And You Will Too!)

1. REGULATIONS

As we dig into why MTRs are a good strategy, the first point that comes to mind is regulations. For many investors looking into unregulated, short-term rental-"friendly" markets, the threat of regulation has felt like a ticking time bomb. It is challenging to buy and plan your returns around nightly stays when that strategy could be taken away from you at any moment. For some, simply understanding the MTR strategy allows them to have a solid plan B.

In most markets, renting more than thirty days puts you in the long-term rental category in the eyes of the city, which might require a low-cost, straightforward license or not require one at all. Lucky for us, MTRs fly under the radar and can tag along with these long-established regulations. Unfortunately, it is a common, frustrating practice for short-term rental operators to call city or county licensing departments only to be met with confused employees and unclear instructions. While cities do not have many regulations directed toward medium-term rentals, long-term rentals have been around longer and are clearly regulated. Those rules apply to MTRS, making MTRs much easier to operate.

---

9 https://www.businessinsider.com/chesky-says-hes-currently-living-on-airbnb-2022-1?r=US&IR=T

10 https://news.airbnb.com/2022-the-live-anywhere-revolution-becomes-reality/

CASE STUDY

"Hindsight is 20/20" by Jasper Ribbers, author of *Get Paid for Your Pad*

When I quit my finance job in 2010, I wasn't planning on early retirement. Instead, I realized that the steadily increasing number in my bank account didn't provide me with enough fulfillment to justify spending nine hours a day in an office building.

I wanted something different, although I wasn't sure what exactly. All I knew was that my most memorable experiences took place during my travels, so traveling seemed like a good place to start. Since I didn't have enough savings to last for more than a few years, I figured I'd go back to a job at some point.

I did have one source of income: my two-bedroom apartment in Amsterdam. I had used the money I made as a trader to pay off the mortgage, so the rent I was receiving, about $1,500 a month, was basically my net income. It wasn't enough to support my travels, though, and I was not too fond of the fact that I could never stay at my place when I was back home.

Two years later, I was in Brazil with a good friend looking for accommodation. He suggested that instead of staying in a hotel, we could try staying in someone's apartment using a new website called Airbnb. The concept immediately intrigued me, and I realized it could provide a better solution for my apartment in Amsterdam. I expected to make more money than renting to my long-term tenant, and I could stay there myself whenever I wanted.

I was fortunate that my renter decided to end his lease and move out soon after I discovered Airbnb. I flew back to Amsterdam, and not long after, I welcomed my first Airbnb guests. I spent the following months reading everything I could find about improving as a host.

As my Airbnb hosting skills improved, so did my income. I was grossing approximately $5,000 a month, and I enjoyed the hosting experience. For the first time since I quit my job, I considered the option of never returning to the corporate world. It felt great.

In recent years, the authorities in many major cities worldwide have been pushing back against the rise of Airbnb and other short-term rental sites. Amsterdam was no exception. Airbnb was blamed for rising real estate prices and rents, as well as disturbances caused by tourists staying in these short-term rentals.

This eventually led Airbnb to strike a deal with Amsterdam, restricting hosts from renting out entire homes in the city. In the spring of 2017, Airbnb enforced a sixty-day minimum on the platform for hosts in Amsterdam. This left me with no other option than to sell my house, as I didn't want to go back to renting to long-term tenants.

Find Jasper's STR hosting tips on Instagram @getpaidforyourpad.

Knowing what we know now about the medium-term rental strategy, we would have suggested Jasper use that with his apartment in Amsterdam.

Jasper is not alone. We know dozens of investors in the same predicament; with their cities or homeowners associations (HOAs) restricting their ability to rent their properties for thirty days or fewer, the MTR strategy is the solution.

2. EASE

This one is a big selling point for us. As constant travelers, we always have a beautiful sunset, new friends, and exciting excursions calling us away from our computers. Having a strategy like MTR with less guest communication and fewer emergencies lets us breathe a sigh of ease. The MTR strategy has less turnover than the STR strategy, which means less coordination with cleaners and less guest interaction in general.

Because new guests are introduced to the space every few days with STRs, it's natural that more questions will arise. Professional hosts try to anticipate these with preprogrammed messages, but things occasionally fall through the cracks. For example, a guest can't figure out a lockbox or the touchpad malfunctions, the toilet is clogged and a plumber can't get there until Monday, or the cleaner messes up the schedule and doesn't show. With MTRs, those guests learn the house in the first few days, and the owner enjoys the blissful quiet of no communication for the rest of the month or more. Knowing we can accept that dinner invite and not spend the whole night trying to find a twenty-four-hour locksmith is one of the many reasons we love this strategy.

3. FEWER EXPENSES

The little-known cash flow killer in STRs is the mountain of expenses. Investors who are used to long-term rentals may forget to account for all the monthly fees—not just the obvious ones like electricity and Wi-Fi but also yard maintenance and snow removal. Then there are supplies that are provided and cleaning fees; it all adds up. We love that MTRs have more predictable monthly expenses that allow us to efficiently run our numbers when analyzing our properties, making bookkeeping a breeze. When people brag about what their short-term rental earns, know that they are likely talking in gross numbers, before expenses. If they are lucky, the net or profit can be 25 percent of that gross number—or less. Another punch to the gut with STRs can be the additional hotel tax, which can be as much as 12.5 percent, depending on your area. Oftentimes you are only able to charge a guest so much, making it difficult to charge the additional hotel tax directly to the guest. Once you add in paying for property management, you may not turn a profit at all.

With MTRs, there is just less. Less communication means lower admin fees and less need for automation software. Less turnover means fewer cleaning fees to pay out and fewer cleaning supplies to replenish. We cover fewer of their supplies with extended stays, instead giving them a starter kit, which we will go over in Chapter Eleven. With MTRs, the rent is a bit less, so it is important to make sure the ratio still works.

4. FEWER TRANSACTIONS

If you are new to short-term rentals, this may seem like an odd category. With STRs, you get paid a few days after the guest checks in, so you may get up to fifteen "rent checks" every month. There are so many transactions going in and out—such as deposits from sites like Airbnb, utilities, supplies from Target, payments to your cleaner through Venmo—that bookkeeping can be a real headache. Receiving a consistent monthly rate gives you a more predictable, steady income and may also allow you to combine all your rentals into one bank account. When Zeona started, she had one bank account and one credit card per house to keep the accounting straight. At about eight properties, it started to become a lot to juggle, until she eventually caved and got a bookkeeper.

5. LESS COMPETITION

One of our favorite things about the MTR space is that the business still operates in a very mom-and-pop fashion, which becomes evident after five minutes on the Furnished Finder site. Many of the homes advertised there are poorly furnished and advertised with low-light photos that make them look more like thriller film sets than cozy, inviting rentals. This leaves a lot of room for you, the novice, armed with our book and the tips you'll learn here, to create a high-ranking listing that will generate a lot of demand. On Airbnb, boutique hotels and professional designers have infiltrated and dominated the space; the competition in Furnished Finder is less than fierce, so it is an easy place to outshine the rest. Between Sarah's incredible eye and stunning furnishing checklist, and Zeona's optimizing tips and automations, you will be equipped to have a high-performing rental.

6. YOU SET THE RATE

By "set the rate," we mean that in this low-competition environment, you can set a higher rate than the norm and test it out. When we name our rates, we list what we suspect is on the higher range and see what kind of bites we get. Zeona loves to say, "It only takes one yes." Then in three months, when the tenant leaves, we try out $50–$100 more per month. Based on seasonality and demand in your area, the rates can swing a lot, so it is essential to test new ones continually.

7. LESS VACANCY

Vacancy—something every landlord dreads. If the property isn't rented, it's costing you money. In the world of STRs, vacancy is seen a little differently. Many STR operators look at the total income for the month over the number of days rented. If you can get a higher price with fewer days, sometimes it is worth it to have some quiet, unoccupied days rather than to rent cheaply to a disruptive group.

In the long-term space, there is often a gap of two weeks or more in rental turnover, which we've never quite understood; maybe it is just the slow pace of managers in this space, but it seems excessive. This may also be because most people are looking to move at the end of the month, and occasionally mid-month, so timing is crucial. In long-term rentals, it is common to tear out the carpet and paint the walls between tenants, which is much less common in the short- and medium-term spaces.

For medium-term rentals, we have been pleasantly surprised to find that tenants are flexible and can move in at all times of the month. They will even get hotel rooms for a few days to wait for our places; this frequently makes our occupancy gaps as short as a few hours to a couple of days.

8. MORE FLEXIBILITY

Medium-term rentals allow for more flexibility than long-term rentals because you do not necessarily have tenants year-round. Want to renovate slowly? Make some improvements here and there as you earn income? You can do that!

9. HAVING A "GUEST APARTMENT"

These are our two favorite words. It's much cooler to offer a friend or family member your "guest apartment" than a guest room. With the flexibility of your calendar, having furnished rentals allows you to stay in the home yourself or share it with friends. We love having the opportunity to make 1.5 times the long-term rental market rate (or more!) so that we can be generous with those close to us, gifting them a free or discounted stay.

10. POPULAR IN UNUSUAL LOCATIONS

In episode 103 of the *Thanks for Visiting* podcast, guest Julie Gates mentions an MTR of hers near a port in an industrial area that does surprisingly well. She had a company rent the space for workers on an extended contract for a high rate. MTRs can work in some of the most unlikely places. While an STR needs to be by an attraction—such as a sports field, downtown area, or vacation spot—MTRs have so many more options—hospitals, universities, office parks, research centers, and more. They also work well in urban areas that are densely populated, where people may visit for work.

11. WORKS IN INEXPENSIVE MARKETS

The MTR strategy is possible to execute in more markets, including less expensive ones. This can be a relief to those investors who had previously been duking it out in highly competitive vacation rental markets, where prices have gone through the roof. While the MTR strategy can work in expensive markets, it also can work in affordable cities like Omaha, St. Louis, and Cleveland. This lower price point could mean a lower barrier to entry for newbie investors. By opening investors up to more markets, the MTR strategy makes going under contract easier. In Chapter Five, we will dive deep into how to pick a market.

CHAPTER THREE
WHO IS THE MTR STRATEGY FOR?

There are two types of people who will tell you that you cannot make a difference in this world. Those who are afraid to try and those who are afraid you will succeed.

—RAY GOFORTH

ZEONA

Furnished rentals have given me so much. As I write this, I am sitting in the popular ski town of Dillon, Colorado, by a toasty fire, cuddling a couple of doggies that are not mine. We are on a pet sit, one of many that my fiancé and I booked this winter to explore the snowboard destinations on the Ikon Pass. Since we returned from six weeks in Hawaii in mid-December, we have enjoyed stunning homes, snowboarding, and wonderful pets in Estes Park, Steamboat Springs, Dillon, and soon Nederland. This life full of travel and adventure is paid for by our furnished primary home that we rent out—all the others are a bonus!

Before I owned a home, I remember people saying they didn't want to buy because they thought it would tie them down like a ball and chain. For me, the experience of homeownership has been the exact opposite. Growing up, my family moved nearly every year when our lease was up. This meant constant packing and unpacking, new neighborhoods, new friends, and new schools. When I struck out on my own during college, I had a similar experience—moving at least once a year, living with roommates, changing cities.

Buying my first property allowed me to truly land. For the first time in my life, I had a place that couldn't be taken away from me: a home base, a launching-off point. I could paint the walls, and I had a place to store my stuff when I traveled. The more properties I collected—and the more income I have collected from renting them out—the more freedom I have had to explore the world, start businesses, change careers, and be generous with others. Owning a furnished rental allows for such incredible flexibility, whether you have one, two to go between (which I did for years and think is the ultimate move), or twelve units (like I do now).

We've gone over *what* the medium-term rental strategy is. But *who* is this strategy for? What type of investors are MTRs best suited to?

Investors Wanting More Profit

Our dear friend Craig Curelop, author of BiggerPockets book *The House Hacking Strategy*, loves to talk about the comfort continuum. It is a rule of thumb that states that the more uncomfortable you are willing to get—or, in this case, the more work you are ready to put in to a deal—the more money you will make. The MTR is the middle porridge that is *just right* in the story of "Goldilocks and the Three Bears." Short-term rentals can be cash flow cows, yet you need to compete to get one in the right market, manage many moving parts, and conduct constant turnover. The long-term rental works in fewer and fewer markets these days, as we are seeing pressure from low inventory (and high demand) lead to sky-high sales prices, driving mortgages much higher than what one would charge for market-rate rent.

The MTR strategy is for those who want to squeeze out a little more profit than would come from a traditional rental. It's for those who are not content with breaking even and hoping for appreciation, those who need a little cash flow to feel safe in their deals—investors who are willing to put in a little hustle and elbow grease to make this business work.

Investors Buying in Rural Areas

In 1900, twelve cities worldwide had populations of 1 million people or more. By 2017, approximately 500 cities exceeded 1 million residents. As the balance of the global population has shifted to cities, so have government resources and business capital, causing a widening gap in economic opportunity between urban and rural areas. As far back as 2017, Airbnb was in the news for bringing economic opportunities to rural communities. Chris Lehane, head of global policy for Airbnb, said, "The Airbnb platform is a platform that is supporting the middle class […] it democratizes tourism, brings tourism to places that haven't benefited from it."[11] He says rural Airbnbs are among the company's fastest-growing segments, with many of the most popular rural destinations near national and state parks. These locations are particularly popular among families and millennials searching for less touristy local experiences.

In June 2020, Airbnb launched the Go Near campaign highlighting stays and experiences within easy driving distance of guests' homes. In response to the campaign, stays fewer than fifty miles away from home grew by 31 percent compared with 2019. Summer travel on Airbnb used to be primarily smaller groups visiting big cities. Still, by summer 2021, families flocking to remote destinations from their big-city homes were the most common travelers. In 2015, rural travel accounted for less than 10 percent of nights booked globally on Airbnb; in 2021, it accounted for more than double, and often triple, that in many countries.[12]

Today, rural hosts make up around a quarter of Airbnb hosts in the U.S. As a result, Airbnb needs more supply in outdoorsy destinations to answer the rising searches for "glamping," "cabins near me," and "farm stays." Building on the Go Near campaign playbook, Airbnb then launched "The Greatest Outdoors" campaign, with the goal to showcase more unique places, camping options, and other rural entire-home stays.[13]

Investors Buying in Urban Markets

When you picture a short-term rental hot spot, images of glittering white sandy beaches and warm sunny days may come to mind. We know St. Louis and Omaha, where we're invested, may not be at the top of anyone's vacation list, yet they work great for MTRs. Places with a strong hospital presence, like St. Louis or, for example, Cincinnati, have a solid flow of tenants due to the high volume of traveling medical professionals and patients in town for treatments. Cities provide several opportunities to find renters: work travelers, students, home remodels, and visiting family members, to name a few. While any densely populated city will do, the smaller or third-tier cities still offer affordable home

11 https://www.cnbc.com/2017/06/27/airbnbs-popularity-grows-in-rural-communities.html

12 https://news.airbnb.com/airbnb-hosts-and-eu-policymakers-discuss-future-of-european-travel

13 https://www.rentalscaleup.com/airbnb-rural-areas-hosts/

prices and lots of multifamily inventory, which is good news for investors.

Though rural destinations are having their time in the sun, travelers are also starting to return to cities for more extended periods, and we see opportunities in both spaces.

Investors Buying in Expensive Markets

These days, being an investor has gotten tricky. Prices are through the roof; the competition from buyers of owner-occupied properties who fall in love and will pay *way* over asking is fierce, making profit margins tight. In most cities, the cost of a mortgage has outpaced market-rate rent. What is the typical buy and hold investor to do? Get creative!

When Zeona got into the short-term rental space, she ran the numbers and couldn't understand how long-term rental landlords were ever retiring. It could take fifteen or more rentals to replace a salary. That's a lot of 20 percent down payments to save up for. With short-term rentals, Zeona saw people "retiring" or making enough to be financially independent with one or two places. But now, as short-term rentals continue to be outlawed, especially in urban markets where many people live, MTRs are the next best option.

Investors Who Don't Mind Furnishing (Or Even Like It!)

We see you. You love to decorate. You are always pinning the latest trends and saving DIY ideas on Instagram. But maybe your family doesn't share your flair for color, prints, or themes. Don't worry; we got you. Your furnished rental can be your outlet. Go crazy, be splashy. Create something that people will have to click on to see more of.

Furnishing a unit can be fun! It can also wear you down to a nub. Make sure to plan some self-care and a dependable meal schedule when you embark on this adventure. If design is not your thing, we also got you. We will teach you how to stay within budget and maximize returns with the right pieces. These days, Sarah flies around the country helping investors furnish their MTR properties, so you could even have the opportunity to have a personal visit from Sarah and her team. In Chapter Eleven, Sarah will show you how furnishing can be fun *and* a good investment.

CASE STUDY

Zeona's Non-Warrantable Condo

I found this property unexpectedly. While I was enjoying an extended stay on Maui, I had a friend reach out, saying that she had just broken up with her long-term partner and was thinking about renting or buying a one-bedroom condo to live in. After a quick search, I found a gem. But she didn't bite. Still, the place just kept calling out to me. I thought, "Maybe I'll just buy it and see if she wants to rent it." It was a building I knew intimately. The unit was two doors down from another condo I owned and had lived in for four years. A little old lady used to live there, and I had heard that there were plans to move her to assisted living. After talking with the HOA president, I reminded them I was a real estate agent and would be happy to help them list it if needed. A few months went by, and I completely forgot about it.

In the end, the condo was listed by another agent. I was honestly thrilled that they didn't have me list it, because the agent who they hired helped them complete an entire top-to-bottom renovation, and the place was gorgeous! If you haven't learned this about me yet, I don't like renovating or dealing with contractors more than I have to, so I am more than happy to pay for a move-in ready space that I won't have to do anything to for a decade. Bliss!

The condo was listed at $269,000, and this was early 2021, when houses were selling like hotcakes. The odd thing was that this place had already been sitting for fourteen days; I couldn't believe my eyes. I called the agent to get the scoop and learned that the building had a low number of owner-occupants, which made it "non-warrantable."

DEFINITION Non-Warrantable Condo

When a condo is labeled as non-warrantable, it does not meet conventional guidelines and will not be bought by government-backed entities like Fannie Mae and Freddie Mac. In addition, many lenders consider financing a mortgage for this type of property to be too risky, making it harder to get a loan.

Some companies have their own guidelines as to what is considered warrantable or not, but the most common reasons for a condo to get flagged include:

- The project is new construction and/or has yet to be completed.

- The developer has not turned over control of the HOA to the owners.
- A high percentage of units are occupied by renters.
- The community allows short-term rentals.
- A single person or entity owns more than 10 percent of the total number of units.
- The building owner or developer is involved in litigation of any kind.

Non-warrantable condos are common in Boulder due to the high rental and student population. I like a challenge, so instead of walking away (I didn't have the cash to buy it outright), I started calling. I called tons of banks, getting leads from those who said no, and had my lender, who brokers with over one hundred banks, check into her resources. Only *one* bank on her roster said yes, and we went for it. But it only takes one yes.

This process of finding a financier took about a week, and during that time, another cash investor had snuck in and started lowballing the seller. The seller's estate was being handled by her daughter, who I imagined was going through an emotional time dealing with her mother's dementia and moving her into assisted living, not to mention managing a remodel and now selling this condo. I knew I had to make my offer more personal and heartfelt.

I sat down and thought back over the four years that this woman had been my neighbor. I wrote a letter about times I had stopped to chat, borrowed a cup of sugar, and played drums with her in a class held in our community house. I also knew she had a cat, so I included a photo of me with a cat I had pet sat for in the past. Her daughter loved my letter and accepted my offer of $255,000, $14,000 off, without a counterproposal.

When I was figuring out what to offer, I played around with the numbers in my spreadsheet and knew I needed to get at least an 8 percent cash-on-cash return to make it worthwhile. Why 8 percent? I use 8 percent as my cutoff mark for any investment because you can earn an average of 8 percent, after inflation, from putting your money in index funds. With the tax deductions that real estate provides and the appreciation potential of our market, I knew that if I could at least meet 8 percent, I would come out ahead. A few doors down, the other unit I owned had been renting for $1,650 through the slow winter season, and my spreadsheet said that I needed to rent the new unit for at least $1,910 per month to make my return. It was a stretch, but I had a strong urge to go for it. We would be closing in March, so at least we would be heading into the high-demand (and higher-priced) summer season.

Since I was an agent and already owned in the building, I made it super easy for them. I didn't need to review the HOA documents, so I removed that contingency. I even decided not to have the property inspected, since it had just been through a full remodel—a risk, but we haven't had any issues since. The best part? You still get paid your commission when you purchase as an agent, so I received a check at closing for over $7,000! More than enough for furniture. If you invest in the state you live in and buy even one place a year, I recommend getting your real estate license.

At the same time, I was brokering the sale of an off-market three-bedroom townhome that had been an Airbnb, and the seller needed to offload all her furniture—fast. The timing was perfect. I sent my right-hand agent, Amy Levine (@amysellsboulder on Instagram), over to scope the scene. She tagged all the necessities for a fully furnished one-bedroom apartment, including the requisite furniture, linens, and kitchen items, giving us the majority of the furnishings for under $3,000. My client sold all the rest, and the day of her closing (two weeks before mine), the sellers let us move it all in. We had movers pack it up and haul everything ten minutes down the road to the cute new condo. Over the next ten days, Amy single-handedly set up the entire space and took some photos that I could use to market it while I played virtual conductor from Maui.

In my final stroke of luck, I had a guest renting my apartment two doors down who wanted to extend. I looked at what she had paid Airbnb in total with taxes and fees, and it came out to a little over $2,400 for the month. I said I would let her continue at the other unit for the same price. We wrote up a month-to-month lease, and I had her move in two days after closing. She rented from me for nearly a year until she purchased a condo of her own (using me as her agent, of course!). And the cash-on-cash return after down payment, furnishing, and closing costs? 16.83 percent!

PART 2
Acquisition

You want your property to bring you cash so you can start living a bigger life, right? That is what the goal is for us all. In the acquisition section of this book, we will cover how to acquire a property. By now you already know why the MTR strategy is the right fit for you in your investing. Investing in medium-term rentals starts with these four steps:

- **Step 1:** Finance the property (Chapter Four).
- **Step 2:** Identify a market (Chapter Five).
- **Step 3:** Identify your deal criteria (Chapter Six) and the type of property you are looking for (Chapter Seven).
- **Step 4:** Master deal analysis (Chapter Eight).

Let's dive in.

CHAPTER FOUR
FINANCING THE DEAL

Buy land; they aren't making it anymore.
—MARK TWAIN

Both of us have quit our W-2 jobs, which may be the end goal for some. Yet, Sarah often hears her investor clients worry about how they will finance deals after leaving their W-2 positions.

If you have a good enough deal, you can find a way to fund it.

Banks are more likely to lend you money when you have a steady and stable income. Investors often cite this as their reason for staying in a job longer than they would like. In Chapter Five, we will cover ways to leverage banks, loans, and mortgages, but first we will share creative ways that you can finance the deal if you no longer have a W-2 income. Quitters and wannabe quitters, listen up.

Speaking of a good-enough deal: The added benefit of the MTR strategy is that it creates more rental income for each property. What would typically be a four-unit property that earns $3,200 per month ($800 per unit) as long-term rentals can now earn $7,100 ($1,775 per unit) using the MTR strategy. (We'll explain more about this later in the chapter.) The higher the property's income potential, the more likely someone is to lend you money or partner with you on the deal.

"Six Deals Before Getting a Mortgage" by Zeona

I can only hope that everyone has a great cheerleader in their lives—someone who wants to celebrate your every success, no matter how small, and grieve every hardship with you. My mother was that person for me. She seemed to believe I could do anything I set my mind to and that I should never, not even for a single second, waste energy on something that didn't nourish my soul. As a single mother, she worked herself to the bone so that we could have every opportunity for something better. She was my best friend, and we spoke most days, even when we lived thousands of miles apart. She was everything to me, and then one day, she fell ill.

In the summer of 2014, maintaining my mother's health became a full-time job. She needed help getting to doctor's appointments, and I wanted to give her access to better care, so I moved her out to Colorado to live with me. The only issue? I knew my lifestyle of constantly moving between two condos—the lifestyle that paid my bills—would not provide the stability she needed. For my entire adult life, I dreamed of owning a home (something my mother never got to do), but suddenly, it felt increasingly urgent.

When my mother received an early payout from her life insurance company to fund her care, we finally had a little extra money that we could use toward a down payment. I knew the stairs at both of my apartments would be a challenge for her, so we temporarily rented a guest studio from a former landlord of mine. Someone I'll call Carl.

Carl had been an investor for the past thirty years and was a great inspiration. He was in his seventies but had a youthfulness about him; he biked around town and played volleyball with the college students in the community. Carl seemed to have it all figured out. He owned seventeen condos in the same complex, and his only work was making sure his apartments stayed rented each year.

I heard that Carl had supplied private loans in the past to help budding investors, so I got up the courage to ask for one. No other lender would have given me the time of day. I didn't have a W-2 job, and most of my income was coming from Airbnb rentals, which was not recognized by lenders back in 2014. This was pretty much my only shot. I practiced my speech in the shower, went over all my talking points, and asked Carl if he could chat one afternoon.

Despite feeling extremely nervous, the talk went comically smooth. Carl asked me my income but didn't verify it, and he came up with the terms. We agreed on 20 percent down (I didn't know there was any other option), and a 5 percent interest-only loan. Then we drafted up a promissory note. I quickly chose between two properties and went under contract. The immediacy that I felt in needing to take care of my mom helped me overcome the hurdle of analysis paralysis most first-timers face, and I landed my first deal. That was her parting gift to me.

That was **Deal No. 1.** Since Airbnb income was not recognized by mortgage companies, I had to keep being creative if I wanted to buy more properties. I bought my first six properties without getting a mortgage in my name. Let's dive into the ways I did it.

Deal No. 2, July 2015: A few months after I purchased my first condo, the market went up, and my home appreciated $100,000. I went back to Carl, the same private lender, and asked if he would do a HELOC on that property so I could buy in St. Louis. He agreed. I did an $80,000, 5 percent interest-only loan, with $0 down, and purchased a $72,000 three-bedroom home for short-term rent.

Deal No. 3, November 2015: I told a friend about how I was buying cheap homes in St. Louis and renting them for three times the market rate on Airbnb; he wanted in. He had recently sold a home in Tampa, Florida, and had a chunk of change from the sale. We purchased a $60,000 two-bedroom home in St. Louis in cash. He lent me $30,000 amortized over thirty years at 4 percent. I paid for all the up-front furnishing fees and low closing costs (which are much less when you pay cash).

Deal No. 4, December 2015: When my mom passed away, I received a $250,000 life insurance payout. But that money was supposed to last forever, as it stood in place of my only supportive parent. I was terrified of losing it. I paid off my $144,000 loan on the property from Deal No. 1 so I would have a paid-off place to live and low monthly expenses. Then I used some of the money for furnishing the property from Deal No. 2. For Deal No. 4, I used my cash and brought on a different partner, who was going to pay me half of the sales price plus furnishings and manage the property. This didn't work out (more on this later in the chapter), and I ended up with the property a few years down the road. I paid $52,000 cash for a two-bedroom home in St. Louis.

Deal No. 5, January 2017: A third friend heard that I had bought homes with two other mutual friends, and he wanted to join the party. This friend had a good deal of cash saved up and a long work history at a high-paying job. We used his W-2 income to get a mortgage in his name alone. By this point, prices were going up, and it was challenging to find a "deal." Finally, we purchased a $69,000 one-bedroom single-family home—guess where? St. Louis.

Deal No. 6, March 2018: I got a tip from my friend Palmer that Colorado Springs was undervalued compared to Denver, and people were flocking there. We decided to see what all the hype was about and take an investment-scouting trip. I contacted a client of mine about a trade—I would give him some feedback on his new Airbnb in exchange for letting us stay in it for one night. When he accepted, we hit the road. My friend got a recommendation for an excellent investor-friendly agent, and we lined up eleven showings. In a blur of tours, we found a funky, recently flipped gem. I pitched the idea to a few potential partners that first evening and saw it a second time before heading home. The person who ended up biting was the partner from Deal No. 5. We again did a loan in his name and split closing costs and furniture. I submitted an offer two days later. This one was a negotiating feat (even in a hot market), which went on for five to six weeks. I'll share in detail in Chapter Seven. We purchased a one-bedroom single-family home for $205,000, which felt like an incredible stretch. At that time, it was, by and large, my most expensive purchase!

Not everyone will have a "Carl" in their life or in their contacts list (yet), so in this chapter we will provide multiple financing strategies for both new and experienced investors, including investors with stable W-2 income and those who are self-employed.

Utilizing Leverage Through Loans

There are other loan products that provide options for investors looking to purchase a medium-term rental.

SECOND-HOME LOANS

This loan allows for buyers to put as little as 10 percent down, making this an attractive loan product for investors. This is one of the most common loan types in the short-term and medium-term rental spaces. The second-home loan, sometimes called the "vacation home loan," allows a buyer to purchase a home with a similar rate to a primary, owner-occupant loan while only requiring them to visit the house for fourteen days during the first year after they purchase the property. These loans can be super helpful if you plan to spend those first two weeks furnishing anyway or know you will visit the unit with your family and friends in the off-season. One con is that you must qualify for this loan based on your income and cannot use the potential income produced by the home to qualify.

Some big things about this loan type:

- It has a similar rate to a primary home loan.
- If married or in a business partnership, each partner can get one loan per area.
- Depending on the lender, the home must be 50 to 100 miles from any other primary or secondary residence of yours.
- You can only own one second home in a market, but you can own multiple second homes, meaning an investor could purchase a second home in as many as seven to twelve different markets.

CONVENTIONAL LOANS

Conventional loans are an incredible option for those who qualify. Rates are lower than commercial financing, and most investors can have up to ten conventional loans at one time. In addition, there is a debt-to-income ratio of 50 percent or below for most conventional loans. For Sarah, her properties' rental income is so much higher than the monthly loan payments that she can use that income to qualify and continue to purchase investment properties using conventional loans. Lenders will consider 75 percent of your rental income as additional income, allowing investors to be eligible for more properties using conventional loans.

DEFINITION Debt-to-Income Ratio (DTI)

A lender looks at a borrower's debt-to-income ratio to see how they manage their debt. Simply put, DTI refers to how much debt a consumer has relative to how much income they have. The lender's main interest is in how much of a borrower's monthly gross income coming in must be set aside to pay debts. Debt-to-income is generally expressed as a percentage. For example, a borrower with a monthly income of $4,000 and $2,000 worth of debt (e.g., mortgages, car loans) would have a DTI of 50 percent.

While the credit score requirement for a conventional loan is 620, higher than the FHA credit score requirement of 500 (more on FHA loans below), you do not have to occupy the property. If you want to buy an investment property, you can put 20 or 25 percent down. However, if you want to live in part of the property, you can put as little as 3 percent down as an owner-occupant. For these low-down-payment loans, there is the additional cost of private mortgage insurance (PMI), which scares some investors. However, the PMI drops off automatically when your home has 22 percent equity in it, or you can request an appraisal at 20 percent equity to have your lender remove PMI. When you are running your numbers and analyzing a property, be sure to include the additional cost of PMI in your loan payments. Most deals Sarah is buying earn so much that it is worth paying PMI.

DEFINITION Private Mortgage Insurance (PMI)

PMI is a type of insurance that your mortgage lender may require if your down payment is less than 20 percent of your home's purchase price. PMI protects the lender against losses if you default on your mortgage.

COMMERCIAL LOANS

When coaching new investors, we always recommend that they only have one person on the loan, even if they are married or have a business partner in the deal. Why? Conventional lenders allow an individual to have ten conventional loans at one time. Meaning, once you have ten conventional loans, investors will look at other lending options such as commercial loans or portfolio loans.

Here are some differences with commercial real estate loans.[14]

- Commercial real estate loans are usually made to business entities (corporations, developers, limited partnerships, funds, and trusts).
- Commercial loans typically range from five years or fewer to twenty years, with the amortization period often longer than the loan term.
- Commercial loan-to-value ratios generally fall into the 65–80 percent range.

DEFINITION Amortization Period

The amortization period represents the amount of time it will take to pay off a loan with regular payments at a set interest rate. If the period is longer than the loan term, you are paying more in interest, which is another way for banks to charge you fees instead of points.

---

14 Jean Folger, "Commercial Real Estate Loan," Investopedia, updated November 30, 2021, https://www.investopedia.com/articles/personal-finance/100314/commercial-real-estate-loans.asp.

DEBT SERVICE COVERAGE RATIO (DSCR) LOANS

Debt service coverage ratio (DSCR) loans have been all the rage recently; in essence, they allow investors to qualify for a loan based on the cash flow potential of their identified rental property. These loans work well for those who are self-employed and may not have two years of income to show on their tax returns. Instead of being based solely on the borrower's income history, DSCR loans focus on their debt-to-income ratio, after factoring in the new property's earning potential.

PORTFOLIO LOANS

A portfolio loan may be a solid alternative for those having difficulty qualifying for a conventional or government loan. These loan products are held by the originating bank rather than sold on the secondary market. In other words, while many lenders sell your loan to government-backed institutions like Fannie Mae and Freddie Mac, portfolio loans are kept by the lender for the lifetime of the loan. This allows for a more flexible, customized experience. Benefits for the borrower include:

- Loan size does not have to be within conforming loan limits.
- Minimum down payment amount is determined by the lender.
- PMI may not be required, regardless of the down payment amount.

203(K) FHA RENOVATION LOAN

Listen up, value-add investors: This is the loan product for you! The 203(k) loan is a type of FHA home renovation loan that lets borrowers bundle the cost of the home AND the renovation into one. This allows you to pay off home updates, amortized over thirty years—essentially financing your property based on its future value. Some 203(k) loan benefits include:

- It can be used for total or partial renovation projects.
- Repairs happen within a designated timeline after closing on the loan.
- The loan is based on the after-repair value (ARV).
- Only the low 3.5 percent FHA down payment is required.
- It can be used for a refinance or a purchase.

HELOC

A HELOC, or home equity line of credit, is a credit line that you establish at a bank (not with your mortgage broker) that gives you access to 75–80 percent of the equity of your home. This equity can be earned through appreciation or debt pay down from monthly payments and can be accessed instantly once you have established the line of credit. They function similarly to credit cards in that you can access and utilize the funds as you choose—up to a specific limit and within a certain time frame. HELOCs are every investor's favorite piggy bank: You can use the funds for home improvements, to pay down your credit cards, or even for a down payment on your next property.

The main benefit of a HELOC over a refinance is the ability to take out only the amount you need and not pay interest on unused capital. Because you must pay closing costs with a refinance, investors feel the need to pull out all available capital, even if they don't have an income-earning place to put it.

CASH-OUT REFINANCE

A cash-out refinance is a type of mortgage refinancing that allows you to take on a larger mortgage to access the equity in your home. Unlike a second mortgage, a cash-out refinance doesn't add to your monthly payment but rather the length of the loan. Once you pay off your old mortgage, you begin to pay off your new one.

Here are the requirements for approval.

- You need to have equity in your home to capitalize on this refinance. Your lender won't allow you to cash out all the equity in your home (unless you qualify for a Veteran Affairs or VA refinance. We will talk more on VA loans later in the chapter). Before pursuing this route, we recommend carefully looking at your home's equity to ensure you can cash out enough to accomplish your goals.
- You typically need a credit score of 620 or higher.
- You will also need a DTI ratio of less than 50 percent.

CASE STUDY

"The Power of Seller Financing" by Grace Gudenkauf

Creative financing is one of the most misunderstood concepts in real estate. Yet it is easily one of the most powerful. When I started investing in 2021, I knew I wanted to learn creative financing to scale my portfolio quickly with little of my own money (because I didn't have much!). That same year, I bought four creative deals. I put $0 down on three homes, and the fourth was just a $3,500 down payment to catch the seller's mortgage up to current.

The biggest key to creative finance is understanding that you target *distressed sellers* rather than the traditional *distressed properties*. This means that a home that might not hold any profit potential under the classic BRRRR or fix-and-flip method could be a great deal if bought on terms. Let me show you what I mean.

DEFINITION Fix-and-Flip

The fix-and-flip method is when an investor purchases a property with the intention of making repairs and renovations, and then selling the property. Unlike the BRRRR strategy and the buy-and-hold method, the investor knows they will sell the improved property to another investor or a homeowner—they have no intention of renting it out.

I purchased a property in a C-class neighborhood, a neighborhood I would not usually invest in. Because I used seller financing with a $0 down payment, I only had to pay the closing costs. I became the owner for approximately $2,500 of capital, and I then turned around and sold it on rent to own (RTO).

DEFINITION Rent to Own (RTO)

Rent to own (RTO) is a type of seller financing where, typically, the buyer is a tenant and the seller is an investor. In RTO financing, an investor sells a property to their tenant and carries the loan like a bank.

With the RTO strategy, I won't have to manage the property, so I was okay with buying in this neighborhood.

I bought another adorable turnkey house with a wrap mortgage. Wrap mortgage is referring to a seller financing deal where the buyer takes over the seller's existing debt. They essentially wrap a new mortgage around the existing mortgage, which is how it gets its name: wrap mortgage. The difference between seller finance and wrap mortgage is that seller finance is with a free and clear property. A wrap mortgage is for a property that has existing debt.

The seller was moving in with her boyfriend and was flexible in getting paid over time. She had owned the home for less than a year, and she knew she wouldn't make any money selling her house on the market after the second round of closing costs and Realtor fees. I would never have paid cash for this property, as my typical purchases are value-add so that I can pull out my capital and use it on the next house. But since I bought this turnkey rental on terms with very little money, I didn't have to worry about how I would get my capital out (because I had so little in the deal anyway!). Once the tenant moves, I will furnish it and list it as a medium-term rental. I'll make all my capital back in less than a year of owning this rental. And with zero rehab costs!

You might be wondering: Who the heck would sell their home on terms for no money down and at no interest?

The answer: plenty of people!

A few situations where someone would be interested in this would be those who:

- Are behind on their mortgage payments.
- Have already moved out of town.
- Don't have money to make repairs to get the home market-ready.
- Don't want photos of their home on the internet.
- Want an "as-is" sale.
- Want a flexible closing time.
- Want a better purchase price.

We can accomplish all of these things when we buy homes with creative financing! The best thing you can do is to truly listen to every seller to understand what their issue is and how you can solve it. Most of the time, it's deeper than "just wanting to sell." Keep your ears open and your creative juices flowing!

How Do I Buy on Terms?

When buying on terms, there are four deal points that you will need to understand. In order of most important to least important, they are:

1. Down payment
2. Monthly payment
3. Term length
4. Purchase price

You might be thinking, "What? Purchase price is the most important!" But this is where I invite you to think a little deeper.

If a seller is willing to give you ten years to pay off a property at zero percent with no down payment, couldn't you pay a little more? Yes, you can. And in fact, I did! I paid almost double what the previous investor offered on a home that I bought with seller financing. And I'm still earning nearly $750 a month on this single-family rental. It's a huge win-win for the seller *and* me. They are almost doubling their money by being flexible and waiting to be paid out over time. They were a busy young family who unexpectedly inherited a home, and they did not have the time or money to get the property market ready. We bought it as-is and paid their closing costs too. And guess what? This couple was ecstatic about the sale.

Tips for Negotiating Creative Financing

When discussing your monthly payment, many sellers will want to know what interest rate you are going to pay them. My favorite line is, "Let's talk dollar amount instead of interest rates. In the end, the numbers are the same, so let's keep it simple." I always tell my sellers that I will give a higher price at 100 percent principal payments (aka zero percent interest), which would, in the end, be the same payout as a lower price *with* interest. Of course, the numbers aren't going to be the same (I want to get a good deal), but you get the idea. You will be surprised how well sellers respond to this. The average homeowner doesn't understand amortization tables, interest-only payments, and how to calculate interest in the first place. Often, they are more than happy to keep the discussion on actual dollar amounts. I took over a seller's mortgage on another deal I did, and we decided on $0 down. Instead of asking about interest, I asked her what she would like for a monthly payment. We decided I would pay her another $150 per month on top of the original mortgage payment. I did let her know that this would chip away at the purchase price on my end (the payment is 100 percent principal), but she was happy to get an extra $150 early every month instead of waiting the whole five-year term.

What This Means for You

At the end of the day, we, as investors, are problem solvers. And creative financing is a problem-solving tool that you can add to your toolbox. Too often, we encounter one roadblock, and we let ourselves give up on a deal. The beauty of creative financing is that it encourages you to keep finding solutions until the deal makes sense. Instead of looking at a transaction as black and white, take a step back and look at the whole picture. What can you do to help the seller and, in turn, help yourself? Do they physically need help moving? Do they need you to be the peace negotiator between them and their siblings? Do they need to be able to leave all the furniture they don't want behind? I have done all of these things to get a deal done!

More on Grace's journey through real estate entrepreneurship on Instagram @grace.investing.

FHA, VA, AND LESSER-KNOWN LOAN PRODUCTS
FHA (Federal Housing Administration) Loan
There is an owner-occupied loan product called the FHA loan. Named the FHA loan because the Federal Housing Administration insures the loan, it is an excellent option for those looking to use the MTR strategy in their home market. You can live in the property and put down as little as 3.5 percent. This allows investors to purchase properties at a higher price because their money goes further. This is exactly what Sarah did with a fourplex in Omaha, Nebraska. Yes, buyers can use an FHA loan on a single-family or a two- to four-unit property, as long as they occupy the property. It is an owner-occupied loan, after all. Keep in mind that the FHA loan does require a strict inspection, so this is not a loan option on a property that does not meet FHA standards.

However, we recommend using the FHA loan on a duplex or triplex. You can live in one unit and rent the others utilizing the MTR strategy while putting only 3.5 percent down.

FHA loans can be helpful for buyers with limited savings or lower credit scores because the minimum credit score requirement is 500, whereas the other owner-occupied conventional loan products require a 620 score or higher.

VA Loan
The VA loan is offered to veterans or those enlisted in the United States military. This is a 0-percent-down product. Yes, you heard that right, $0 down. Of course, this makes your mortgage higher, but if you intend to combine it with house hacking, your cash-on-cash return can be infinite. In addition, this is an owner-occupied loan, meaning you must live in the home yourself for at least a year.

While there is no official maximum loan limit, lenders usually won't make a no-down-payment loan larger than $417,000 or $647,000 in Alaska, Hawaii, Guam, and the U.S. Virgin Islands. In addition, a person can only qualify for one VA loan, although the Navy Federal Credit Union offers a similar product, allowing veterans to get a second $0-down loan.

One con with these loans is that, similar to an FHA loan, there is a strict inspection at the time of appraisal, requiring certain items to be repaired before the loan can be issued. It can be challenging to find a seller willing to make the repairs in a seller's market, especially with competing offers not requiring that same stipulation. In general, when someone is putting $0 down, they may also be tight on cash and not willing or not able to complete the repairs on their end either. This can make these loans more complicated to get as a buyer, but not impossible.

Physician Loans

Did you know there are loan programs designed specifically with doctors in mind? Physician loans are a unique home loan option for doctors that can help them buy a house before they otherwise could.

Like a VA loan, this is an owner-occupied loan product. It often has zero down payment required with no PMI. Physician loans are meant for new medical professionals just entering the field. While a doctor's high student loan debt would often make it difficult for them to get a loan, this product looks less at their debt and more at their high income or income potential.

While these, unfortunately, do not extend to nurses, some lenders offer loan programs for other medical professionals such as dentists, orthodontists, chiropractors, and veterinarians.

Young Professionals Loan

The mortgage company that Zeona is a partner in offers this unique loan product. It was designed for professionals who come out of school with good incomes but little cash. It is another excellent owner-occupied loan that can be used with the house hacking strategy. The young professional loan:

- Is 100 percent loan to value (or zero percent down).
- Is a fixed-rate loan amortized over fifteen or twenty years.
- Allows funds gifted from family.
- Requires a credit score of 700 or higher.

CASE STUDY

"Delayed Financing and the BRRRRnB Strategy" by Shelby Osborne, *BiggerPockets Real Estate Podcast* No. 406

My favorite strategy is the BRRRRnB. Never heard of it? It's when you combine a BRRRR and an Airbnb (or any short- or medium-term rental). It takes two of the most effective strategies in real estate and creates a "best of both worlds" scenario. You recycle funds to grow your portfolio quickly *and* increase your revenue ... win-win!

Since this is a section on financing, I'll explain an additional layer I add to my BRRRRnBs to speed up the process. It's called delayed financing.

Delayed financing is, quite literally, when your financing is delayed. For example, instead of purchasing the property using a loan, you initially purchase using cash or a form of cash and delay the financing until after the renovations are complete.

Why? Delayed financing allows you to circumvent the standard six-month seasoning period with a traditional BRRRR.

DEFINITION Six-Month Seasoning Requirement

Fannie Mae guidelines require six months of "seasoning," or on-time consecutive payments, on a home (regardless of type) before the loan is eligible for a cash-out refinance. They will also require a minimum of 20 percent equity to be left in the home.

You refinance (or rather, finance) the property as soon as the renovations are complete, regardless of the seasoning period and/or having a tenant in place. This allows you to establish a new loan at 75 percent loan-to-value (LTV) or the total cost you put into the project as shown on the closing disclosure (whichever is less), which is why you need to include all costs associated with the project on the initial closing disclosure.

DEFINITION Loan-to-Value (LTV)

Banks use loan-to-value as a way to determine how much they are willing to lend on a property. It is a ratio, usually expressed as a percentage, that dictates the amount a bank will require a buyer to put in a down payment. The higher the LTV, the more risk the bank is taking on and more expensive the loan product might be for a buyer. If an investor buys a home for $100,000 with a $20,000 down payment, their LTV is 80 percent, since the bank is financing 80 percent of the purchase.

I'll use a real-life scenario.
- **Deal:** Courthouse foreclosure in Fayetteville, North Carolina
- Initial closing disclosure (acquisition) included:
- **Purchase price:** $52,129.71
- **Renovations:** $14,000
- **B and B furnishing/setup:** $8,000
- **Additional closings costs:** $2,347.20
- **All-in at initial closing (with attorney fees, etc.):** $76,476.91
- **Funding source:** Line of credit (form of "cash"; no lien against the property)

At this point, I closed with all costs associated documented on my closing disclosure and had cut the checks for renovation and furnishing/setup to my contractor and my Airbnb designer so they could immediately get started on the project.

Note: *If you don't have a solid relationship with your vendors, you can have the attorney set up a draw schedule or keep the checks yourself until the work is complete.*

In a month, the project was complete, and I began the delayed financing process to pull out everything I put into the project and recycle the funds into the next one.

- **Appraised Value:** $110,000
- **Loan Amount:** $76,476.91 established thirty-year fixed loan (again, you cannot pull out more than is documented on the closing disclosure)

Then I used the funds received from the new loan to pay off my line of credit and use it again on the next project.

How's the property performing, you ask? Like any short- or medium-term rental, it depends on the month. However, it usually looks like this.

- **Income:** $2,000–$3,000 per month
- **Mortgage payment:** $600 per month
- **Monthly expenses:** $400–$500
- **Cash flow:** $1,000–$2,000 per month

And that's it, folks! The BRRRRnB strategy in action.

Learn more on Instagram @realtestatewithshelby.

Private Money

Private money and hard money are often used interchangeably, but they are not the same thing. In short, a private lender is an individual. Sarah likes to call it "your rich uncle." What we love about private money is that the terms are negotiable. Unlike a federally backed loan, private lenders have no rules, regulations, or guidelines that they are obligated to follow. Everything is negotiable. Some lenders may require points paid up front, while others may not. The loan terms, including the interest rate and term length, are all up for negotiation. A private lender may require interest-only payments each month, each quarter, or even at the end of the term period.

HARD MONEY LOANS

Hard money is more regulated and set in stone. Hard-money lenders can be private investors, but often they are companies that lend to investors. Thus, their term may not be as negotiable as a private money lender. Some hard-money lenders now also offer thirty-year products. Sarah has used a hard-money lender to refinance a property with a 3.875 percent interest rate when she could not qualify for a conventional loan. As a result, she quit her W-2 just before refinancing a BRRRR. The thirty-year product allowed her to stay on track.

DEFINITION Points

"Points" is a lending term that simply means a fee paid. Not all lenders require this, but many do.

Sarah King, the investing genius behind the Instagram @nerdsguidetofi, often uses private money to fund the down payment on value-add rental properties she purchases. She has a lender who allows her to pay all the interest at the end, when she returns the principal. King has also borrowed money from a private lender who requires her to pay the interest on a monthly basis. These are just two examples of how you can negotiate different terms.

Documentation can be an individual guarantee, a promissory note, and a mortgage. At the same time, some lenders do not require all three. Others will ask that they be put as a second lienholder on the property, and others are satisfied with a single promissory note.

The critical thing to remember is that all is up for negotiation. You do not have to offer 12 percent interest to all lenders. Some are happy to receive 6 percent interest on their borrowed money. If you are one of these lenders, call us!

CASE STUDY

"Getting Creative with Private Money" by Sarah King

It was the time to be creative, and I was starting to be good at it.

Sarah Weaver hooked me on the medium-term rental strategy. After hearing about the strategy at her retreat I attended, it made me focus on getting my cash flow up. Cash flowing $200 per door is excellent for slow and steady long-term wealth-building, but I realized I could pivot the same properties to MTRs and get $800 to $1,000 per door if I adjusted my investment market.

Before I take you through a deep dive on my first MTR (which I purchased specially for MTR, for $130,000 to bring in $4,200 per month in rent!), let's take it from the beginning—when I first used private money and became hooked.

It was the spring of 2020, and I had just filed for divorce. You may be thinking this is a weird place to start, but divorce touches so many people's lives. After finding the strength to leave a toxic marriage, I starter a newer, happier chapter. As you can imagine, though, I had no money. What does one do when they have minimal cash, no prospect of that changing in the near future, and experience self-managing four units? I swallowed my fear and any misplaced pride, and I started to ask for private money.

I like to be the most prepared person in the room, so here is what I brought to my pitch.

1. Personal financial statement (net worth statement)
2. Rent roll of current properties (which were all to be sold)
3. Rent comps
4. Deal analysis on my target property (cash flow, NOI, cap rate, CoC)
5. Credit score (almost 800!)

I received verbal offers from two individuals—one family member and one friend from Instagram. The Instagram friend's hard-money rate was 10 percent with 2 points. Appalled at this rate, my family locked me in at 4.5 percent for one year of interest-only monthly payments, with a balloon payment due at the end of that year. We wrote it all up using a promissory note template I got from another investor friend on Instagram and did not record the note, as the private-money lender was agreeable to not.

What could I have done better? I would later learn that some people do not make monthly payments to their private-money lenders and instead pay back the principal and all interest at the end of the term. I was so used to banks structuring their money in monthly payments that I didn't think twice about it until my friend Sarah noted that there are other ways to do it. In the world of private money, everything is, in fact, negotiable.

I bought my first house hack for $280,000 and offered all cash. Yes, my first private-money deal ever involved me getting $280,000 in cash. Once I learned the power of an all-cash offer, I was hooked on private money. We would do two more duplexes together. But soon it was time to find more money sources.

For my MTR, it was time to branch out into other private-money sources. This is where, as cliché as it sounds, your network is your net worth. How did I build my network with people who ultimately *love* to lend me money? Instagram. I build relationships using the "know, like, and trust" factor. There are more people out there than you think who have money they would be willing to lend, but you must be credible and take action to ask for it.

I put together a formal presentation using Google Slides for this MTR private-money pitch. I already had the property under contract, but I should clarify I don't think that is necessary. However, it *is* necessary to know your market and where you plan to buy.

Here is what I included in my pitch:

- **My experience:** number of deals, private-money experience, doors managed
- **The property details:** beds, baths, square footage, list price, deal source (the MLS!)
- **The financials:** purchase price, down payment needed, rehab costs, furnishing costs, ARV, timeline
- **The numbers:** 1 percent rule, cap rate, CoC, NOI, and cash flow
- **The market:** Furnished Finder screenshot with comps circled and several slides with full screenshots of comps used to set MTR rents
- **The ask:** amount of money requested, interest rate, timeline/term
- **The details:** All terms that would be laid out in the promissory note, with a link to the promissory note

I always buy when the deal makes sense and ignore the market, media, and my relatives all trying to push an impending sense of doom. If the numbers work, I buy. If the numbers ever stop making sense in my target market, I will find a new market. For me, the deal needs to work as a long-term rental if the market changes. I run the numbers, and I do my homework.

Significant changes are happening in health care right now, and burnout is high. Travel nurses are in high demand. People think you have to live in cities to do medium-term rentals, but I don't find that to be true. There are travel nurses at smaller hospitals or urgent care facilities. I hear people say, "Well, I went on Airbnb or Furnished Finder, and there were only two properties. Clearly, I'm not in a good market for medium-term rentals." But why write off a strategy before doing your homework? In my area, for example, there was not an overwhelming number of MTRs. But I started networking and talking to the people who had listings, and it turns out there is a shortage, and they have next-to-no vacancy. So, before you write off a strategy, do your homework! Send some emails and make some calls. The population of my current town is 3,575, and there is an MTR shortage. Local market data and research are critical!

As an investor, it is also important to work smarter not harder. I saw many people, like Sarah and Zeona, doing short-term and medium-term rentals on Instagram, so I started reaching out and networking with them. I gathered information on what systems I needed to be more success-ful out of the gate. For example, I stressed constantly about forgetting to buy something critical for the unit. I then changed to shopping with Sarah Weaver's furnishing list, and it was such an anxiety eliminator.

Finally, it is important for investors to keep networking with lenders. Get to know both conventional and portfolio loan lenders. Shop *small* and shop *local*. If you bank with a big national bank, rethink that. Relationships matter when it comes to lending. Trust matters. So start building it. And start your LLC immediately, so you are eligible for portfolio lending options in two years. Even if you don't end up using commercial or portfolio lend-ing, it's good to have options. When I work on funding deals now, I have an array of lenders and private money to choose from. And that has been the secret sauce to scaling faster.

Follow along with Sarah's MTR journey on Instagram @nerdsguidetofi.

PARTNERSHIPS

Another option for those who either lack capital or are not lendable is partner-ships. You, as an investor, can bring in an equity partner to fund the deal. Similar to private money, everything is negotiable. Some equity partners may fund the entire down payment, up-front renovations, and closing costs, while others may ask that you bring some money to the deal as well.

Sarah has done both. She purchased a fourplex in Omaha, Nebraska, with a partner. Sarah's partner, Mary, took out the loan in her name and paid the down payment because she could not accept funds from an outside party for the down payment. After closing, however, both Sarah and Mary split costs—as well as management duties—50/50 from then on. They decided to furnish three of the four units and rent those units to traveling nurses. The other is an inherited tenant who is, at the time of writing, three months behind on paying rent.

Sarah and Mary tell themselves that they are earning their PhDs in real estate and see the eviction process as a learning opportunity rather than a huge setback. The power of mindset is essential as you invest in real estate, especially initially. It is not a matter of "if" you will need to evict a tenant but rather a matter of "when." We cannot stress enough the importance of a powerfully positive mindset.

The property brings in $1,875 per furnished unit, bringing their rental income to $7,500 against a monthly payment of $2,003. The power of the MTR strategy with small multifamily is incredible. Each of the four units would rent for $750 if unfurnished and rented to long-term tenants.

- **Purchase price**: $328,000
- **Annual Property Taxes**: $4,001
- **Annual Insurance**: $1,699
- **Monthly Rental Income**: $7,500 ($1,875 per unit)

An investor-friendly agent found this fourplex off-market. While Mary and Sarah agreed to split both costs and duties 50/50, and then cash flow and equity 50/50, this is not the only way.

Sarah is currently under contract on a duplex in Urbandale, Iowa, a suburb of Des Moines. Sarah is using a different equity partner on this deal. Her terms with him are different. Because she found and will manage the deal, Sarah will bring no money to the closing table. Her partner is acting more like a silent partner. The partner will obtain the loan and pay the down payment, closing costs, and up-front renovations; Sarah brings the hustle without having to bring any capital. Sarah's partner receives 50/50 on equity and 50/50 on cash flow.

Zeona calls this "hustle equity." With hustle equity, one partner does the work—either they find the deal, analyze the deal, manage the deal, or sometimes all three—while the other partner secures the loan and finances most (or all) of the down payment.

In 2021, Zeona leaned into partnerships, and she has been carrying on with that theme through 2022. Not only did she purchase a home with a partner but she also partnered on the *Invest2FI* podcast, this book, all her real estate sales (with a referral agent team she built nationwide), a monthly meetup event, a Facebook Group, and a mortgage branch. This girl is busy! We mention all that just to illustrate that partnerships can come in many forms and span many ventures. In short, you are only limited by the terms you can dream up!

As previously discussed, Zeona has purchased seven homes with five partners over the years. Let's go into the partnership breakdowns in depth so you can see all the terms available for negotiation.

#1. Purchase Price: $60,000

Found On: MLS
Method of Payment: Cash

Partner's Value:	Zeona's Value:	Splits:
• Silent equity partner (lets Zeona manage the home in peace) • Full $60,000 in cash • Lending $30,000 amortized over 30 years at 3% • Flew out to help move, furnish	• Found the deal, negotiated, got under contract • Paid inspection, closing costs • Paid for furnishings • Lead on design • Sole manager of the property	• Expenses: 50/50 • Equity: 60/40 • Profit: 60/40 (accounting for 20% management fee to Zeona)

#2. Purchase Price: $52,000*

Found On: MLS
Method of Payment: Cash

Partner's Value:	Zeona's Value:	Splits:
• $10,000 down payment • Manager of the property, with a little coaching from Zeona • Flew out to help move, furnish • Reimburse for 50% of furnishings	• Full $52,000 in cash • Lending $26,000 amortized over 30 years at 4% • Found the deal, negotiated, got under contract • Paid inspection, closing costs • Paid 100% of furnishings • Lead on design	• Expenses: 50/50 • Equity: 50/50 • Profit: 50/50

As you will learn in the case study below, this deal did not work out like this, but this was the original negotiated structure.

#3. Purchase Price: $69,000

Found On: MLS
Method of Payment: Mortgage

Partner's Value:	Zeona's Value:	Splits:
• 50% down payment, closing costs • Got the mortgage in their name • Flew out to help furnish • Paid for 50% of furnishings	• Found the deal, negotiated, got under contract • 50% down payment, closing costs • Paid for 50% of furnishings • Lead on design • Sole manager of the property	• Expenses: 50/50 • Equity: 50/50 • Profit: 50/50

#4. Purchase Price: $205,000

Found On: MLS
Method of Payment: Mortgage

Partner's Value:	Zeona's Value:	Splits:
• Majority of down payment, closing costs • Got the mortgage in their name • Drove out to help furnish	• $10,000 cash toward down payment • Lent Zeona $23,000 toward down payment, closing costs, amortized over 30 years at 4% • Found the deal, negotiated, got under contract • Paid for inspection • Paid for 100% of furnishings up front (later split 50/50) • Lead on design	• Expenses: 50/50 • Equity: 50/50 • Profit: 60/40

#5. Purchase Price: $650,000

Found On: Off market, home next door to rental
Method of Payment: Mortgage

Partner's Value:	Zeona's Value:	Splits:
• Market knowledge • Experience owning in market • Found the property undervalued, off market • Coordinated furnishing • Coordinated remodel • 50% remodel/furnishing • Managing property • Paid for inspection • Drove out to video tour the property	• Got the mortgage in her name • Found an agent to coordinate the paperwork • 100% of down payment and closing costs through 1031 exchange • 50% remodel/furnishing	• Expenses: 50/50 • Equity: 50/50 • Profit: 50/50

#6. Purchase Price: $440,000

Found On: MLS
Method of Payment: Mortgage

Partner's Value:	Zeona's Value:	Splits:
• 100% down payment, $0 interest for 3 months, then repaid • Split furnishings & cost of furnishing help 50/50 • Mortgage in his name	• 50% furnishing/down payment • Found the deal, negotiated, got under contract • Flew out to furnish the home with hired help	• Expenses: 50/50 • Equity: 50/50 • Profit: 60/40

#7. Purchase Price: $277,020

Found On: MLS
Method of Payment: Mortgage

Partner's Value:	Zeona's Value:	Splits:
• 50% down payment, closing costs (this is Zeona's fiancé. She owed him money back from a loan, so she put him in this deal instead) • Paid for 50% of furnishings + help	• Found the deal, negotiated, got under contract • Fronted 100% down payment through 1031 exchange, closing costs • Mortgage in her name • Paid for 50% of furnishings + help • Lead on design • Manages the property	• Expenses: 50/50 • Equity: 50/50 • Profit: 50/50

CASE STUDY

Zeona's Epic Partnership Fail: A Lesson on Contracts

It was the fall of 2015, and I was still on a high, returning from St. Louis with Property No. 2 in the can: furnished and fully rented out. My excitement was infectious, and I already had a friend interested in partnering on my next deal! One day, I stepped into a deli to grab lunch when I ran into an acquaintance who I had coached a few months back on turning his first investment into an Airbnb. Let's call him Keith.

As Keith and I were catching up, I was bursting about my recent success and told him how I was already looking to acquire the next one with our mutual acquaintance. He said he would love to partner on a deal, too, and that he had $10,000 he could provide up front, with more on the way.

Even though my last buy was $72,000, I had my eye on two-bedroom properties (instead of three) in the $60,000 range. I had $50,000 in the bank, but because it was the last of the life insurance money I had received from my mother's passing, I felt a huge responsibility not to squander it. Even though I had not relied on my mother financially for some time, the money held an incredible weight once that safety net was gone. It essentially had to provide for me for the rest of my life. Oh yeah, no pressure. A partnership seemed like a good option so I could keep the additional $25,000 as a reserve.

Keith and I made an informal handshake deal, and I was off on the hunt to identify properties. In the days leading up to the purchase, we had a few discussions to hash out the details of the ownership split: who would manage the property, profit share, etc. We detailed a partnership agreement and a promissory note—one he conveniently never got around to signing.

I quickly found two homes (three minutes from each other), and I coordinated the closings to be the same week. Why fly out to St. Louis to furnish twice, right? It will be easier to do two at the same time, right?

Since both were to be cash closings, Keith and I were able to close quickly in just fourteen days. Inspections flew by without major issues, and we were booking our flights. However, as our travel dates neared, a hiccup with the title gave us an unknown settlement date. Instead of letting this ground us, I had a genius idea to take the risk and rent the property from the owner (then furnish and put it on Airbnb for short-term rent) in the hopes it would eventually clear. We rented the home for two months for $420 total and made over $1,600 the first month and $1,700 the second! It finally closed at the end of the year.

Since I was the most flexible party and wanted to hit the ground running, I flew out early and stayed late, totaling a grueling two weeks of nonstop, sixteen-hour days—shopping, furnishing, and fixing—that almost broke me. Up until this point, I had paid for all the inspections, and when we landed in St. Louis, Keith decided it would be "easier" accounting-wise if I just covered all the furnishings (around $4,000). I took the bait. When it came time to close, without warning, he pulled the rug out from under me and told me that he didn't have the $10,000 he had initially promised.

This put me in an uncomfortable position. I scraped together all the cash I had to pay the entire $52,000 purchase price, on top of all the inspections, closing costs, and furnishings. Keith assured me not to worry; the money was on the way.

Luckily, the home was off to a great start and rented well and steadily. He was doing a decent job managing with my guidance, and I was free to manage the rest of the homes in my portfolio. I followed up with him regularly, but he always conveniently had an excuse as to why he didn't have the money. I knew his Airbnb property had experienced an 18 percent equity gain, as had everything in Boulder at that time, and he was talking about selling it, so I set him up with an agent and nudged him down that path. I was hoping that he would finally come up with not only the $10,000 but also pay back the entire $28,000 to pay for his half of the house plus up-front costs. I was looking forward to building my emergency fund back up.

Months went by, and I decided to check in with my friend who was the Realtor selling Keith's home to see how it was progressing. She was surprised to hear from me because it had sold *three months prior*. What?! Of course, I had not heard a peep from Keith, despite him guaranteeing I would be reimbursed. When I confronted him, he made more excuses about having to give money to his family. It got heated. At this point, it had been a year since we purchased the home, and this influx of funds seemed like my last opportunity to get a large chunk of money from him. To add insult to injury, he said I wouldn't understand because "I had money." Although I had busted my tail to create a successful business, I did not come from money, and now, with my mother gone and my father never being a support, I no longer had a safety net and felt the strain of its absence.

I told him that I could no longer honor his 50 percent ownership of the home if he was never planning to put a dime into it. When he refused to give me control of the listing and management, I had to get creative.

First, I gathered the paperwork to change the name on the deed to remove him, which was surprisingly easy. Next, I went to Airbnb to get them to remove his listing, which they wouldn't do, even with my documentation. Instead, I created a new, duplicate listing and, when the next guest checked out, I got the handyman to go in and change the door code. Extreme, I know. But it worked. I let him know, and at this point, he was forced to give up, cancel his remaining bookings (which I offered to honor), and take the listing down—a short moment of relief.

I should have known this wasn't the last I would hear of him. A month or two later, I received an email from his lawyer. He was going to sue me for half ownership of a home he never paid into. Really? I didn't think he had a case, but I also didn't have a lawyer, and I was terrified of losing a home that I'd invested nearly $60,000 into. Over the next two months, I enlisted the best law firm in Boulder, and while I agonized and stressed, my lawyer assured me that it would all be fine. I spent countless hours poring over emails to gather any proof or documentation. It was terrible, and yet I knew I had to do everything in my power to save this.

In the end, I was able to deduct much of the last year of profit in maintenance, startup costs, operating expenses, etc. I only ended up shelling out $2,000 to him as a concession for management help. With a bruised ego, I bitterly handed it over, upset that he ever got a cent but grateful beyond words that the home was 100 percent mine and no one could take that away from me now. I knew this home was a great deal, and it was an incredible waste for him to have burned the bridge of our relationship and partnership, on top of losing the income stream. This home consistently profited over $10,000 per year, and in 2021, I sold it for $100,000—nearly double its purchase price.

The takeaways I want to share:

1. **Always have everything in writing.** Contracts are essential. Make sure they are signed. I was lucky to be able to use the promissory note, even though he neglected to sign it, but in the future, I will make sure to have everything signed before moving forward.

2. **Partnerships are great—you just have to pick the right partner.** Don't let this story tarnish your desire to work with friends. Throughout this process, many people wanted to say, "You can't do business with friends." I don't believe it. I now own five homes with friends, and we have easy, positive communication between us. Partnerships can make the stress, responsibility, and weight of investing shared and therefore easier to bear.

CHAPTER FIVE

MARKET CRITERIA: IS YOUR LOCATION RIGHT FOR MTRS?

*Success is not the absence of failure;
it's the persistence through failure.*
—AISHA TYLER

This chapter will cover how to know if a market is a good fit for the medium-term rental strategy. Nearly any market can utilize MTRs, but, as with any investing strategy, some markets are better than others.

Analyzing a Market for Medium-Term vs. Long-Term Rentals

Keep in mind that both of us analyze and purchase properties out-of-state and often sight unseen. The amazing tools and information available online allow us to do all of this remotely, from anywhere in the world. At this very moment, Sarah is writing from San Pancho, Mexico, and Zeona is writing from the south of France. To find data on a region and to get a sense of the area, we use a number of resources, including www.city-data.com, AirDNA, Google Street View, and Furnished Finder.

When analyzing a long-term and medium-term rental, we look at six metrics.
1. Population growth
2. Job growth
3. Wage and income growth
4. Rental rates
5. Home values
6. Crime rate

POPULATION GROWTH

As a general rule, we want to see a population growth of 20 percent over the most recent ten-year period in a market. Cities with population decreases over the past decade tend to have lower rents and higher vacancies, making them less attractive to invest in. When investing, we want to ensure our properties will be fully occupied and investing in the right market can help ensure that.

We have noticed that population growth as a sole metric is becoming less and less reliable. We are seeing two things happen in the United States. First, there have been massive migration shifts, with hundreds of thousands migrating to states such as Texas or Florida, where there is no income tax. Second, we are seeing the remote worker workforce increase. Both are causing inaccurate numbers when we rely only on population growth as a metric to analyze a market.

In addition to creating inaccurate population count, these migration patterns, paired with the increased ability to work remotely, have created a demand for furnished, temporary housing. All of this combined is making population growth less of an important metric when analyzing medium-term rentals, or even long-term rentals.

Lastly, be aware of oil cities, as they will show significant population increases and may entice investors to purchase investment properties in that area. However, when the price of crude oil dips, those towns can decrease in population significantly and quickly.

JOB GROWTH

We want to see a 2–3 percent increase year over year. More jobs in an area means more employed tenants who will pay rent on time. More tenants also creates more of a demand for your unit, ensuring increased occupancy.

WAGE AND INCOME GROWTH

When choosing a market to invest in, you want to see that your tenant pool is earning enough money to pay rent on time. We like to see wage and income

growing at least one percent year over year. Wage and income gr[...]
can be hard to quantify because, in many U.S. cities, we are no[...]
increase that is outpacing inflation. In certain sectors, we are seein[...]
"real income," which is wages adjusted for inflation. Because of re[...]
inflation increases, some U.S. workers are earning less year over y[...]

If wage and income growth is not happening across the count[...] ~qually or
at all in some U.S. sectors, why include wage and income growth as a metric to
analyze a market?

You have likely heard of the famous proverb: "Give a man a fish, and he eats
for a day. Teach a man to fish, and he eats for a lifetime." We want you to walk
away from reading this book with the ability to analyze any deal in any market.
Thus, wage and income growth is worth keeping top of mind. You want your
tenants to be making more money year over year, because you will want the
ability to increase rent over time. If your tenants are not making more money,
you cannot continue to raise their rent. Across the U.S., lack of wage and income
growth continues to be an issue, especially as inflation hits over 9 percent in
2022. We will continue to keep an eye on this metric because if you can discover
a market with increased wages, you can continue to charge top-of-market for
rent in addition to increasing rent over time. Just know that most U.S. cities are
not keeping up with inflation.

RENTAL RATES

In addition to increased wages, we want to see increased rents in the market we
invest in. This means other landlords are raising rents, making it possible for
us to also raise rents. When analyzing a city you want to invest in for long-term
rentals, a good rule of thumb is to see rent rates increasing by 1–3 percent year
over year. This affects medium-term rental rates as well. If an unfurnished unit
in Cincinnati can rent long term for $850, that very same unit may be able to
rent medium term for $1,600. As rent rates increase for long-term tenants, rents
for medium-term tenants will also rise.

Nationally, the United States saw year-over-year rent increases 14 percent in
2021, with some markets, such as Austin, Texas, seeing upwards of 40 percent
rises.[15] Landlords who already owned in those markets are rejoicing as they cash
flow now more now than years prior. But these rents are rising at unsustainable
levels, and experienced investors will tell you not to expect this type of year-over-
year growth. Rest assured that 14 percent—and especially 40 percent—yearly

---

15 https://www.redfin.com/news/redfin-rental-report-december-2021/

th is not standard. And while rising rents are a boon for those collecting them, it's important to remember that, as we mentioned above, unaffordability and stagnant wages can make this a double-edged sword.

All this it to say that just because you aren't seeing 14 percent rent increases in a market, that doesn't mean it's not worth investing in. Sarah analyzes properties so they can work as long-term and medium-term buy-and-hold. Thus, her main concern is knowing that she can increase rents 1 to 3 percent to keep up with increased property taxes and inflation.

HOME VALUES

Similar to rent rates, home values increased substantially during 2020 and 2021. Over the last decade, a solid market to invest in should have seen a 40 percent increase in home values. (For those who put away their mathematical hat after high school, a 40 percent increase over a decade is 4 percent year over year, which is in line with the national average.) When we invest in real estate, we are doing just that: investing in real estate. We want to know that our assets are increasing in value over time. Thus, appreciating home values are crucial to the success of our investments.

It's worth reemphasizing that the priority of our investing strategies is cash flow. Investing for cash flow allowed both of us to leave our day jobs to focus on real estate full-time. Appreciation does not pay your bills month to month; appreciation builds *wealth*. This is why cash flow, paired with appreciation, is the right combination for us. Some investors have different strategies and are willing to take minimal cash flow if a property has an appreciation upside. If you run the numbers and feel that home-value appreciation beyond inflation is at the forefront of your investing goals, pay careful attention to fast appreciating markets, as well as markets where the home value is below the national average (meaning it has room to grow, provided the other metrics are satisfactory). RealWealth is a great resource for this.[16]

CRIME RATE

This is the only metric on this list that you want to see going down. You want crime rates low not only for the safety of your tenants and their community but also to ensure insurance rates don't increase over time. Essentially, you want criminals to leave, and you want tenants and low insurance rates to stay.

---

[16] https://realwealth.com/markets/

Pay Attention to Regulations

In addition to those metrics we have mentioned, when considering a market, pay attention to real estate policy. Cities across the country are tightening their short-term rental regulations. Anyone running a short-term rental without permits in these cities will need to look for alternative strategies for their investment properties. These short-term rental bans are becoming increasingly common and likely will only continue to present a threat to STR investors. Unlike a short-term rental, medium-term rentals house tenants for thirty days or more, making them more like a long-term rental—cities are regulating MTRs as such.

Locations

Every market is unique. A metric or factor that is make-or-break to one investor may barely register to another, depending on their investment strategies. For example, short-term rental investors are less concerned than long-term rental investors with metrics like population growth or wage growth. Short-term rental investor Rob Abasolo, founder of the Robuilt YouTube channel and cohost of the *BiggerPockets Real Estate Podcast*, speaks often of the value of proximity to amenities such as tourist attractions, a convention or event center, an airport, or even sports stadiums. Properties next to a university can attract short-term tenants as well as medium-term tenants. When Zeona was first starting out, she admits that location and proximity to amenities was her main consideration. She also paid attention to crime, as she wanted to invest in low-crime areas. It wasn't until she started investing in long-term rentals that she broadened her criteria. Know that you may want to change rental strategies over time as your cash flow needs and desire for involvement evolve.

These factors are important with the MTR strategy, but if you plan on renting to traveling nurses, one of the more common tenant types for MTR, nothing is as important as proximity to a hospital. We find the MTR strategy works best when you have two or more major hospitals within a five-mile radius. Be mindful of driving times to the hospitals. Know that driving five miles in Manhattan, New York, is different from driving five miles in Manhattan, Kansas. We have found that nurses are willing to commute up to twenty minutes, though anything shorter is preferred. The closer to a major hospital the better; even higher rents are possible in units that are less than half a mile from a hospital.

Now, not all MTR tenants are nurses, and some investors have MTR units that are not near hospitals. The location of your rental will depend on the type of tenant you are seeking. Thus, there are several key elements we look for when investing in an MTR. They include:

- Hospitals (traveling health professionals)
- Corporations (corporate relocation, industry)
- Research centers (temporary scientists and researchers)
- Universities (graduate students, professors, students)
- Filming destinations (see Julie Gates's case study later in this chapter)

Personal reasons can also factor into this decision. For example, Sarah purchased properties near her parents not only because she wanted another reason to visit them but also for tax purposes. Now every time she visits her properties (and her parents!), the expenses are business expenses. Next, she purchased in Omaha and Des Moines because her grandparents live in a small town about an hour or two from both cities. Sarah was flying into Omaha every year at Christmas time. Now, each trip to Kansas City and Omaha is a business expense.

We know other investors who do the same thing: They purchase properties in places they frequently visit to utilize tax write-offs. You may want to consider doing the same thing.

Whatever you decide, be sure there are also demographics and data that support your decision to invest there. If you cannot rent the unit for enough money to cover your expenses and profit, we do not recommend purchasing it.

CASE STUDY

"Attracting the Movie Industry to Your MTR" by Julie Gates

If you're looking for an industry where the rules are clear and the path is wide, you might want to choose a different investing model than STRs. Short-term rentals are the Wild West of real estate investing. There are general rules, but, for the most part, you make them up as you go.

My hometown is Savannah, Georgia. We have STR regulations that are pretty specific, and STRs are only allowed in the tourist area of town. When I initially got into the STR space, I started in a small town outside of Savannah, where short-term rentals are allowed. I loved the model, loved the guests, and loved decorating. I started looking at houses that could be rented as STRs in the tourist district but could not stomach the asking prices as a new real estate investor. However, since I had been running several houses at that point and was turning down requests for extended stays,

I already knew there was a demand for medium-term rentals in my town. I expanded my search for properties just outside of the tourist district. I found an older neighborhood in a great location and pounced.

The house I bought was inexpensive and small. This type of property wasn't well suited for a growing family, but it was the perfect size for one or two travelers to enjoy for a months-long stay in Savannah. I'm still renting that house today and have added many more on the same street. As they say in real estate—location, location, location!

If you have any large industry in your town, there is probably a significant need for your furnished properties. The most important advice I can give you on this subject is that you need to make sure your place is available for longer stays. If you allow someone to book a two-night stay eight months from now, this will stop a professional from securing your home for a multi-month visit. This could be costly, especially in lean months.

An example of this is attracting snowbirds to your location. If you live in a warmer climate, January and February are slow in the tourism industry. Still, they can be very profitable for hosts attracting people wanting to get out of the cold. Make sure that your calendar is wide open two to four months in advance to attract these stays.

When attracting guests for these longer stays, it's vital to get your name in front of the department that handles housing for industry professionals. This is typically the tourism office in your town (or the larger town nearby). If you think you don't have one, you're probably wrong. I have been amazed at how many small towns have a tourism office in my area. It takes only a little time to stop by and introduce yourself. I take business cards to them every year to ensure they have my info, which has proven to be an effortless way to get business. Medium-term rentals are not easy to come by; you are solving a problem for them even if you only have one house available when they need it.

The movie industry, like many others, is in constant need of temporary accommodations. I've honed in on this niche. I started offering MTRs with only one property, but I never told my contacts that I only had one house. I just said that if anyone needed a place for more extended stays, I was their girl. These contacts soon learned that I was the best person to call when they had a need. The phone calls I got drove me to get more houses—I knew I was onto something! This relationship and number of listings didn't happen overnight, but I made a name for myself with the local housing contact as someone who always worked hard to get them housing. They will always call the person who makes their life easier first. Who wouldn't?

I have many great stories of working with the film industry, but I'll tell you my favorite. Whenever a studio notifies me that they need housing, they first look at my website. Location and size matter, but film people are visual: the actor, producer, or director often chooses a house based on the decor. They work very hard, and they want to stay in a home that they feel matches their personality or helps them relax. I have heard about houses being fought over many times. One actor, coming for a production, decided he wanted to stay in a particular home that I manage, which was already booked for half of the dates. I gave him several other options that were available for his stay. The response was no; none of the other houses would work. He wanted that house. This was not good.

The original booking was through Airbnb. I had to honor that; I couldn't just cancel on a guest, and moving guests between houses on Airbnb is incredibly difficult. The studio told me to get it done. They would pay the guest 20 percent over what they'd paid for my house to cancel the booking. I asked them to put that in writing on the studio letterhead, and then I reached out to my Airbnb guest, letting them know the situation. Would they consider canceling the reservation? I would give them a full refund, plus the movie studio would drop 20 percent more into their bank account. The guest agreed and canceled the reservation, and the actor had the house for several months.

Keep up with Julie's property management company on Instagram @sidwashere912.

CHAPTER SIX
DEAL CRITERIA

It takes as much energy to wish as it does to plan.
—ELEANOR ROOSEVELT

SARAH

This chapter will cover why your deal criteria matter, as well as how to craft them. But first, let me tell you a story about how I saw firsthand the power of having and sharing crystal clear criteria.

I was living in a van in New Zealand (and no, not down by the river).

At that time, I owned and self-managed a single-family home in Prairie Village, Kansas, and a duplex in Kansas City, Missouri. All three units were fully occupied, bringing in $4,250 in rental income, and my two monthly mortgage payments totaled $2,651. I knew I wanted to own more real estate to fund my ideal lifestyle and international travel, but something was not working.

In 2020, I wrote seventeen offers in six different states and nine different markets within those states. At the time, my criteria ranged from a $400,000 short-term rental in Phoenix, Arizona, to a $70,000 BRRRR in Columbus, Ohio. I wanted to do it all! Does this sound familiar to any of you?

I had investor-friendly agents, or so I thought, in all nine markets. I had given them an idea of what I was looking for, but I was not clear enough. As a result, I was frustrated and wearing myself thin analyzing deals in multiple markets day in and day out.

A trusted mentor sat me down to dive deep into my investing strategy. During a one-hour call with them, I discovered that I was trying to do too many things at once. Looking back, I can see now that doing too much was an obvious issue. But in the thick of it, I could not see what was right in front of me.

I wanted to see results. So I pivoted.

Directly after the meeting, I listed the different strategies I could try in order to determine what my next step should be.

Strategy 1: Find a small multifamily property where I could use the house hacking and MTR strategies in tandem. This appealed to me for two main reasons.

First, I wanted to finance through an owner-occupied loan. The FHA loan requires a lower down payment, leaving me more capital to invest in other deals. I knew I wanted to leave my salaried W-2 job soon, and I wouldn't qualify for an FHA loan without income from a W-2. Once I stopped working at my W-2 job, it would be nearly impossible to qualify for an owner-occupied conventional loan for up to two years. This would be my last chance at it for a while, as I saw it.

Second, I was eager to purchase a small multifamily property. My investing strategy includes maximizing cash flow. While some single-family homes provide high returns, multifamily units give you the ability to live in one unit and rent out the others for maximized cash flow. Renting small multifamily properties using owner-occupied loans is a strategy I recommend to many of the investors I coach for the same reason. You can use the FHA loan on a single-family home, duplex, triplex, or fourplex. When you start to invest in buildings with five units or more, you will use commercial loan products, which tend to have higher interest rates and require a greater down payment.

Strategy 2: Complete my first BRRRR.

At some point as a new investor, you struggle to accumulate (or not spend) enough savings to have funds available for the 20 or 25 percent down payment required for conventional investment property loans. That is why the BRRRR (buy, rehab, rent, refinance, repeat) strategy is attractive for several reasons. With BRRRR, you can:

- Use other people's money to secure the property.
- Renovate the property to increase the property's value, creating equity.
- Create cash flow.
- Recycle your capital.

For more on the BRRRR strategy, I recommend reading David Greene's definitive work on the subject, *Buy, Rehab, Rent, Refinance, Repeat,* also published by BiggerPockets.

While I did not use the BRRRR strategy on this deal, it is exactly what I did with the following two deals.

Strategy 3: Short-term rental using a second-home loan.

The other option I was weighing was using a 10-percent-down second-home loan to finance a short-term rental property in a city like Phoenix.

The second-home loan strategy appealed to me for many reasons, including:
- The lower down payment requirement left more capital in my pocket.
- The cash flow from an STR in this market exceeded anything I could get from house hacking or using the BRRRR strategy.
- The cash-on-cash returns were 30 percent or more, pairing 10 percent down with the cash flow from the STR.
- I like the idea of investing in Phoenix, a city where my grandparents live during the winter months. Owning in a town they live in would mean a trip to Phoenix could be a tax write-off every time I visited my grandparents (I mean, my rental property).

Arguably, all of these were great strategies for me at the time. However, I quickly learned it is hard to focus on many moving targets simultaneously. I was analyzing properties in multiple markets and communicating with nearly a dozen real estate agents. Trying to keep everything straight was exhausting, and I was dropping the ball. This was causing anxiety for me and for the numerous agents who were bringing me deals. Plus, I had little to no results to show for my efforts.

I decided I would focus on two strategies instead of three and no more than two markets. This meant my second home in Phoenix would have to wait.

Here is the beautiful thing about focus: When you focus your efforts, you see more results. Within twenty-four hours of the call with my mentor, I sent a text message to two agents in:
- Omaha, Nebraska
- Des Moines, Iowa

Four days later, the agent in Omaha texted me.

"I have a fourplex for you…"

I quickly and confidently analyzed the fourplex once the agent sent me the following information:

- Suggested offer price
- Current rents
- Market rents
- Estimated rehab
- Property taxes
- Estimated insurance
- Property management fee percentage

I plugged this information into my deal analysis spreadsheet calculator. I liked the returns, and I wrote the offer. The next day, I went under contract—all from 8,000 miles away. Within five days of the conversation with my mentor, I was under contract on a fourplex that my agent found off-market using an FHA 3.5-percent owner-occupied loan.

How did I get what I wanted so quickly, after spending the last several months unable to see the forest for the trees? Let's take a moment to discuss the power of crystal clear deal criteria.

The more specific you can be, the more likely an investor-friendly agent will find the deal and send it to you. It is then your job to analyze the deal and write the offer.

As David Greene explains on the *BiggerPockets Real Estate Podcast* in episode 563, if you want your friends to help you find a boyfriend, you should tell them exactly what you're looking for in a mate. Then, when they go out searching, they are more likely to find a good match rather than just bring you any eligible bachelor. The same is true in investing.

The more specific you can be with your criteria, the more likely your agent is to bring you a deal that fits your criteria. Many of my investor consultation clients worry that they could be missing out on other deals if they are too specific. Why should they be specific if they are open to investing in "any" good deal?

Plain and simple: They are *not* open to any good deal.

Let me show you.

An investor looking to use a 10-percent-down second-home loan on a turnkey single-family property with a 9 percent cash-on-cash return will not magically overnight be open to investing in a $2.3 million value-add multifamily property. Very few investors are open to purchasing just "any" good deal, because most investors are constricted on some combination of time, money, and financing capabilities.

Being specific will better serve you. It did for me, and it will for you too.

I know that many investors consider purchasing a single-family and a multifamily property simultaneously. I am doing the same thing. However, I'm confident that an agent is more likely to find you a deal if you tell them precisely what you are looking for.

I am also confident a great investor-friendly agent will sling you some deals that do not fit your criteria. And you may also end up writing offers on those too. As an agent, Zeona occasionally sends her clients deals that stretch their criteria, educating them on different perspectives or strategies that they may not have considered yet.

Here are the key elements of crystal clear deal criteria:

1. Purchase price
2. Renovation budget
3. Class of neighborhood
4. Investing strategy to be used
5. Cash-on-cash requirements
6. Desired cash flow per unit
7. Location

Do not get stuck here. I urge you to avoid analysis paralysis.

I beg you to take action.

THE EDUCATION-ACTION EQUATION

Multifamily investor Jake Stenziano gives the perfect rule of thumb for this topic: "Education times action equals your results."

Education × Action = Results

For us, this means sometimes you need to stop educating yourself and start taking action. Other times, we understand that education is required, but I have seen many investors over-educate themselves.

Now, we all know that anything multiplied by zero equals zero. Thus, results do not come if you are either not taking action or not educating yourself.

It may seem obvious that in order to get results, you must take action. Yet there are investors I have known since 2017 who, despite wanting to invest and having the funds to invest, are still in analysis paralysis. As a result, they have not written an offer since I met them.

This is where Stenziano's equation comes into play.

Education x Action = Results. If your education is at ten, you have read the real estate investing books and listened to the podcasts. You have the knowledge, but if you have written zero offers and only analyzed a handful of deals, you have not acted. Your results, then, are (yes, you guessed it) zero.

Education times zero equals *zero*.

Let's say you finished reading this book, but you have not picked a market. You have not written your crystal clear criteria, and you have not contacted any investor-friendly real estate agents. Likely, you also haven't analyzed many deals, if any. Thus, you haven't written any offers, so you inevitably have not gone under contract. As a result, you have yet to collect rental income and build wealth through the MTR strategy.

But here's what is so cool. If you educate yourself, even just a little bit, and you then take one small action step, you have some results. But if you take big actions steps, you now have multiplied results!

Now, let's say you finished reading this book, and you took action and picked a market. As a result, your deal criteria are clear, and your trusted investor-friendly real estate agent knows it! Because of this, you analyze deals with confidence every day.

When you find a deal that matches your deal criteria, you write offers, and you are then under contract. When you close and stabilize the property, you begin to collect rental income, and now you are building wealth with the MTR strategy.

All because you did what? You took action!

When you feel as though you are not getting what you want, ask yourself, "What am I lacking?" Is it education or action? For many investors, it is often action. For some investors, it is, in fact, education. For many, it's a combination of both.

Here's where crystal clear criteria come in. When I was deal shopping and not finding what I wanted, I was taking action, but my activity was scattered. I needed to concentrate my efforts so I, too, could start seeing results.

First, I laid out crystal clear deal criteria for each strategy.

I had one criterion for each of the following.
- Primary house hack
- Long-distance BRRRR
- Short-term rental

I focused on house hacking my primary residence, because it was my first and foremost area of expertise. After sending my deal criteria for that strategy to an investor-friendly agent in Omaha, Nebraska, I was under contract in five days. From there, I went from owning three units to owning fifteen units in ninety-three days. I want the same thing for you.

I credit my success to three things.

1. Relationships with investor-friendly agents
2. Crystal clear deal criteria
3. Confidence in analyzing deals (read more on this in Chapter Eight)
4. Now let's cover the elements of crystal clear criteria.

1. PURCHASE PRICE

Two things are essential when determining price point: Your price range must be realistic, and you must be able to finance the deal.

Financing the property may be the first determining factor in determining your price range. For example, when I was making less than $60,000, a conventional lender would not approve me to purchase a property worth $600,000. In addition to your salary determining your financeability, a lender may also consider 75 percent of the property's rental income as income. This meant that I would qualify for a $350,000 fourplex but not a $350,000 single-family because the rent from the other three units contributed to my monthly income, allowing me to qualify for a higher purchase price.

Part of setting an achievable purchase price is first educating yourself on the market. It is not realistic to ask an agent in the Phoenix market to find you a fourplex for $320,000, yet that is the price I paid for my first fourplex in 2021 in Omaha, Nebraska. It is also impossible to buy a duplex for under $150,000 in Boise, but in Milwaukee, you can pick up a duplex for under $100,000.

Thus, educating yourself on prices in a market is the first step. Use reliable websites to look at active listings to get a sense of what sellers are asking in the market you have selected. Keep in mind that just because the seller is asking for $439,000 does not mean you or someone else will pay that. While you can do this with online research, my favorite way is to network with other investors and investor-friendly agents. By asking them, you can cut down on research time by more than half. You can read more on finding investor-friendly agents in Chapter Nine.

After determining your price range, you must find out how you will finance the deal. We covered financing in Chapter Four. Again, be realistic with how much you can afford and give this criterion to your agent.

2. RENOVATION BUDGET

"Money does not grow on trees" is a famous adage, and for a good reason. If you are targeting properties that will need rehab, you need to have a plan to finance those renovations. Be realistic about what you can afford and specify the renovation budget to your agent. If you do not have a way to finance a $150,000 renovation, tell your agent not to send you those types of deals.

Keep in mind that you do not have to use your own money when financing a property or a property's renovation. For me, I have used private lenders to finance both the down payment and the renovation costs knowing that I could refinance after the repairs were completed. After I refinance at a higher price point, I would be able to pull out cash and pay my private lender back plus the interest I owed him for lending me the money for the renovation. I know other investors who use private lenders for short-term loans for things like a large-scale renovation.

For some investors, money may not be the hurdle. Instead, they may not want to manage a costly renovation from afar—or at all. In that case, the investor should specify in their deal criteria how much renovations they are willing to do, if any at all.

If an investor prefers no renovation, they would prefer a turnkey property. "Turnkey" means that the property needs little to no work to be rent-ready.

The Real Estate Food Chain by Zeona

As an Airbnb investor, my mantra has always been "Get it furnished; get it rented." I would arrive at my out-of-state property the day before closing and start shopping. I wanted to have pictures up by the end of the week and have it booked before I boarded the plane back home. I understood that the money I was targeting in my strategy was from high rental rates, so I did not slow myself down by trying to squeeze in a renovation. This is a common mistake I see new investors making when wanting to combine a BRRRR with private financing and then throw Airbnb in the mix, too—because why not? This can be a massive trap for new or savvy investors. They have usually overeducated themselves and want to squeeze in too many strategies at once.

The key was knowing where I stood on the "real estate food chain." This "food chain" is a concept I like to illustrate when I am talking to budding investors about whether to buy value-add properties versus move-in-ready properties. The way I see it, there are investors in every step of the deal. Sure, someone made money on renovating the home before me, but I knew where I excelled was in the make-ready and management. So why not skip ahead and move on to the next property? When I was starting, money was tight, so even though I bought turnkey, renovated places, many of them were over one hundred years old. Since then, I've started buying some new construction and aim to have all my homes be from the 1950s or newer to limit my maintenance. The moral of the story? Just get started without overcomplicating the situation. Then, as you become more proficient, take a small bite out of the next strategy like updating a bathroom or bringing on a money partner. As you learn and develop your strengths, it will become more and more obvious where your energy is best spent.

---

3. CLASS OF NEIGHBORHOOD

In real estate investing, neighborhoods—or even markets—are often categorized as A class, B class, C class, and D class. While there is no specific measure to directly indicate a variance in classes, your Realtor or other investors should be able to show you the difference.

A Class

When we talk about A-class properties, we are referring to those located in the most desirable areas for tenants. A-class areas attract tenants who tend to be high-income earners; thus, these properties tend to be more expensive and, in turn, command higher rents. These areas often have low crime rates, high occupancy, and modern or premium finishings.

B Class

Properties in B-class areas may be less desirable than A-class properties, but they still have low crime rates and tenants want to live there. On the whole, B-class properties are well maintained but can be improved and updated through minor renovations. I tend to invest in B-class neighborhoods because that is where I find value-add opportunities, and they tend to be excellent locations for the MTR strategy.

C Class

Properties in a C-class area will demand lower rent rates than those in B-class or A-class locations. This may be because there is more crime in these areas, or the neighborhood may just be more run-down or in a less desirable location. Some C-class properties are older or have a good deal of deferred maintenance and so may need more work to bring them up-to-date or to rentable standards.

D Class

Properties in a D-class area do not match the market criteria we mentioned in Chapter Five. A D-class neighborhood is high crime, often deemed as dangerous, and may even have a declining community. D-class properties are run-down and generally in need of large-scale repairs. This is a neighborhood class we do not invest in with long-term rentals, although that is not true for all investors. Regardless, it is crucial that everyone using the medium-term rental strategy avoid D-class properties.

4. INVESTING STRATEGY

Your agent must know what investing strategy you plan to use. Some would argue that the agent should be experienced in said strategy, but I don't agree. My agent who sends me the best off-market deals has never furnished a unit or owned an Airbnb or MTR. Yet, he is great at finding those types of deals. Why? Because he knows what I am looking for. I educate him on what I need.

If you plan to rent the property as a short-term rental, your agent should not send you properties in a county or city that does not allow short-stay furnished rentals. If you plan to use the property as your primary residence, there may be certain parts of town where you would prefer to live versus avoid.

Some investing strategies include:

- Long-term rental
- Medium-term rental
- Short-term rental
- Live-in flip
- BRRRR
- Fix-and-flip

Keep in mind that a property could be suitable for multiple strategies. This is actually what we prefer! I like purchasing a property that can cash flow as a long-term rental. Then, as an MTR, it simply cash flows even more. Meanwhile, I own two duplexes where I have one unit running as an MTR and the other unit runs as a long-term rental. Diana Ossa, an investor in Missouri, also employs this same strategy. "I like that my long-term tenant keeps an eye on the property for me, like if the lawn needs to be mowed or if something seems off with an MTR tenant," Ossa said. "It definitely helps me feel more comfortable moving away from my units eventually knowing I have eyes on the property at all times."

When choosing your strategy, the "education" piece of the results formula becomes crucial. There is a wealth of resources out there—books, podcasts, YouTube videos, boot camps, and more—that you can use to self-educate and select the best strategy for you. If your agent knows that you are looking to rent to traveling nurses, they are more mindful of the location and condition of the property. We recommend educating your agent on the medium-term strategy; maybe even give them this book!

5. CASH-ON-CASH REQUIREMENTS

Similar to purchase price, the market will determine the cash-on-cash (CoC) most properties in your desired area will yield. For example, I can find a duplex in Des Moines that produces 12 percent CoC, even as a long-term rental. We haven't seen that high of CoC in Austin, Texas, in years. (We will discuss more on cash-on-cash return in Chapter Eight; for now, understand that it is a ratio that describes your cash flow relative to your cash invested.)

Some investors are willing to invest in a property that produces 9 percent cash-on-cash if it is in an area that appreciates or if the property is turnkey and requires little work. Personally, I want at least 14 percent cash-on-cash. If the property yields higher CoC, I am willing to purchase a dilapidated property that requires a significant amount of work.

If you plan to use the house hacking strategy paired with a lower down payment, you will see higher CoC returns. For example, my fourplex is 82 percent cash-on-cash because my initial investment was an $11,000 down payment plus the $10,000 in renovations and furnishings. It cash flows more than $1,800 per month and has the potential to cash flow twice as much when I furnish all four units and move out. With that being said, it is not realistic that you or I will house hack our way to a huge portfolio—nor is it what many of you want. How does moving every twelve months sound to you? Maybe you're happy to move that often, but you do not want to live near your tenants. And that's okay! I have learned that there are many paths to financial independence. I have chosen real estate investing paired with delayed gratification.

6. DESIRED CASH FLOW PER UNIT

You must know your investment strategy before you determine your cash flow requirements. For example, if I rent my fourplex to all long-term tenants, I will cash flow approximately $220 per unit. However, by moving to the medium-term rental strategy, I can cash flow closer to $720 per unit. My agent would look at me like I had two heads if I told him I was looking for a long-term buy-and-hold property that cash flows $720 per unit. However, when my agent knew I would use the MTR strategy, that number became more realistic and easier to accomplish. Read Chapter Eight to see how to calculate cash-on-cash returns and cash flow.

7. LOCATION

Location is key with medium-term rentals. For example, if you plan to rent to traveling nurses, be sure your agent knows to look for properties within five miles of two or more major hospitals. Ideally, your property is less than a mile from one major hospital. We talked more about location in Chapter Five.

It's Not Your Agent's Job to Find You a Property, But It Can Be

In some markets, like the Smoky Mountains, agents will often prepare their buyer clients by telling them that they, the investor, are the ones who need to find the deals. Whereas in Des Moines, I have an investor-friendly agent who sends me deals consistently. How an agent will want to work with you depends on a few factors.

We recommend navigating this by having an expectation conversation with your agent from the beginning.

In the very first conversation with them, I ask agents I work with how they find deals. This allows me to understand if I can expect consistent deal flow from an agent.

Often, if an agent is going to set me up on an automated MLS search and nothing else, I will politely decline and move on. I am looking for an agent who finds both on-market and off-market deals. Also, I want an agent who is working hard to find properties, not one who sets me up with an automated search and who I never hear from again.

There is also a misconception that agents do not get paid a commission on off-market deals. First the agent negotiates with the seller to earn a commission for bringing them a buyer. Then, if that does not work, I, the buyer, offer to pay my agent's commission. They are saving me both time and money; they deserve to be paid on each deal they bring me that I close on.

CHAPTER SEVEN
MTR PROPERTIES AND STRATEGIES

> Focus is a matter of deciding what things
> you're not going to do.
> —JOHN CARMACK

SARAH

Both of us have used the house hacking strategy to build our portfolios.

I started investing with a single-family home in Kansas using a conventional loan that required a 3 percent down payment. Remember, the HomeReady loan is available to some first-time home buyers or those who make under a certain wage requirement.

After close, I furnished the common areas and rented each room individually to long-term tenants. Those tenants brought their bedroom furniture and signed individual leases for twelve months. This is called the rent-by-the-room strategy. I chose to do this because I could charge $750–$800 per room, making my total income $2,300, whereas if I were to rent out the entire house, I would only be able to charge $1,700.

After my first purchase, I knew I wanted to do what David Greene calls "the Stack." According to David, the Stack is when you purchase a single-family home, then you purchase a duplex, then a fourplex, and after that, you purchase an eight-unit apartment complex. So on and so forth; you get the picture.

I purchased a duplex thirteen miles from my single-family home and moved into the upstairs unit with a roommate. I rented the bottom unit to a family who would later also occupy the top three-bedroom apartment. When my roommate and I both moved out of the top unit, the unit was left vacant. As a result, I would have had to spend $10,000–$13,000 renovating the unit, including completely gutting the kitchen. Mathematically, it was worth it to spend the money on the upgrades because the unit would demand higher rent. Yet, I thought there might be a better way.

"What if I could rent the unit as-is for $750?" I thought.

I made a phone call, and, within days, that's exactly what I did.

My tenants in the bottom unit are a four-generation family. The great-grandmother, the grandmother, the mother, and the son lived together in the three-bedroom, one-bathroom unit. When they moved in, they told me there was plenty of space. I believe it was, until COVID-19 hit, and everything changed for them. The mother lost her job at the events stadium nearby. Her 12-year-old son switched to virtual learning and needed to occupy an entire bedroom while he attended school. And the grandmother's job also became virtual. What once was a cozy apartment was now crowded. I came to them with a solution.

While it was an added expense, they gladly accepted my offer to rent out the top unit in addition to the bottom unit. I discounted the top unit and rented it below-market, meaning I did not need to renovate the kitchen. The tenants did not mind an outdated kitchen, because the great-grandmother cooked dinner in the bottom unit nearly every night for the entire family. I did not have to stop what I was doing to coordinate a long-distance renovation or write a $10,000 check for a new kitchen. Plus, the turnover was so quick that my unit was only vacant one night—just enough time for my cleaner to deep clean.

This is just one example of how being creative can create a win-win scenario for both you and your tenants.

The Infamous House Hack

I first heard those sweet two words, "house hack," when Brandon Turner published a blog in June 2019 called "Beginners Guide to Hack Your Housing and Live for Free." In it, he explained the concept of what many living with roommates over the years had already figured out: You can rent out a portion of your home and have it pay all or a majority of your share of the "rent." With Brandon's investor mind, he thought beyond the roommate, applying it to multi-unit buildings, which worked better for his growing family.

The concept caught fire, and in October of that year, BiggerPockets author Craig Curelop released *The House Hacking Strategy*, a deep dive on the rent-by-room strategy in book form. We highly suggest checking it out, as we believe house hacking combined with any other rental strategy only supercharges it!

CASE STUDY

"The Short-Term, Medium-Term Combo" by Merrily Matthews

In the summer of 2019, we decided to turn the mother-in-law apartment in the basement of our house from a long-term rental (which it had been for sixteen years) into a combination medium-term and short-term rental. This way we could take advantage of the summer tourism in Seattle with a short-term rental and know the unit would be filled with stable, well-paid nurses on three-month leases during the rainy winter months. The best of both worlds!

Our house is located in Seattle's safe, walkable Greenwood area, with easy bus access to downtown and its hopping restaurant and shopping scenes. I felt it was the perfect place for traveling nurses due to its safety and proximity to local hospitals and amenities.

When we bought our house in 1998, we were house hacking before even knowing there was a word for it. The basement apartment with a separate entrance was always part of our plan, since I knew I would not be working while our children were young. While not replacing my income entirely, it has provided extra money.

The numbers as of 2022 are as follows: The last long-term renter was paying $1,200 per month. The Airbnb calculations we ran were conservative at $3,000-plus per month, and medium-term Furnished Finder rents were $1,900 per month. Since we were "trying on" Airbnb to see if we liked it, we knew we could keep the furniture investment and turn it into an MTR and still get great returns if we decided we didn't like the constant turnover and cleaning of an STR.

Our biggest hiccup was that we went live right before COVID-19 hit. As a result, all Airbnb reservations evaporated immediately, and traveling nurse activity came to a standstill. One of our last Airbnb guests was a traveling nurse waiting to go back to her own house, which she had sub-leased out to another nurse.

My husband is a Seattle firefighter and was still going to work during the early days of the pandemic, when we didn't understand how it was spreading. Initially, he stayed in the basement apartment to separate from the rest of the family. After we felt it was safe, he moved back upstairs, and we filled the unit with my husband's colleague who was going through a divorce. Since he and my husband were already in the same COVID-19 bubble, it helped ease my fears. Once he left at the end of the year, we opened back up to a nurse and then Airbnb.

Last month, I bought a duplex that I'm turning into a short-term/medium-term rental that I will manage long-distance. My system creation has been much quicker for these units because I have already had several years of understanding how to run it. For the rest of 2022, I hope to add long-term rentals and medium-term rentals to my portfolio that add $2,000 cash flow per quarter.

Here's what I recommend folks should know: Understand demand and pricing in your neighborhood. Understand how your competition decorates, and research the costs to do the same. Look into all the technology that helps run your place automatically and remotely. Also be sure to verify the insurance requirements for an MTR and look into how security technology can get you discounts.

Things I love about MTRs:

- The great, stable, well-paid tenant who is often working, and therefore "lives light" in your unit
- Not subject to the same regulations as an STR (verify based on your location)
- Less cleaning and communication needed compared to an STR

Follow Merrilly's outdoor adventures and real estate forays on Instagram @merrilymatthews.

ZEONA
MTR STRATEGIES

In the past ten years that I have been an investor, I've had the opportunity to test out four strategies for furnished rentals extensively.

1. Renting out a room, or my whole personal home (I still do this)
2. Airbnb arbitrage/master leasing (renting a home and subletting on Airbnb)
3. Cohosting or being an Airbnb property manager
4. Buying homes to be full-time Airbnbs

Rent-by-the-Room

Since Craig wrote an entire book on the subject, we'll keep it brief. The math for this strategy works best with larger homes, as more rooms bring in more income. When I help clients find these properties in the Denver area, they look for four-plus-bedrooms and over 2,000 square feet of finished living space. The more spacious the home is, the easier it will be for roommates to cohabitate. The basic math works out that the rent from three rooms pays the mortgage, the fourth room is for you (the owner), and the fifth room, if you have it, is for cash flow.

House Hacking, according to Craig Curelop

House hacking is the strategy where you put zero to 5 percent down on a one- to four-unit property. You live in it for a year, and while you're living there, you rent out the other bedrooms (or units) such that the rent covers your mortgage, and you live for free.

Ways you can use the house hack strategy and MTR strategy together:

- Rent out a room in your primary residence.
- Rent out your basement in your primary residence.
- Rent out a unit in your primary residence (if it is a multifamily unit).
- Rent out an ADU (accessory dwelling unit) or in-law suite.

The Makeshift Separate Unit by Zeona

Before we dive into all the benefits of house hacking, I wanted to share a sneaky hack that I have helped some clients achieve in their homes. It's a primary bedroom turned separate unit. Let me explain.

A short- or medium-term rental studio needs four things: a bedroom, a full bath, a kitchenette, and a separate entrance. When the primary bedroom is on the main floor, it often has access to the outside—this can be via a sliding door or back door, which becomes your separate entrance. Primary bedrooms usually have an ensuite, which becomes the unit's full bathroom and sink for the "kitchen." Usually, a walk-in closet or section of the room can become a small kitchenette with a Keurig, tea kettle, microwave, and toaster oven. The last benefit of using a primary bedroom is that they are usually large, so they can accommodate a small writer's desk or sitting area. Mount a TV, and you now have a separate unit!

One of the main benefits of house hacking is that it is owner-occupied, so you can take advantage of a low-down-payment conventional loan (generally

3–5 percent). However, the issue many investors are experiencing is that a low down payment requires private mortgage insurance (PMI), which makes the mortgage payment higher.

Don't let PMI discourage you! We always say, if the numbers work, go for it! You will want to look at your total cash-on-cash return and make sure it meets your standard. With house hacking, it usually does.

I like to take house hacking a step further by adding Airbnb into the mix, boosting cash flow potential. For example, if you rent out rooms medium-term, you can often get 1.5 percent of the market rent, which can help you cash flow over a larger mortgage payment.

Renting Out Your Home

My fiancé and I continue to rent out our home when we travel because we are addicted to the concept of house hacking. Why pay a mortgage when you can live for free and travel the world?

To illustrate what this looks like, let's break down our numbers.

We have a three-bedroom townhome in Boulder, Colorado, with a monthly payment of $2,200, including our mortgage and HOA fee. Airbnb demand is seasonal, so we rent it out for $1,200 per week in the low season and $1,800 per week in the high season. We could take the profit after paying our mortgage and use it to cover our travels. Instead, we use another life hack to supercharge our earnings: pet sitting.

In 2012, when I began renting out my room on Airbnb in Boulder, I quickly realized that I could make the most money when I was out of my space. While sleeping on a friend's couch might be a short-term solution for a night, I needed a more permanent solution. Enter pet sitting. Traditionally, with pet sitting, a sitter stays in the pet owner's home while the owner is traveling. This can be for short stays, like a few nights to a week, but I have also seen extended opportunities spanning many months.

CASE STUDY

"Pet Sitting" by Zeona

By far, my favorite house hack is pet sitting. It offers a slew of benefits. My preference isn't usually for pet sitting through friends or a recommendation (although trust me, I've done plenty of that). That type of sitting usually happens through a text or email introduction and generally isn't accompanied by photos. If you live in the same town, you may be able to go over to meet the owner and the pet and see the home, but I've done many long-distance sits where it's a little more challenging to know what you are getting yourself into.

Using Trusted Housesitters truly elevated my game. This app allows pet owners and sitters to create profiles and leave reviews, giving more transparency on who the people are, what pets you'd be looking after, and what the space is like. It also provides incredible sitting opportunities—so much so that a subset of folks (for example, Amy and Tim from the You-Tube channel "GoWithLess") have sold their homes and travel from pet sit to pet sit full-time.

I heard about a woman in New York City—one of the most expensive places in the world to rent—living rent-free full-time by pet sitting and then making money on the side dog walking. Trusted Housesitters is from the U.K., so it is very established in Western Europe. But it is incredibly popular in the U.S. as well as with expats in popular destinations, like Mexico City. Not only can pet sitting help you get out of your home so you can rent it out, but it can also take you on some incredible staycations. In 2020, after quarantine eased but air travel still felt iffy, my fiancé, Ben, and I used Trusted Housesitters to explore Colorado. I actually wrote this from an incredible "writing cabin" in Nederland. I now have pet sat in Colorado, Hawaii, Mexico, and the Virgin Islands.

Airbnb Arbitrage

People love to say "It takes money to make money." My favorite thing about Airbnb is that when you are renting a space in your own home, it actually doesn't.

When I was getting started with Airbnb, I was a penniless college student. I had $50,000 in student loan debt, was working for $15 per hour, and was going to massage school full-time. I bring this up to show that anyone can give furnished rentals a try if they have a spark of inspiration and the will to put in the effort. Since I was operating on a tight budget, I couldn't exactly go out and purchase a home to be my first short-term rental; I had to get creative.

I got my start by renting a room in my apartment. At the time, I was leasing a two-bedroom condo in central Boulder, near the densely populated University of Colorado area. I furnished the apartment (to collect the most rent possible) and then got a roommate for the second room. It was August when I decided to try out Airbnb, and I knew my roommate was planning to move at the end of the semester in December. What did I have to lose? If it worked well, my guests could cover the rent and I'd have the apartment to myself in between, and, if it didn't work out, I would get another roommate.

Even though it was heading into the slow season, it worked! When my roommate moved out, I rented both my room and the empty room individually. Looking back, it was very little money; I was barely breaking even on the rent, but I was awestruck that I could have a two-bedroom apartment to myself AND live for free. I worked out a few trades (e.g., massage therapy, babysitting) to stay with friends when both rooms were rented, but I quickly realized that if I wanted to scale, I needed more places.

I borrowed $4,000 from my dad to rent a second apartment; I needed the first month's rent, deposit, and money for furnishings. I made sure that the landlord allowed subletting, and I was off to the races (this is well before needing a short-term rental license). Over the next three years, I maintained two apartments at a time, living in whichever one wasn't rented. I kept up this strategy until I saved up enough to buy my first condo.

Cohosting

When I first started renting furnished apartments on Airbnb, very few people had heard of the website. Year over year, the popularity grew, and by 2016, people were beginning to talk about it. I started receiving a lot of questions about running an Airbnb business, which organically turned into inquiries about me managing furnished rentals for others. For what started as 18 percent of the revenue and grew to 25 percent, I would manage all the marketing and logistics of other people's listings. I built out their ads and house manuals. I then hired cleaners, created an automated scheduling system, and communicated with guests. Even though it sounds like a lot, with the help of automated software, I was able to keep up a rotation of five units with three to five hours of work per week. This put about $500 per unit, per month in my pocket.

In 2017, during a Camp FI retreat, I decided to start a blog on my website (www.zeonamcintyre.com) and began to grow my cohosting portfolio steadily. Since I had been managing out of state since 2015, with my St. Louis property, I wasn't limited by location. Shortly after that, I started receiving invitations to speak on podcasts like the *BiggerPockets Real Estate Podcast* (episodes 229 and 300). That platform gave me global reach, and I got a request to host in Cape Town, South Africa. Why not? Since then, I have co hosted more than sixty rentals in five countries (the United States, Greece, Spain, Mexico, and South Africa) and have perfected the skills required to do this from afar. In Chapter Sixteen, we go over all the tips and tricks to self-manage from anywhere in the world. While I no longer co host for other investors, I still manage my furnished units across four states.

Buying Homes to Airbnb

During my first two years of Airbnb arbitrage, I often worried that my landlords would decide that I could no longer sublet their units and I would have to find another arrangement. By this point, Airbnb rentals had become my livelihood, and I felt a strong pull to own property to be more in control of the process.

For the past two years, my mother had been battling cancer and was nearing the end of her fight. I knew my lifestyle of living between two condos (whichever wasn't booked at the time) would not provide the stability she needed. We were fortunate to receive an early payout from her life insurance company that provided a windfall to put a down payment on a condo.

When my mother passed, I entered a thick haze of grief that settled over my life for the next two years. During that time, Airbnb was such a blessing for me. The timing is rather remarkable; I began my Airbnb journey shortly before learning that my mother was diagnosed with cancer. Thanks to the power of furnished rentals, I built up a new support system that has been able to carry me through my life, filling the financial security gap left by my parents.

I continued my dwindling massage practice through the haze while living between my arbitrage property and my newly owned property. I was profiting over $2,500 per month between the two properties, just like I had set out to do after reading Mr. Money Mustache's blog a few years earlier. At 28 years old, just two years after welcoming my first Airbnb guest, I hit my financial independence number.

DEFINITION Financial Independence Number

A financial independence number tells you when you no longer need to earn income. It usually relates to the amount of money you would need to have saved in compounding assets (like index funds) to earn more in growth and dividends than you spend annually.

To calculate your own financial independence number, you need to know approximately how much you're currently spending each year. Take your total monthly expenses and multiply that number by twelve. You have reached your FI number when your passive income is more per year than you spend.

If you are using real estate as a passive income source, you can look at it in terms of cash flow and often get to your financial independence number much quicker. For example, if you need $5,000 per month to live off (remember you would no longer need to save half of your income), you can buy five houses that produce $1,000 in cash flow per month.

Sometimes I think Airbnb saved my life; if I hadn't had these furnished rentals in place, I don't know how I would have supported myself through that period of grief.

In the summer of 2015, a friend (I will call her Amanda) invited me out to St. Louis, Missouri, for her wedding. I was still in a difficult place emotionally, but I accepted, feeling the pull to be around her family, who I had known for over ten years. While I was mixing and mingling at the wedding, Amanda's friends asked me what I did for a living, and I brought up my furnished rentals. Many of them mentioned that they had a friend who was using Airbnb with great success or that they had been thinking about trying it out themselves. I remembered Amanda mentioning how affordable St. Louis was, but my jaw nearly hit the floor when her friends said that their three-bedroom home with a garage and backyard had only a $300 monthly mortgage payment.

My wheels began turning, and I decided, right then and there, that I would purchase a rental property in St. Louis. The apartment I had been renting in Boulder was $1,100 per month and earned nearly $100 per night. I thought, "If I could rent just three nights a month in St. Louis at the same price, I would break even." I couldn't lose! When I returned home, I took two weeks to calm myself and weigh the options. Was I being too hasty? Would I have the energy to pull this off with the emotional ups and downs of grief? Then I dived into the research, and the idea took on a life of its own. I found a great property, and then put in a cash offer. They accepted! After a brief closing period to negotiate a discount, I was back in St. Louis to furnish my new home.

Gross Income versus Net Income

Some investors have gone to social media to complain about STR investors only talking about gross rent, so we want to touch on that here. We are not attempting to make our deals sound better than they are. We use gross income because this figure is easily found on sites like Airbnb and Apartments.com, whereas calculating net income requires looking at monthly utilities, cleaning fees, maintenance, and repairs. Bookkeeping is admittedly our least favorite part of real estate investing. We will continue to share our gross income with full transparency.

Geoarbitrage

Another form of house hacking that we have both taken advantage of is living in cheaper countries while you rent out your place back home; this is commonly called "geoarbitrage." For example, in the winter of 2015, I flew to Spain for three months when a friend was looking for a house sitter. I then rented out the spare room in my friend's house on Airbnb and hosted travelers while splitting proceeds with my friend to cover her rent. All the while, I managed my rentals in Colorado and St. Louis from afar.

OTHER CONSIDERATIONS

Value-Add versus Turnkey

Remember the "real estate food chain" I mentioned earlier? Every investor has their place in the food chain, along the life cycle of a property. For example, someone buys a condemned home from the city for $1 and then tears it down to the studs and rebuilds it to be sold for $50,000. Then the next investor comes in, paints it a trendy color, adds Luxury Vinyl Plank (LVP) flooring, and then puts it on the market. Maybe it's now worth $100,000. That's where I come in. I move in the furniture, put it on Airbnb, and voilà!

Who is overpaying? I would argue no one is. We are all just buying at our level of convenience or willingness to do the work. As a furnished-rental operator, I don't have any issues buying a home off the MLS in a fixed-up, move-in-ready condition; all I want to do is furnish it and then rent it immediately. I don't want to deal with carrying the note, making mortgage payments while undergoing a renovation, or paying for repairs with my precious and limited cash. I want to roll all that work into a mortgage, paying the price for those who came before me.

Multifamily versus Single-Family

Both multifamily and single-family properties can be profitable in the medium-term rental space; it just comes down to the investor's preference, criteria, strategy, and goals. For example, all of my medium-term rentals are single units, and all of Sarah's are multifamily. Is one better than the other? Not exactly, but they each serve us differently.

The main benefit of a single unit is autonomy. People tend to prefer the feel of living in a stand-alone home and will pay a premium for it. The one caveat about that is that traveling nurses are often women who are traveling alone, and their safety is a big concern. For them, sometimes being in a condo complex or in a multifamily property gives that extra comfort of not being alone.

The benefits of multifamily are savings in numbers. Despite having multiple units, you've got one roof, one walkway to shovel, and one lawn to mow. Medium-term rental managers enjoy other benefits over short-term rental ones—a big one being less worry about trash, snow removal, and mail. For someone on the outside, trash may sound like a silly problem—it's not, especially if you live in a bear-prone area. It's the little-known thorn in most STR owners' sides. The great thing about MTR guests is that they are invested; they are staying a while, so they learn the trash routine and take it to the curb each week. They are fine with shoveling the walkway or recycling the junk mail. It's easier to find a property manager (if you decide to go that route), since all the units are in one building, and more convenient for a cleaner. One downside for multi-unit properties might be that monthly in-and-out movement may attract negative attention from neighbors.

Beware of homeowner association (HOA) regulations. HOAs can set arbitrary minimum lengths, like ninety days or even six months, that you need to rent out your space. Even though it *could* work, I'd give most strict HOAs a hard pass. Month-by-month rentals allow you to charge more than by a six-month agreement, just as charging week-by-week brings higher income than month-by-month. In addition, some HOAs restrict your ability to rent a unit even if it is your primary residence. Be sure to read the HOA rules and bylaws before purchasing a property! You do not want to find out after closing that the strategy you planned on using does not work.

Size of Unit or Number of Bedrooms

In the traditional, drivable vacation rental markets, which are the bread and butter of short-term rental operators, "the bigger, the better" is the rule with home size. The idea is to have four or five bedrooms and sleep ten or more guests, meaning you can attract two or three families who can pay more per night. Medium-term rentals are a different game. We have found that one- and two-bedroom units are the sweet spot. (Although, with families traveling for extended stays, three bedrooms can work as well.) Our reasoning behind one to two bedrooms is that nurses often travel alone or with a partner, child, or another nurse. Most of these scenarios can be covered by a maximum of two bedrooms. We believe sticking to the one- and two-bedroom units will give you the most expansive tenant pool (and at a lower purchase price).

A little aside about one-bedroom units: One-bed properties often get a bad rap as not being as easy to rent or market. Therefore, they tend to sit for sale longer and can often be scooped up for a discounted price. This is my favorite weapon because they are dreamy for medium-term rentals. Fun fact: I owned two one-bedroom single-family homes (didn't know they made these, did you?) and two one-bedroom condos. Let's jump into my story about negotiating a one-bedroom home.

CASE STUDY

Zeona's Colorado Springs Negotiation

It was the winter of 2018, and my friend Adam Palmer gave me a call one day and said he heard a tip that Colorado Springs, Colorado, was undervalued compared to Denver. He insisted there was also a lot of potential for appreciation. "Let's go scope it out," I said.

Adam lined up a referral and appointment with a local investor-friendly agent, and I hooked up the accommodations from a generous former Airbnb client in exchange for some feedback on their space. We were off! When we arrived at the agent's office, she pulled out a map and gave us the grand tour, showing us which neighborhoods were areas of opportunity. We searched extensively through the MLS and chose eleven properties to see. It was a whirlwind!

Toward the end of our long day, we saw a quirky little one-bedroom house on the edge of a gentrifying neighborhood. It looked like it was right out of an HGTV special: barn door, shiplap walls, and a brand-new open kitchen. It was top-to-bottom remodeled and so cute! I was enamored. I always tell my clients not to fall in love, but this property and I were connected —it had its hooks in me, and I had to find a way to buy it.

The only problem? It was listed for $239,000, which was almost $100,000 more than I had ever paid for a property. To top it off, I didn't think I could get a loan because all of my income was from short-term rentals, which was still not widely recognized by banks. I spent the afternoon calling a few potential partners and negotiating terms. Finally, I had one bite. It was a partner that I owned another home with, so he trusted me and already knew what it was like to work together. On our way out of town, I swung by the house I wanted again. I took some videos for my business partner, and I told the home that I'd be back.

It took me a few days to get my ducks in a row to offer. This home had already been sitting on the market for a few days, likely because of the B-minus area, proximity to the train tracks, and size (not many people want a one-bedroom house in family-focused Colorado Springs). And yet all these things work fine for a furnished rental. It is across the street from Colorado College, on a greenway path to downtown, and is a perfect size for a short stay, especially with its finished basement.

My hunch was that another reason it was sitting was because of the price. I had just been reading *Never Split the Difference* by Chris Voss and knew I needed to give a low anchor: a lowball price that would make anything above that seem reasonable. I offered $197,000 and held my breath, hoping it wouldn't offend the seller, and we never heard back. I thought, "Okay, I don't *need* this place, so let's play the game." I told my agent that I wanted to write an offer every Friday but come up less each time. I wanted those sellers to sit through the weekend with no offers and see how appealing my offers would start to look.

My agent told me it would never work, that "the market was on fire" and it was "a buying frenzy," but I knew this home was being overlooked. Even my partner thought we had no chance. I didn't care; I was having fun.

After four weeks of playing, we settled on $215,000, and they accepted. The best part? As we went through inspection, I realized the seller had only fixed the cosmetic stuff, and the house needed a roof and furnace. He credited us $10,000 to cover both, so we got those and paid just $205,000 for the property! When there's a will, there's a way.

CHAPTER EIGHT
HOW TO ANALYZE
AN MTR DEAL

Much effort, much prosperity.
—EURIPEDES

SARAH

In Chapter Six, we talked about the three things I credit for my success.

1. Relationships with investor-friendly agents
2. Crystal clear deal criteria
3. Confidence in analyzing deals

We showed you that finding an investor-friendly agent and knowing your deal criteria are critical. However, having an investor-friendly agent sending you deals does not do any good if you don't know how to analyze them.

NO MASTER'S IN MATHEMATICS REQUIRED

There is no math degree required to analyze real estate properties. The last time either of us touched a TI calculator was in 2007. I have bachelor's degrees in journalism and international studies, and Zeona has an associate degree in merchandise marketing from a fashion school. Trust us when we say that nowhere along the way did anyone mention cash-on-cash return or capital expenditures.

This chapter will show you how you, too, can analyze deals in any market with confidence.

I find confidence in the numbers. Whenever my mind starts to wander and I question a purchase, I fire up my computer, open my deal-analysis spreadsheet, and run the numbers backward and forward. Investing can take a toll on your emotions, but the numbers should determine your investing decisions—not your emotions.

Before we show you how we analyze an MTR, there are two things we must cover first.

1. Know when to walk away.
2. Always trust but verify.

WHEN TO WALK AWAY FROM A PROPERTY

Often, it is emotions that keep investors from closing on a property, but I have also seen many cases where emotions lead investors to buy bad deals. I encourage you not to get caught up with what others are doing. You must focus on your goals and your investing strategy. Do not get distracted, including getting caught up in your own emotions.

If a deal is no longer a deal, walk away. Do not purchase something just because you want to buy something. Another deal will always come.

TRUST BUT VERIFY IS CRITICAL

Investing in real estate is like dating. You can trust, but you must verify. How often have I showed up to a date thinking the guy I'm meeting was six-foot-one (because that's what he says in his profile), only to find out we are eye-to-eye? I am five-foot-five.

If the agent says the deal has 12 percent cash-on-cash returns, run the numbers through your calculator to ensure that is the case with the capital expenditure (CapEx), maintenance, vacancy, and property management fees all included.

If the seller says that the utilities are all paid for by the tenant, you need to verify this with the lease. If the lease says the tenant pays for the water, you need to call the city and verify. Trust but verify.

CASE STUDY

Zeona's Trust but Verify Lesson

In July 2015, I was in deep. I was buying my first property in St. Louis, Missouri. It was my first out-of-state investment property.

A friend had referred me to an agent in Boulder who was licensed in both Colorado and Missouri. The agent said he could help me with the paperwork for the purchase in Missouri; this was my first mistake.

I found a place that looked move-in ready; it had been sitting on the market for a few months. The list price was $89,000. From some quick research online, I saw that homes in the area were selling way under asking, so I offered $70,000. With a bit of haggling, we landed on $72,000. And just like that, I was under contract on a three-bedroom home that I had never laid my eyes on—let alone driven by.

As I went through the inspection report, I noticed that the inspector couldn't get the air conditioner to blow cold air, so I had my agent ask the seller to fix it.

"The seller says it works," my agent said.

He advised me to move on to the next item, and I listened. We had a significant sewer repair that the seller had agreed to fix, and that repair became the distraction that won my attention.

Now that I have become an agent myself, I am adamant about making sure that the home's major systems are working for my clients. If the inspector can't get it to work, I am meeting the seller there to show me, or we are getting a professional out to take a look. This incident with the AC unit in Missouri was a lesson for me to not blindly trust someone's word.

Of course, when I arrived in St. Louis the day after closing, it felt like the beginning of a heat wave. (Although, it may have just been a regular July day in the Midwest!) It was more than eighty degrees inside the home and incredibly humid. This confirmed that the AC indeed was not working fine.

With the high demand for HVAC technicians at that time of year, plus the need to order parts, it took weeks to get the AC back up and running.

In the meantime, I bought window units because I had the rooms rented. Unfortunately for the guests and for me, this caused a lot of issues. It was not ideal for anyone.

The broken part was a $1,200 compressor. Fortunately, I had negotiated that the seller pay for a home warranty, which covered half of the repair.

As a new investor, I was super sour about that $600 for years, but looking back, it was just a drop in the bucket.

The lesson here? Verify that *everything* works before close, and don't let a lazy agent convince you otherwise.

We like to be conservative when analyzing our deals for two reasons.

1. We only want to purchase exceptional deals.
2. We want our actual numbers to be better than our analysis.

THE ABILITY TO ONLY BUY THE BEST

I have spent years building relationships with investor-friendly agents in my markets and finding other ways to increase deal flow. As a result, I have created a consistent stream of deals from trusted sources. Having constant deal flow means I can be pickier when it comes to investing, but it also means that I can pass on a 7 percent cash-on-cash return and wait for a deal with 10 percent or more cash-on-cash return. That is my investing strategy. But, of course, if you invest in an expensive market or use an appreciation play, your deal requirements will be different.

I believe it is dangerous in the real estate investing education world to tell students that they should invest in a deal for more than 6 percent cash-on-cash or that has $200 of cash flow per unit per door. Steadfast rules or lines in the sand do two things: (1) they ignore other factors that apply in investing and (2) they eliminate the need for investors to think. In my opinion, thinking is one of the most important things an investor must do. Allow me to further explain.

EVERY INVESTOR IS DIFFERENT. AS IS EVERY DEAL.

Every investor is different. Your investing strategy and your tax strategy are likely different from mine. Your reason for investing is not the same as mine.

In the beginning, Zeona focused on increasing her cash flow as much as possible, which meant investing in one-hundred-year-old properties in Missouri that required a lot of upkeep. Zeona was also doing the work of self-managing the properties to keep costs down. Now Zeona is happy to park her money in a turnkey, new construction property in Florida. That's because her investing strategy, and even her tax strategy, has changed. Every investor is in a different stage in their investing, and they, too, will change over time.

ONLY GOOD SURPRISES

I want to be pleasantly surprised when I review my profit and loss (P&L) statements for my MTR units each month. To ensure that happens, I will:

- Analyze deals conservatively.
- Ensure current tenants are satisfied to increase lease renewal and extensions.
- Respond quickly to tenant inquiries on sites like Furnished Finder and Airbnb.

I will purchase an MTR property using the following metrics (more on these shortly).

- 8 percent vacancy
- 5 percent CapEx
- 5 percent maintenance and repairs
- 10 percent property management

Often, my actuals will end up being closer to:

- 3 percent vacancy
- 3 percent CapEx
- 4 percent maintenance and repairs
- Zero percent property management

Note: *I still self-manage the units from afar, which allows me to keep property management fees to zero. But I like to make sure any deal I buy works with property management factored in, in case I decide to stop self-managing.*

There are a few terms every investor should know when analyzing an MTR deal.

- Vacancy
- Cash flow
- Cash-on-cash return
- Landlord-paid utilities
- CapEx
- Maintenance

VACANCY

First, do not be fooled by local real estate agents and property managers who tell you that vacancy rates are always 3 percent or lower. There is always a chance that vacancy rates could be higher. Thus, I am using 8 percent vacancy when underwriting my deals. I don't care how good you are at furnishing your MTR, finding and placing tenants, and managing your properties; your unit will be vacant at some time. Make sure you have enough rental income and cash flow to cover the times it is vacant.

There are two types of vacancies.
1. Physical vacancy
2. Economic vacancy

Physical Vacancy

Physical vacancy is when your property is—you guessed it—physically vacant. This means there is no tenant occupying the property, and, as a result, you are not collecting rent. This occurs for numerous reasons.
- You purchased the property vacant, and you need to secure tenants.
- You need to complete renovations before scouting tenants.
- There are maintenance issues during turnover.
- You want to make cosmetic upgrades during turnover, such as deep cleaning the carpets or removing the carpets and installing LVP.

A unit being vacant is not always a negative. If you can spend $2,000 on cosmetic renovations and then increase rent by $350 per month, I would suggest you allow the unit to sit vacant while you make those renovations. Be sure not to allow construction delays to result in unnecessary vacancies. Always check references and push for a short timeline when working with contractors.

With medium-term rentals, vacancies will happen every three to six months as a nurse's contract ends or a tenant's lease ends. Our goal is to limit vacancies as much as possible, but they will happen, so we account for those when analyzing a deal. *We typically use 8 percent as the portion of the year the unit will be vacant.* That is approximately one week of vacancy every three months.

So far, I have kept vacancy down to one to five nights in between stays. In addition to shorter vacancies during turnovers, I also have had 47 percent of my traveling nurses extend from three months to six months. This results in higher occupancy, which in turn also means less administrative work. Less turnover = fewer leases.

I often see investors become lazy when it comes to asset management. If you allow for seven days or more of vacancy between stays, you are leaving a lot of money on the table. I see 3 percent vacancy on average, which is a little less than five days every three months. Yet 60 percent of my MTR units are vacant three days or fewer a year, which is a 0.8 percent vacancy.

We will talk more about ways to decrease vacancies, but let me be the first to tell you: If you are willing to allow your unit to sit empty for no reason, why are you investing in real estate? If you, like me and most other investors, are trying to maximize cash flow, don't leave that money on the table.

We will cover ways to limit vacancies in Parts 4 and 5.

Economic Vacancy

I describe economic vacancy as there being a butt in the seat, but the butt is not paying. You have a tenant in your unit, and they are refusing to pay rent. There are a number of reasons this occurs, and there are a number of solutions when it happens. Many of you will invest in different states, markets, and counties. Each state, county, and city has different laws to protect you and the tenant.

CASH FLOW

As you've probably guessed by now, cash flow is the net income from an investment property, factoring in all operating expenses and debt payments.

Medium-term rentals command a higher rental rate, making it much easier to create money-making properties in an otherwise difficult city. As home sale prices continue to soar around the country, it is becoming increasingly difficult to find homes on the MLS that will cash flow as long-term rentals. This is especially true in first- and second-tier cities. In addition, many investors, especially first-time investors, may not be comfortable investing out of state in cheaper markets. Thus, the medium-term rental strategy allows investors to cash flow in cities where it would otherwise be impossible.

Know that cash flow is not the only reason to invest. Many investors in higher-priced markets such as Seattle, New York, San Francisco, and Los Angeles invest for appreciation. This may mean that the properties they purchase cash flow very little or nothing at all. Instead, these investors are anticipating that the properties will increase in price over time, making their investment worthwhile. Some investors are also primarily interested in real estate for its tax benefits, such as depreciation and tax write-offs.

CASH-ON-CASH RETURN

You've heard us mention cash-on-cash return (CoC) a few times so far. Let's dig into what CoC really means.

In essence, cash-on-cash return is the cash flow earned by the cash you invested versus how much money you had to put into the deal to create that cash flow. It is a rate-of-return metric that can be calculated by dividing your annual cash flow by your initial up-front investment.

$$\text{Cash-on-cash return (CoC)} = \text{Total annual cash flow} \div \text{Initial cash investment}$$

Think: How much money did you put out, and how much do you get back every year?

For example, if I put $100,000 into the stock market, I would anticipate a 7 percent return on my investment year after year, on average, across thirty years. That is how I think of cash-on-cash return.

Now let's apply the example to real estate investing. If I put an $80,000 down payment on an investment property, the property required $15,000 in renovations, and I spent another $5,000 in closing costs, that's a $100,000 initial investment into the property.

- $80,000 down payment
- $5,000 renovations
- $10,000 furnishings
- $5,000 closing costs, up-front loan points, and fees
- **$100,000 initial investment**

Remember, you want to account for furnishings in your initial up-front cost too. Read more on furnishing in Chapter Eleven.

I like to have at least 8 percent cash-on-cash from a property. Otherwise, I like what I call "lazy money," which is what I call investing in the stock market. Let me show you what this would look like.

Let's say I invest the $100,000 into the stock market. Experts say 6 to 8 percent is the expected average return if you were to invest in the stock market for thirty years. For every $100,000 I invest, I can expect $6,000–$8,000 in return each year.

This return sounds nice to some, but not for me. I don't typically purchase property with a 7 percent cash-on-cash return. Instead, I tend to buy properties with 26 percent or higher CoC. Yes, you are reading that correctly.

Here's what a good deal looks like to me.

Cash Investment
- $55,372 down payment
- $3,000 up-front renovations
- $12,000 furnishing and decor (two two-bedroom units for $6,000 each)

Income
- $3,800 monthly rent ($1,900 per unit)

Expenses
- 8 percent vacancy ($304 per month)
- 5 percent CapEx ($190 per month)
- 5 percent maintenance and repairs ($190 per month)
- 5 percent management fee (I self-manage with a virtual assistant) ($190 per month)

That leaves me with $2,926 per month after vacancy, CapEx, maintenance, and management.

My principal, interest, taxes, and insurance are $996 per month, leaving me with $1,930 in cash flow per month. Before tax, that comes to $23,160 in annual cash flow.

$$CoC = \text{Total annual cash flow} \div \text{Initial cash investment}$$

$$CoC = \$23{,}160 \div \$70{,}372$$
$$CoC = 32.9\%$$

These are the numbers I ran on a duplex I closed on in March 2022, which, as you can see, has a projected cash-on-cash return of 33 percent.

CASE STUDY

"Making the Switch from Long-Term Rental to Medium-Term Rental" by Ashley Gallacher

My MTR is located in Tacoma, Washington, thirty minutes south of Seattle, where I live. I purchased this property in March 2020 as the state of Washington was beginning to shut down due to COVID-19.

I purchased in this market because, in May of 2019, Redfin released a study saying Tacoma was the hottest housing market in the nation. I already knew the area and how attractive it was. I found the home on the MLS and was instantly attracted to it! It has a very large backyard that I would like to eventually build a DADU (detached auxiliary dwelling unit) on. The home is two-bedroom, one-bathroom, and 728 square feet. When I purchased it, it was fully remodeled on the inside and out. Even though I wasn't familiar with the MTR strategy when I purchased it, luckily for me, the property is five miles from three major hospitals in the area.

I was able to purchase the property at list price ($270,000) with a conventional investment loan and 20 percent down. The down payment and closing costs were roughly $65,000, which I funded with personal savings. When I first purchased the property, my strategy was to rent it out as a long-term rental. I found a couple to rent the house for $1,700 per month.

As a long-term rental, the cash flow was just shy of $200 a month. I did have lower CapEx and maintenance reserves, as the property was fully remodeled. Going into the deal, I knew the CoC would be lower, given the high cost of the market. But I also knew the appreciation would be really good. Almost two years after purchasing the property, it's valued at approximately $380,000, giving me $110,000 in appreciation in less than two years. As a long-term rental, the CoC return was 5 percent.

The Numbers
- Purchase price: $270,000
- Down payment: $54,000 with a conventional loan with 20 percent down
- Long-term market rent: $1,700
- Cash-on-cash return: 5 percent

During the pandemic, I began to fret. Uncertainty gripped the nation, and my long-term tenants decided not to renew their lease. I started researching other strategies, and quickly found the MTR strategy. I did a lot of analysis to determine if the strategy would work for me. To help determine the demand and pricing, I used Furnished Finder data as well as information from local Facebook groups. Shifting my property to an MTR was very attractive due to the higher cash flow and tenant base. I market my property to traveling nurses primarily, and I know they are already vetted through the agencies they contract with, so the risk of them not being good tenants is low.

Once I decided to move forward, I managed to furnish the entire two-bedroom home for $3,000. I used Facebook Marketplace, thrift stores, and Target to purchase almost everything. Now I rent the property for $2,500 a month (including internet and utilities). As you can see, I was able to increase the rent by $800 and increase my CoC return to 14 percent! I will be increasing the rent this summer to help offset property tax and insurance increases. The summers are highly desirable in this area, so I have no doubt I will be able to rent the property for slightly more.

The Numbers
- Purchase price: $270,000
- Cost of furnishing: $3,000
- Medium-term rent: $2,500
- Cash-on-cash return: 14 percent

Medium-term rentals are a very good way to increase your cash flow and still have a relatively passive income stream. Being in the Seattle/Tacoma market, where home prices are high, allowed me to significantly increase my CoC return while still getting the appreciation benefits. There are so many resources available to learn more about them! Don't be hesitant to start this strategy; just educate yourself and make sure the numbers make sense.

More of Ashley on Instagram @rei.ashley_pnw.

LANDLORD-PAID UTILITIES

When calculating your recurring expenses, be sure to include landlord-paid utilities. For the MTR strategy, it is the landlord's responsibility to cover all utilities. These include:
- Trash
- Sewer
- Water
- Gas
- Electric
- Lawn care and snow removal
- HOA dues when applicable
- Internet

We no longer provide cable services in our MTRs, so that is not a monthly fee we have. Instead, we provide high-speed internet and purchase smart TVs (or devices such as a Roku or Amazon Fire TV Stick), allowing the tenants to log in to their favorite streaming services on their own.

During the due diligence process, Zeona and I call all utilities providers and verify charges. When investing in a new market, it is important to understand that their seasons may not be the same as yours, so account for more snow in some places or higher air conditioner usage in other areas. This may sound like common sense when reading it. However, I have seen investors purchase a property assuming natural gas is $80 per month on average, only to find out it is $350 per month. Even with high cash-on-cash returns, that kind of surprise is not welcomed! Protect yourself and your investment by properly handling the due diligence process.

You may also find out that trash services are included in your property taxes or that the gas and electric bills are combined. Not only is every market different but also every unit can differ. For example, I own a duplex where the water is sub-metered, meaning we can calculate water usage, allowing the tenants to pay their own water. One unit in the duplex is a long-term rental and the other unit is a medium-term rental, where I pay the water. I own another duplex in the same town and the water is not sub-metered, so even though not both units are furnished, I pay the water bill for the entire building.

Meanwhile all of my other multifamily properties have water all together on one meter, making it difficult to charge the long-term tenants automatically.

Ways to Decrease Utilities

When you rent a furnished unit, utilities are covered by you, the landlord. Let's keep more money in your pocket with some tips to decrease utilities.

- Ensure your property managers change the air filters on your properties.
- When you replace appliances, replace them with more energy-efficient appliances.
- Caulk all windows and ensure there are no ways for cold air to come in or to escape, especially when investing in colder climates.
- Add weather stripping around all windows and doors to ensure the house is efficiently heated and cooled.
- Install water-efficient showerheads. (Some municipalities will give you these for free or at a discount.)
- Change light bulbs to LED or another energy-efficient light source.

CAPITAL EXPENDITURES (CAPEX)

- Foundation
- Roof
- HVAC
- Electric
- Plumbing

I tend only to count these five as CapEx because they are the systems that will cost me a pretty penny (plus, it is easier to memorize five things than twelve). Different investors' lists may vary, but a CapEx list might include any expensive fix such as:

- Windows
- Siding and exterior facade
- Replacement appliances
- Flooring
- Additions to the property like an accessory dwelling unit (ADU)
- Bathroom and kitchen remodel
- Concrete placement or paving an entire driveway

The difference between CapEx and maintenance can seem subjective at first. Replacing parts on your air conditioning unit or replacing the thermostat is a maintenance line item, whereas completely installing HVAC into a house would be a capital expenditure.

Like most things in investing, an investor's comfort level is going to determine how much they set aside for CapEx. Your CapEx amount is determined by the number of repairs needed for a property over time.

When I initially analyze a deal, I use 5 percent for CapEx. To clarify, that is 5 percent of the monthly rental income that goes into a savings account for each property each month. Some are more conservative. Maria and Lane Koch are investors in Kansas City who take on large-scale renovation projects. If they know a house has a CapEx item that needs to be replaced eventually, they save 8 percent for CapEx until they replace some items during renovations. After rehabbing the properties, they set aside 5 percent.

Every investor is different, and every property is different. For example, a friend recently purchased a new construction property. She is only anticipating needing 2 percent for CapEx, since the property is brand-new. Then, we have Sylvia, an investor who invests in Texas. Sylvia has completely gutted and renovated some of her units, while other units are in dire need of repairs. Thus, her CapEx percentages are different for each property she owns.

Once you have a certain amount of properties, you will likely change the amount you set aside each month again. For example, Soli, an investor in Cincinnati, owns twenty-six units. She has a large enough nest egg set aside for repairs that she no longer sets aside 5 percent of the rental income each month. That comfortable dollar amount changed as she owned more properties, and some investors' definitions of "comfortable" may vary. For example, a savvy investor recommended Soli set aside $30,000, but Soli feels better with a minimum of $50,000 in accessible cash for repairs.

Keep in mind that when the CapEx account is spent, it needs to be replenished. You may want to keep a higher cash position if your CapEx funds would take considerable time to replenish after an expensive repair.

I have mentioned before that steadfast rules are difficult in investing, so writing a book for the masses challenges me to create guidelines. As always, I encourage you to put tools in your toolbox that allow you to determine what CapEx percentage is best for you, your properties, and your investing strategy.

MAINTENANCE AND REPAIRS

No matter how well a house is built, things will break. When they do, you want money in the bank account to cover these costs. This is why we recommend setting aside another 5 percent each month for maintenance and repairs.

Preventative maintenance is something Zeona resisted for a long time. She was trying to save money but found that she was instead "stepping over dollars to pick up pennies." She has since learned that the longer she waits on a maintenance project, the more it costs.

First, she started to fix things the moment issues came up. Now she has taken it a step further and even looks for ways to take preventative measures. For example, most HVAC companies have a program that offers maintenance subscriptions. You join their program, and they come by twice a year at a discounted rate to service either the furnace or the AC. In places like St. Louis, where broken AC is a health risk, you don't want to take the chance of having down days waiting for a repair. Instead, with a simple biannual appointment, make sure systems are functioning well. Have a professional replace the furnace filters routinely and get ahead of any needed repairs.

Smart Thermostats

ZEONA: Tenants do not always realize that it is unnatural for the AC unit to be down as low as sixty-five degrees. Plus, when utilities are included in your monthly rent, and you want the home icy cool, who cares?

This is a problem because it can freeze the line and cause a costly repair. This issue comes up more often in older homes that don't have thorough insulation ductwork or a strong unit. As a preventative measure, we recommend having smart thermostats and locking a high and low temperature setting. You can move it upon request, but it is a nice feature to control from your smartphone— not to mention the cost savings.

Plumbing

ZEONA: Our best advice to you? Unless it's a one-bedroom, one bathroom, don't invest in a unit with just one toilet. You have been warned! We know this sounds silly, but some of our most stressful events have been toilet emergencies. If the only toilet is nonfunctioning late on a Friday night and you can't get a plumber out until Monday, you can imagine the drama that can ensue. We aren't sure why most of these issues happen in short-term stays, yet we've had all kinds of weird things removed from toilets, from wipes to menstrual pads to a full-on diaper! A kitchen sink that doesn't have a disposal is another item that guests can be hard on. Zeona's plumber once pulled an entire sandwich out of the sink!

We have found that a stylish, framed sign with dos and don'ts can go a long way. We recommend those for your bathrooms and kitchens to prevent some recurring issues.

ADDITIONAL EXPENSES WITH FURNISHED RENTALS
- Supplies such as towels, soap, and cleaning supplies
- Cleaning turnover
- Small maintenance repairs with wear and tear
- Occasional furniture updates or replacements

OTHER TERMS TO KNOW
Real estate is a world full of jargon, but fret not; we want to bring you into the inside circle! The terms we've discussed (and those below) are not an exhaustive list, but they are the most common terms you'll come across in your real estate investing career.

Gross Operating Income

Gross operating income = Rents – Vacancy + Other income

Other income includes items that tenants pay you for in addition to rent, such as laundry, parking, pet rent, renting storage on the property, or a shed in the back.

Gross Operating Expenses

Gross operating expenses are the total routine incurred expenses that come with ownership of a rental property. These include:
- Property taxes
- Insurance
- Maintenance and repairs
- Utilities
- Property Management

Net Operating Income

$$\text{Net operating income (NOI)} = \text{Gross operating income} - \text{Gross operating expenses}$$

To calculate NOI, simply subtract all operating expenses from all revenue earned. NOI is used to calculate capitalization rate (cap rate), which tells us how valuable a property is. Remember, you are investing in real estate to make money, so you must measure the profitability of the property somehow.

Remember:
- Gross refers to what you earn.
- Net refers to what you take home.
- And the NOI metric does not include capital expenditures (CapEx).

Capitalization Rate (Cap Rate)

You can calculate cap rate by dividing the NOI by the current market value. Most investors can use cap rate to compare similar real estate investment properties' values.

Capitalization rate = Net operating income ÷ Current market value

Example: $100,000 per year NOI ÷ $1,000,000 current market value = 10% cap rate.

You may also see cap rate calculated with the following formula: Capitalization rate = Net operating income ÷ Purchase price. We do not like this equation for several reasons. First, if there is no purchase price—such as if a property is inherited—it makes it impossible to calculate the Cap Rate. Second, for properties purchased decades ago or even a few years ago, the purchase price is not reflective of the current value and misconstrues the Cap Rate.

We hope you take the time necessary to master both deal analysis and due diligence. We still stand by our first statement that you do not need to be a pro at mathematics to master this skill. That being said, deal analysis is a crucial skill for every investor. It seems obvious to say "do not buy bad deals," but we feel it is important to reiterate that point here.

If, during the due diligence process, the numbers no longer make sense and the deal is not actually a good deal, it may be best to walk away. However, that does not mean that a messy inspection or higher CapEx costs are always reasons to walk away from a deal; there are scenarios where higher expenses or more headache in some areas can pay off in spades. Instead, let the numbers guide you in your decision-making.

PART 3
Your Team and Why They Matter

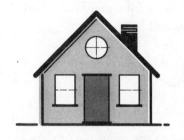

CHAPTER NINE

KEY PLAYERS

"Alone we can do so little, together we can do so much."
—HELEN KELLER

As you certainly know by now, both of us place a significant emphasis on travel. We have both traveled to more than forty-five countries on six continents. Plus, we have no plans to slow down, even as our real estate portfolios grow. Even if travel is not a priority for you (or perhaps it is not possible with where you are in your life), we want you to think about what you want to make more time for in your life.

Maybe you want to spend time riding your bike, and that means three to four hours spent on the saddle on a Saturday without worrying about checking your phone or even being in the range of cellular service. Or maybe you want to spend more time with your young children without distractions constantly pulling you away during those precious years. We want you to figure out what you want from life. If it's not spending time with family, on a bike, or in an airplane, what is it?

Before you put together your team, be thinking about *why* you are investing in real estate in the first place. Get in the right headspace. That way, if you have a unit that needs to be turned over, you are not quick to head over there yourself. Instead, you consider hiring things out. To do that, you need an on-the-ground team you trust. That is where this chapter comes in. We will show you how we have done all of the following from thousands of miles away.

- Created consistent deal flow
- Analyzed properties
- Completed the due diligence process
- Closed on properties
- Furnished units
- Screened tenants
- Managed the move-in and move-out processes
- Completed massive renovations
- Scaled our portfolios

We can both travel as much as we do because we have developed systems and processes that allow us to be hundreds and even thousands of miles from our properties. We want to make it very clear that we are not doing any of this on our own. Our on-the-ground team and virtual assistants make this possible.

Let's quickly review the five steps to acquiring a property.

- **Step 1:** Decide how will you finance the property (Chapter Four)
- **Step 2:** Identify a market (Chapter Five)
- **Step 3:** Identify deal criteria (Chapter Six) and the type of property you are looking for (Chapter Seven)
- **Step 4:** Master deal analysis (Chapter Eight)
- **Step 5:** Build your team (Chapter Nine)

Investing in your market may seem easier than investing from miles away. But we disagree.

We have found it easier to invest long-distance. Investing in your nearby market makes it more hands-on. Investors say they will hire out renovations, repairs, and even furnishing a unit, but they end up driving out to the property time and time again because it is "easier" or "saves money." It may be cheaper to put in some sweat equity, but you have to ask yourself: Does this align with my goals?

SARAH

As I am writing this chapter, I am sitting in Mérida, Mexico. I am staying here for one week with thirteen friends who all invest in real estate. Owning real estate allows us additional income, but it also allows us to say yes when friends invite us abroad. This morning, I reviewed an inspection report on a duplex that I am under contract on. Afterward, I emailed my agent my concerns and sent a list of what I wanted to negotiate with the seller to repair. I did all of this from my computer in Mexico. I have never seen this duplex, nor have I ever visited the part of town it's in, and I will not see it until after close.

This chapter will show you how we grew an on-the-ground team for our medium-term rentals from afar and how you can too. Chapter Sixteen will cover management.

Let's begin by saying who needs to be on your team.

- Investor-friendly real estate agent
- Mortgage lender or loan officer
- Property manager
- Real estate attorney
- Real estate–focused CPA
- Contractors and general contractors
- The cleaner (This is your MVP, so we have dedicated the entire next chapter to them)

As I outlined in Chapter Six, I was able to invest from 8,000 miles away only because I had built trust with an investor-friendly agent. Likewise, your agent can be the foundation of your trusted on-the-ground team. Let's dive into how to find an agent you can trust.

FINDING AN INVESTOR-FRIENDLY REAL ESTATE AGENT

What Is an Investor-Friendly Agent?

An investor-friendly agent is a licensed real estate salesperson who understands investing. They likely invest themselves and own rental properties. They will know the basic terms of real estate investing and have a good understanding of investing strategies. An investor-friendly agent is going to make your investing much easier, saving you hundreds of hours and thousands—if not hundreds of thousands—of dollars in the long run.

Key characteristics of an investor-friendly agent are:

- Communicative
- Outstanding negotiator
- Understands your investing strategy
- Finds off-market deals
- Confidently analyzes deals
- Offers connections through the market

Now, we want to clarify a few things. Your investor-friendly agent is not the same as your residential real estate agent. Here is how an investor-friendly agent can stand out:

Communicative

Being communicative does not mean that an agent answers every time you call. A great investor-friendly agent is busy looking for deals and negotiating contracts. They may not answer every time you call them, and that's okay! Their job is to take you, the client, from contract to close. Their No. 1 skill is in negotiating the contract and ensuring you make it to the closing table with agreeable terms. With that being said, the market and the seller often dictate what we can get a property for—if prices in a market increased 17 percent in 2021, that is neither the agent's fault nor yours.

When I coach real estate investors, I often hear my clients complain about the agent not being responsive. A lack of communication is a problem, but a lack of responsiveness is not. Here's why.

I want an agent who is always "on the hunt." Instead of answering me all the time, they are looking for opportunities for me to invest in. This means the agent is often finding off-market properties through a number of marketing campaigns and networking. If my agent doesn't answer my call because they are out knocking on doors, and they call me back later that evening, I understand and am excited to have an agent who works hard to find good deals for me.

Outstanding Negotiator

In my opinion, being a top negotiator is the best trait in any real estate agent. I like kindness, too, but let's not try to ask for too much. Everything is a negotiation. Securing an off-market property requires negotiating with a distressed seller or an owner of a distressed property. Negotiating terms on purchase agreements also requires ninja-like negotiating skills. The inspection period includes another round of negotiations on seller-required repairs or price adjustments. An agent's negotiation skills can mean a difference of tens of thousands of dollars or, often, you winning on the property at all.

Understands Your Investing Strategy

If you are looking to invest using the MTR strategy, give your Realtor this book! Seriously. Be willing to educate them on what you're looking to do. Not every flipper will find an agent who also flips, so not every MTR investor is going to find an agent who is also using the MTR strategy. Instead, find an outstanding investor-friendly agent and be willing to train them on what you are looking for in a property.

Finds Off-Market Deals

Finding good deals is key. This is where I get a lot of pushback from my agent-coaching clients. Some agents believe it is the investors' job to find the deals. This can be true in some markets. But in many markets around the country, great investor-friendly agents send deals to their clients each and every week.

Finding off-market deals can be hard, especially in certain markets. That doesn't make it impossible. I teach my agent-coaching clients how to find on- and off-market deals. As a result, they are closing more transactions than before, and their investor clients are thrilled. If you are looking for an agent who works with investors, ask them how they find deals. This will quickly tell you if they have a consistent deal flow.

Confidently Analyzes Deals

Whether the investor or the agent finds the deal, it is key the agent knows a good deal when they see one. Analyzing deals should be a top skill for both the investor and the investor-focused real estate agent.

I do not have a mathematics degree, nor do I particularly like math. But I like money, so I learned how to analyze deals and calculate things like annual cash flow and cash-on-cash returns confidently. If you have a real estate agent who is excellent at finding deals and negotiating contracts, but they are weak in calculating estimated repairs or cash-on-cash returns, I advise you, the investor, to train them or send them in the direction of someone who can! I didn't know how to calculate gross operating income when I first started in real estate, yet I was a tremendous asset to my clients because of my ability to communicate clearly and find off-market deals. Now that I understand the numbers behind real estate, I have even more value to offer.

I am confident that anyone smart can learn how to analyze deals in a matter of weeks, if not days.

Offers Connections through the Market

Behind every great investor is a great on-the-ground team. Having an agent with a solid network they can refer you to allows you to buy sight unseen and manage from afar. I have been able to complete a long-distance BRRRR because my investor-friendly agent introduced me to everyone I needed to make this possible.

Not All Agents Are the Same

I recently taught a class to a group of residential real estate agents. They sell upward of $100 million in real estate each year. I was teaching on investing in real estate, with a focus on buying money-making out-of-state rentals.

One of the real estate agents raised their hand to ask, "What is cash-on-cash return?"

I was glad they asked. The truth is, an agent does not need to know CoC to take a residential buyer or seller successfully from contract to close. However, you do need to know CoC to invest in real estate successfully and work with investor clients.

When you are looking for a real estate agent to help you grow your real estate portfolio, remember that you are not simply finding the No. 1 agent by sales volume or listings. Often, these No. 1 agents are not going to be the best match to find you your next value-add small multifamily that you rent to traveling nurses.

When It Rains, It Pours

Let me tell you a story of how knowing an investor-friendly agent changed my investing strategy altogether.

"If you find a good enough deal, you can find the money," a mentor told me back in 2019. Unfortunately, I was not in the place to hear it at the time. I was frustrated that none of the twelve offers I had written had been accepted. Of the four times that I did go under contract, I had to terminate every time. I terminated after finding mold, exaggerated rent estimates, inaccurate rehab estimates from inexperienced agents, and seller-exaggerated leases. After months of not going under contract, I was emotionally exhausted, frustrated, and nowhere closer to my cash flow goals of ten months prior.

When I heard yet another experienced investor essentially say, "Money just appears," I was not believing it.

"Easy for them to say," I thought. "They own 120 units and have a net worth of $10 million."

This scarcity mindset was not serving me. I will be the first to say that this scarcity mindset stunted my portfolio growth and my personal growth—no doubt!

In April 2021, I had an offer accepted on a fourplex in Omaha, Nebraska. After reviewing the inspection and leases, I was confident this one would stick and I would make it to the closing table. Then, under contract and doing a happy dance, I was surprised to see my phone buzzing from Des Moines, Iowa. I compare this event to something that happens in dating. Stick with me.

When you are single and dating, you have to kiss a lot of frogs (or, in my case, swipe on a lot of duds). Then, one day, you find someone worth your time, and you start to see this nice suitor exclusively. You may even go so far as to delete the dating apps altogether. You have a good feeling about this person.

But when it rains, it pours.

A "Sarah-is-happy" Bat-Signal shines bright in the night sky, alerting all previous suitors. Duds and studs alike start to text you. It was quieter than a school library two months prior, but now that you are moderately happy with someone new, they swoop in to ruin it. It's like they have Spidey senses and think, "Sarah's happy. Let's stir up some trouble."

More or less, this is what happened in my real estate investing life, and it's not an uncommon occurrence. (After all, this book is not about my dating life.)

I was elated when I went under contract on the Omaha fourplex. The seller accepted my 3.5-percent-down FHA financing, even though everyone in my investing circle was convinced this would be an impossible feat.

That's when my agent in Des Moines texted me, "I found you a deal."

"A little too late, my friend," I thought. "You snooze; you lose."

But then I saw the numbers on the deal in Des Moines.

These are two duplexes next door to each other, comprising four units in total. To recap the numbers:

- $385,000 purchase price ($193,500 each)
- $25,000 estimated rehab ($12,000 each)
- $520,000 ARV ($245,000 each)
- $4,400 ($1,100 market rent or after-repair rent per unit)

I realized if *I* snoozed on this deal, *I* would lose. But how would I pay for this?

I thought back to the saying that had annoyed me so much two years earlier: "If the deal is good enough, you will find the money." I was determined to shed my scarcity mindset and try something new.

At this time, I had never used the BRRRR method (let alone a long-distance BRRRR), hard money, or private money.

It is essential to reiterate the power of the investor-friendly agent. This agent texted me directly about the deal. He'd found this BRRRR deal on the MLS. It was a duplex listed by a tired landlord, a seller wanting to move to Florida—along with the 2 million others who migrated to Florida in 2021.

When my agent spoke to the seller, he asked, "Do you own anything else?"

Real estate agents and investors alike: Listen up.

You should *always* ask, "Do you own anything else?"

Do not ask, "Are you selling anything else?" or even, "Are you willing to sell anything else?" These questions will immediately put the investor on the defense.

Instead, ask, "Do you own anything else?" Investors have one thing in common: We are proud to talk about the real estate we own. If you can get an investor talking about their portfolio, you may be able to convince them to sell part of it to you. That is exactly what my agent did. It turns out the seller owned the duplex next door and was willing to sell me both simultaneously. When it rains, it pours.

But how was I going to fund this?

It is not an exaggeration when I say that my whole world changed when I read Matt Faircloth's book, *Raising Private Capital: Building Your Real Estate Empire Using Other People's Money*. It gave me a step-by-step process on using private money and how to ask for it. Like Zeona, I used private lending to fund one of my deals. Let's call him Josh—because that's his name! Josh and I went to undergrad together, and to my surprise, he had been watching my real estate investing journey from afar. Josh reached out to me on Instagram.

His message to me went a little something like this: "Sarah, what the f*** do you do?"

"Excuse me? Hi to you too," I replied.

"What do you do for a living? You're always posting about traveling the world but you're also posting about investing in real estate. So really, what do you do?"

After I explained that I was a long-distance real estate investor buying real estate in the Midwest while traveling the world as I pleased, he replied, "Great. I want to lend you money."

It turns out that Josh had been lending money to flippers in Baton Rouge, Louisiana, where he lived. However, as home prices increased, the flippers were starting to take their foot off the gas pedal. Josh was happy lending his money to the flippers at 9 percent interest, but now the flippers were not needing Josh's money. With inflation on the rise and Josh's cash piling up in low-rate savings or, even worse, a checking account, he needed to find a way to make money on his money.

I realized that I could pair four strategies on these Iowa duplexes.

1. **Hard money:** I would borrow 80 percent loan-to-value from a hard-money lender at a 9.1 percent interest and two points.
2. **Private money:** I would use a private lender for my down payment, the 20 percent down required by the hard-money lender.
3. **The BRRRR strategy:** I would use my own money for the renovations, rent the units out as quickly as possible, and refinance into a thirty-year product that the hard-money lender offered at the higher appraised value with the goal of getting all of my money out.

4. **Medium-term rental strategy:** I would furnish the units when the current tenants moved out and rent them to traveling nurses.

Even though I had just closed on the fourplex in Omaha, I now had a way to fund this deal in Des Moines.

Here are the actual numbers.

- $385,000 purchase price ($193,500 each)
- $77,000 down payment required (borrowed at 9 percent from my private lender, Josh)
- $23,436 actual rehab (I put this on a new Chase credit card to earn 120,000 points, and I paid it off every Friday using my own money.)
- $525,000 ARV ($260,000 and $265,000)
- $4,950 rent collected per unit ($1,325 + $1,325 + $1,450 for long-term tenants; $850 for inherited tenant)
- $2,879 monthly PITI

I plan to furnish the units once the current tenants move out and charge $2,000 per unit ($3,000 more per month across all four) using the MTR strategy. The power of combining these strategies should not be ignored, and the power of having relationships with investor-friendly agents in any and every one of your desired markets should also not be ignored.

MINDSET CHECK-IN

Sarah didn't think, "I can't afford this." Instead, she thought, *"How* can I afford this?" The power of mindset continues to play a vital role in her investing success. We cannot stress enough how crucial it is to think positively, especially when investing in real estate. Things tend not to happen when they are most convenient.

Now that it's clear that finding an investor-friendly agent can expedite your success as an out-of-state investor, let us show you how to find one (or ten). Keep in mind that not every investor-friendly agent will want to work with you, so in this chapter, we will also cover ways to be an ideal client for your agent. There are multiple ways to find an investor-friendly agent.

How to Find an Investor-Friendly Agent

- **BiggerPockets agent marketplace.** (www.biggerpockets.com/agent/match) This resource allows investors to search for and connect with agents in a specific market who identify as investor-focused.
- **BiggerPockets forums.** (www.biggerpockets.com/forums) Investors can post on the forums asking specifically for investor-friendly agents.
- **Facebook groups.** I use Facebook groups to network with both investors and agents in the market I invest in.
- **In-person networking events.** Attending in-person events can be a great way to build relationships with agents in your area.
- **Calling on listings.** When you see an investment property for sale, I recommend calling the listing agent to build a relationship with them. If this agent is listing this investment property, they may have other investment properties available now or in the future.
- **Networking with other investors in the area who own rental properties.** I find some of my best referrals from savvy investors in the area. Leaning on others who are two or ten steps ahead of you is a great way to save time and build your network. Network with other investors who have MTRs and STRs and become known around town as someone who helps with housing. Share tenant opportunities that are not a good fit for you with your newfound friends. This will open many doors for you as people will want to help you out in exchange.

How to Interview Investor-Friendly Agents

First, you want to build rapport with these agents. You are not getting on the phone to quiz them or grill them. I highly recommend you read *How to Win Friends and Influence People* by Dale Carnegie if building rapport does not come naturally to you. If an agent likes you and wants to do business with you, they are more likely to send you deals. If they don't, you can expect to not hear from them.

A couple of things to avoid when working with investor-friendly agents:

- **Not being preapproved.** If you are not lendable or you do not know how you will finance a property they will send you, you run the risk of dropping to the bottom of the agent's investor buyer list.
- **Asking them to spend an hour on the phone talking about the market or the state of the market.** You are not to use them as a human Wikipedia. As an investor, you should do your own research and come to the conversation educated and ready to act.

How do you know if an agent can analyze deals? And if you've met them outside of an investor-specific resource (like the BiggerPockets agent match), how do you know if they're investor-friendly?

It's often not realistic that a prospective agent will find a viable property on demand, so instead, I ask them to send me the last two to three deals they sold to an investor. I run the numbers, and if the deal is a deal, I proceed with the relationship. I generally ask them what deal analysis spreadsheet they use and if they're willing to use mine. To my surprise, most of the agents I work with now are willing to run the numbers through the same spreadsheet I use, which eliminates back-and-forth between the agent and me.

I also always ask an agent about their portfolio and what they are looking to invest in too. This helps me decide how savvy they are and if we are looking for the same deals.

Red Flags

- **Not sending deals.** I can forgive an agent for not being responsive. Remember, I will first assume they are out looking for deals. But if an agent has not sent me a deal in months and I am constantly checking in with them, then they are not the agent for me.
- **Lying.** If an agent is dishonest at any point in our relationship, they are gone. Honesty and integrity are key in this industry.
- **Making (and not saving) mistakes.** Mistakes will always be made in a transaction. But it is the great agents who find a way to save a deal and get a client to the closing table.
- **Not learning from mistakes.** It is okay if an agent sends me a deal that's been analyzed with a small mistake. But if they keep making the same mistake and are not willing to take action to grow, they do not belong on my team.

Ways to Be an Ideal Client for Your Agent

Always be thinking of ways to add value to your agents' lives. When I invested in Omaha and was living in a van in New Zealand, I started looking at tax records in the town. I wanted to know who owned the multifamily properties next door to the fourplex. I sent the owners' names to my investor-friendly agent. My agent then started calling sellers and sending mailers to those owners to see if they would be willing to sell their properties. I saved my agent time by providing information, making her life easier. I view my relationship with her as a partnership. If I pass on a deal my agent sends me, I am referring my agent to other investors I know. I want my agents to close on every deal they find.

FINDING THE REST OF YOUR TEAM

Once you have found your investor-friendly agent, you can start building out the rest of your team. Again, I recommend getting recommendations and referrals from your real estate agent and other investors.

Finding other investors is pretty much the same as finding real estate agents.

- BiggerPockets forums
- Facebook groups
- In-person networking events
- Calling on listings
- Looking up who owns the most real estate in your town

For Facebook groups, I suggest typing in "real estate investing" plus the city's name in the search bar. Facebook will suggest a number of investor-focused real estate groups. Join them all. I recommend spending time searching within the group. At some point, an investor has asked for a plumber or an attorney or something else that you also need. It is nice to see that you are not alone, and also get the resources you need with a click of a button.

Another great resource is Meetup, a website that can connect you with local events in your area. You can also find local investor meetups through the Bigger-Pockets "events and happenings" forum.

Once you have built a network of other investors, they can help you find the rest of your team. Never underestimate the power of a referral.

Finding a team takes time. I like to tell my coaching clients, "It isn't hard, but it also isn't easy." Have patience, and remember that people want to be treated with kindness. Be sure to always be thinking of ways to add value for others, and good people will start to ask to be on your team.

CHAPTER TEN

YOUR MOST VALUABLE ASSET—THE CLEANER

"You can only become truly accomplished at something you love. Don't make money your goal. Instead, pursue the things you love doing, and then do them so well that people can't take their eyes off you."

—MAYA ANGELOU

Our rental businesses are successful because of the team we have built around us. In the previous chapter, we outlined how to find (and keep) your Dream Team. This chapter will focus on the most important person on your team: the cleaner. Frankly, nothing would be possible without our MVP.

This chapter will teach you how to find, interview, and maximize profits with the right cleaner.

New investors always ask us about the terrible-no-good-awful things that happen in a furnished rental. Here are two:

1. My cleaner texted to notify me that there was human urine in the hall closet. My cleaner has seven children, so she cleaned it up without a complaint but wanted to inform me before I left the guest a review. Lucky for me, the guest booked through Airbnb, so with a few clicks, I had charged the guest an extra $100 cleaning fee, which I immediately gifted to my cleaner for her trouble.

2. My cleaner texted me photos of my blinds, letting me know it looked like a dog had chewed them. Sure enough, the previous guest had a dog. Again, the booking was through Airbnb, so I sent a payment request. The guest apologized profusely and sent me the money. Meanwhile, my cleaner went to Home Depot, purchased the same blinds, and reinstalled them for me.

A great cleaner will go above and beyond for you, even when you don't ask for it. They are also your eyes, ears, and nose on the ground. On another occasion, my cleaner let me know that the hallway was smelling. I shipped air fresheners and deodorizers to her personal house, and she delivered them to the unit at her convenience.

You can have the perfect location, a well-appointed, gorgeous home, and guests lining up around the block to stay there. But without a great cleaner, you've got nothing.

A lot of investors just starting out will try their hand at cleaning themselves. They soon find it can be a tedious task over time, and if you decide to leave town or want to scale your business, you will need someone to tag in. If you want a successful MTR business, having and keeping a great cleaner is an essential skill.

Where to Find Cleaners

How do you find this incredible person who will care for your property like their own? Get to know it inside and out and recognize when something is off or out of place?

- **Agent recommendation**—We love a good recommendation. If your agent has some experience or is on a long-standing team, they will have a spreadsheet full of vetted referrals. Get that immediately; your dream cleaner may be on it! (But agents don't deal much with having places cleaned, so if you strike out, fret not.)
- **Property managers**—Property managers should have a lot of recommendations for you. They deal with move-in and move-out, which entails the work of painters, cleaners, handy people, and the like. However, they may not know a "vacation rental" cleaner, and the regular weekly house cleaner is a different animal, as is the move-in, move-out cleaner. Keep that in mind as you vet recommendations. A vacation rental cleaner is partially a stager; they need to pay close attention to details and know how to make a hotel-worthy bed and fluff pillows like a champ. A move-in/-out cleaner is working in a vacant space; they are detailed enough to wipe down shelves

and baseboards, but they still might not be your person.

- **Other STR and MTR hosts**—Okay, we need to vent a little here. We know you love your cleaner, but some furnished rental hosts are stuck in the scarcity mindset and need to learn to share. We share our best cleaners widely and encourage them to build out a team to train others to do what they do so well. It all comes back to mindset. Because some hosts can get territorial, you likely don't want to message them on the booking platforms—they will get annoyed when they realize you are not inquiring about a stay. You will have much better luck at an in-person meetup event or through a platform like BiggerPockets, where you can connect with investors in your market.

- **Facebook groups**—If you search Airbnb as a keyword, dozens of groups will come up. You can also join Zeona's nationwide Facebook group, "Airbnb Investing." In those groups, people are constantly swapping contacts and advice on running their businesses.

- **Apps**—Taskrabbit is an excellent app that allows you to hire out odd jobs, such as moving a heavy piece of furniture, hanging some art, and cleaning. It can come in handy for furnished-rental owners like us who have found ourselves trying to move a couch or assemble a bed frame alone. The only thing to beware of is cancellations.

  Zeona had terrible luck trying to hire someone to help get a new couch up the stairs in St. Louis when she was orchestrating a purchase from Hawaii. It was an icy day, and she had three people cancel on her. Luckily, she had posted the old couch for free, and those people were picking it up just as the new couch arrived. She was able to throw them $20 to move it in place—thank goodness.

  Another excellent app is Properly, but it requires a paid subscription. This app has digital cleaning checklists with photos that allow the cleaner to check in when they arrive so everything is time-stamped. In addition, they have access to notes about things like the Wi-Fi code and where the trash goes, as well as a way to report damage right in the app. Properly also allows you to find cleaners in your area and submit job requests. Zeona has found at least one good person this way.

- **Google**—Zeona used to hire individual cleaners from Craigslist, but things have evolved quite a bit since she started in 2012. If you are turning to the World Wide Web, the first thing we'd suggest is googling "Vacation Rental Cleaning Service." Sure, a cleaning company may charge a little more overhead for hiring, training, and scheduling staff, but there are benefits. For example, a service can have more than one cleaner if someone is sick, there's more flexibility/availability in scheduling, and a company can fix or finish the work in case the person does a poor job.

If those options don't work out for you, we would also suggest posting an ad on Craigslist (we've gotten loads of applicants overnight). Just know that it's a wild card, and those people are largely unproven. I would vet them like a tenant. Ask for references and talk with them over the phone or meet them at the home to get a vibe.

Now let's dive into the hiring process.

Hiring Your Cleaner
THE CLEANER INTERVIEW

Whether you are making an ad or just inquiring over the phone, it's essential to set expectations. Here are some critical questions to ask to see if a prospective cleaner is a good fit for your needs.

- First, do they have experience with STRs or furnished rentals? (This is a must.)
- Are they available every day of the week?
- Can they be available during the cleaning window? (Typically, 11:00 a.m. to 3:00 or 4:00 p.m., depending on the size of the home.)
- Can they do a job on short notice? If not, how much lead time do they need?
- Do they have a team (alternates to cover if someone is sick or out of town)? If an individual cleaner, would they be willing to hire and train a friend to help them if you give them more business?
- Are they comfortable with technology? Can they sync to automation? Are they familiar with self-scheduling?
- If not, can you schedule with them by text or email? (This is important for automation.)
- Can they invoice you to get paid? This makes it easy so that you don't have to keep track of when they cleaned and if they have been paid. Make sure you set an expectation of how often you will pay; some people are antsy to be paid the same day, which doesn't work for us. (We pay once a week, but we let them know we can do weekly, biweekly, or monthly payments. Then we let them choose.)
- Can they be paid via credit card (for an opportunity to rack up points and miles) or PayPal/Venmo? We are often not in the same state as our properties, so we must make payments digitally (rather than cash or check). This way is also much easier to keep track of for taxes.

- If it's a team, what type of training do they do, and what is their policy around deep cleaning?
- A team Zeona used to use in Boulder would rotate deep cleaning rooms of the home, depending on the week, so that the house was not just surface cleaned. The team lead left a laminated sheet in the homes (functional, though not exactly tech-forward) and had the cleaners sign it with a dry-erase pen next to what they did and send photos of the house after each clean. That team lead was on top of it! We love it.
- Do they prefer to come to the home to give a quote, or can they do so over the phone?

PRICING

Part of setting expectations is discussing the money part of the equation. Some people get squirmy here, but it is important to be firm and confident. Always look people in the eye when discussing payment or commission; if you look around the room, you can give a nervous, untrustworthy vibe. Here are some points to go over during your interview call.

Make sure they understand you need a set price for every turn. The reason for this is there is only one price for cleaning on all the booking sites—cleaning fees are not a sliding scale on whether the guest stayed a month or six. We advise overshooting what you think it will cost (just in case) while aiming not to make it outrageous. After months, the home generally needs a deep clean, so plan for that. More often than not, we find someone won't clean once their entire stay, which is why we generally don't allow pets.

We tend to stay away from hourly pricing. But, even though our price will be a set rate, you will want to calculate that set rate based on an hourly wage. Here's an example: A one-bedroom generally takes two hours to fully clean, a two-bedroom takes three, a three-bedroom takes four, and so on. By hiring single cleaners, you can pay $25–$35 per hour. For cleaning companies, $45–$55 per hour is standard. Beware of predatory companies that charge more.

Underpricing

Beware of paying too low or negotiating hard to the point where the cleaner feels slighted. Cleaners will cut corners if they don't feel valued. You get what you pay for. This is not an area to skim.

Laundry

This price also needs to include laundry. Whether they do it at the property, take it home, or do it at a laundromat, it is the cleaner's responsibility, and we don't want items mixed with other homes'. Unless it is a luxury home, the items can be left in the dryer if it's too time-consuming to wait (just make sure to tell the guest). There should always be enough towels left in the house for the number of maximum guests. If there is an air mattress or pull-out couch, there needs to be bedding there for that, too, just in case. (We recommend you have three sets of towels and three sets of sheets per bed, just in case the cleaners get backed up on laundry.)

Oh, laundry. Laundry is the nemesis of our industry. It is ideal to have a washer/dryer in the home. But if you have larger homes, you may want to get a laundry service for the extra sheets and towels because a load can take a while. I have also heard of owners getting a second dryer to speed up the process. While a laundry service may sound convenient, it can be expensive, and the cleaners have to pick it up and drop it off, resulting in higher fees. It may be more cost-effective to pay the cleaner to sit with a book and wait for it to dry.

Inventory

Depending on the size of the home, you may ask the cleaners to inventory the number of sheets and towels in the house and, if laundry is not taken offsite, to have them count it every time. This may sound excessive, but sheets and towels disappear, and it allows you to know which guests to charge. This is worth it, even if you have to pay a little extra. Your cleaner should also notify you when the house is low on supplies (toilet paper, trash bags, etc.) so you can order more.

Training

Depending on where you hire your cleaner from, they may require more or less training. By managing MTRs from afar, we have had to hire and train cleaners from afar as well. Don't worry, it's doable. A good standard to set from the beginning is three complaints, and you're out. The great thing about running a furnished rental is that your guests will tell you when a clean is unsatisfactory.

Suppose we are managing more than one property in an area. In that case, we like to have a head person in charge, whether they are a contact at the cleaning company or someone we hired as a solo agent who has proven their dependability and skill, and agreed to hire and train the newcomers. We work with this person to decide how we want to track the cleans.

Here are some options.

- **Have checklists.** Some places have a checklist in a binder that is kept in each home that cleaners can reference. There are also online and digital systems, like the app Properly.
- **Require photos.** Zeona's Boulder head cleaner requires pictures of every room for every clean. She uses Slack to track that. We think it's handy to have photos to reference if there is an issue with a tenant.

Deep Cleaning

Sure, your cleaner will make the bed, wipe the counters, and scrub the toilet each time. But what about cleaning the windows, wiping the fan blades, and dusting the floorboards? It's essential to come up with some way to track this. You can have deep cleaning checklists, thorough regular checklists, or brainstorm other methods with your team.

Another thing that helps in this department is having different cleaners service your property. If it is the same person every time, they may get in a groove and always do it the same way; another person may deep clean different areas.

Prepping the Home

Make sure a part of your checklists or training explains how you want the home to be left. Do you leave towels on the bed? Do you like them folded a certain way? Chocolate on the pillow? Wine and glasses out? House manual on the coffee table? All these instructions are important to detail specifically; leaving items for the cleaner to figure out will allow more room for error. In Properly, Zeona has photos from the listing in the checklist so they can stage it precisely as it is advertised.

Most importantly, your cleaners must understand that the home is always to be left "guest ready," even if they think a handyperson is coming or they might come back later. Leaving a place unfinished can cause problems.

Gratitude and Respect

Cleaning is backbreaking work. Pay some respect to the people who do this sweaty work to allow your business to prosper. Pay them what they are worth, pay them on time, and always be kind. If you treat people right, they can be a part of your life and, most importantly, your property's life for years to come.

The right people will be dependable and loyal; build these relationships and long-lasting partnerships.

Our cleaners save us both money and headaches, and for that, we are eternally grateful. We make sure they know how much we appreciate them by sending small bonuses of $20–$75 here and there. We also make sure they get a holiday gift around that time of year. Never forget that you are running a business, and your cleaner is a large part of your success.

PART 4
Listing Strategy: Implementation and Management

CHAPTER ELEVEN
FURNISHING

A lot of hard work is hidden behind nice things.
—RALPH LAUREN

This chapter will show you how to furnish your unit for maximized profits and fewer headaches. We are not here to tell you exactly how to furnish your unit, but we will go over some tips and tricks. Every market is different, and every investor has a different taste in interior design. That's one reason why it is so fun! If your market demands more luxury, we recommend choosing higher-end finishes and decor. However, keep in mind that medium-term rentals still do not require the same level of luxury that a short-term rental might.

CASE STUDY

"Creating Remarkable Spaces" by Travis and Heather Sherry

"That's the place with the _____."

We've all said it. In fact, I'm guessing you do it every time you look for a place to book; I know we do! When we're sifting through one hundred tabs of different homes, there's often one defining characteristic that makes a property stand out. That property becomes "the place with the _____." Pool, hot tub, game room, sauna, amazing views, swing chairs, funky leopard-print wallpaper, etc. (Hint: Maybe don't be the funky-leopard-print-wallpaper house.) The list goes on and on. There's always one thing that sticks out about a house.

The key to success is making sure that you know *exactly* who you are renting to and then making your major defining characteristic speak to that person.

Most people say, "Oh, I'll take whoever."

Wrong!

Small families have different needs from traveling nurses, who have different needs from business travelers, who have different needs from a group of friends. You get the idea. So instead of going after everyone, go after your niche of traveler. So many people hate niching down, but they are wrong to.

Listen, you'll get other types of travelers too, but if you become the best for one kind of traveler—if you speak directly to them—you'll never have to worry.

When we first started doing rentals in Philadelphia, we did it wrong. We didn't know it at the time, but hindsight is 20/20. We bought all four-bedroom houses and went after "groups." You're probably aware that "groups" is a pretty wide demographic. Because of that, our listings did just average. Not great, not terrible. Average. And who wants average?

We decided if we were going to continue in the real estate game and put the time in, we might as well start being remarkable. That doesn't necessarily mean spending more money, but it does mean being more deliberate.

With our next house, which was also a four-bedroom, we decided that instead of going after groups we would go after "families with two or more kids." We put things in that families with two or more kids would want—custom bunk beds, swing chairs hanging from the ceiling (not one, but two!), and a playroom with kids' toys.

Our place booked...and booked...and booked...and now it is the No. 1 property in our entire zip code and has been featured by Condé Nast. We make over twice the rental income of an average four-bedroom in our area ($190,000 vs. $90,000). All because we are the "house with the swing chairs" or "the house with the custom bunk beds."

Pick who you are going after, get super specific (even though you are afraid to), give them exactly what they want, and you'll flourish. This applies just as much to medium-term rentals as to family-friendly STRs.

Learn more about Heather's remarkable designs on Instagram @extrapackofpeanuts.

Many investors will have the same first question about furnishing a rental: Should you do it yourself or hire it out?

Geography doesn't have to dictate this decision for you. If you are investing out of state, you have a few options for furnishing from afar. You can do it yourself, which we will cover later in the chapter. But first, consider when it is best to hire out the furnishing rather than do it yourself.

Let us tell you that it is both physically and emotionally tiring to furnish a unit without support. No matter how much you enjoy decorating, the physical strain of carrying furniture up stairs is exhausting. Likewise, simply putting together a bed frame that was delivered in a box thinner than your forearm is backbreaking work. Ever put together an IKEA bookshelf on your own and wanted to throw that little Allen wrench at the wall?

Whether you like decorating or loathe it, this will be a challenge.

For those who love decorating, you will constantly be restraining yourself from overspending and overdecorating—which can both happen, especially with the MTR strategy. On the other hand, those of you who do not love furnishing will lose patience with the copious number of minute decisions that must be made.

"Do I choose these throw pillows or those throw pillows?"

"Why do I even need throw pillows to begin with? You just put them on the floor every time you get into bed."

What it takes to furnish a unit is something unmeasurable. It requires patience and organization skills. We will do our best to paint you a vivid picture of the amount of time and money required to furnish a unit.

Sarah enjoys furnishing rentals so much that she founded a company that helps investors do exactly that. Arya Design Services has furnished units all across the country, both in person and remotely. Furnishing from afar is possible, and we will show you how.

Should You Hire It Out?

To decide whether you'd be best suited hiring out the furnishing of your rental, you need to ask yourself the following questions.

- Am I the best person to do this?
- Is my time worth doing something else?
- Is this why I got into investing in real estate in the first place?
- Would my money go further if I hired a professional to do this?

AM I THE BEST PERSON TO DO THIS?

If you have no eye for design, furnishing an MTR unit is not for you. Plain and simple. You don't have to be a professional interior designer to furnish an MTR, but if you genuinely struggle to grasp what makes a space look appealing and what doesn't (and if you don't want to learn), this is not the job for you. Add the additional service cost when you are analyzing deals. You may need to pay an interior designer or furnishing company $3,000 to $10,000, depending on their level of the service. Paying for help may be worth it to take this off your plate. If you're looking for permission to spend this money, here is your permission slip: Hire this out.

IS MY TIME WORTH MORE DOING SOMETHING ELSE?

Simply put, think about what your time is worth. Investors often ask how long it takes to furnish a unit. Furnishing one two-bedroom unit in Des Moines took Sarah approximately seven hours of just ordering things online (about a third of what it used to take her). This does not include collecting measurements of the property, visiting the property, installation, or tracking orders. It took seven hours to simply order the items needed to furnish the place. Plus, Sarah owns a company that does this for clients, so it is safe to say she knows a thing or two about ordering for a furnished rental.

If you hate picking out rugs and do not know what a duvet is, and if you have the money to spare (but not the time), add $5,000 to your furnishing costs and up-front renovation budget when analyzing deals. If you've gone for a good deal, the cash flow from your MTR units should more than cover the additional cost. Think of your time like this: If you are a whiz at finding off-market deals, the twenty-plus hours you will agonize over furnishings are better used for finding and securing your next deal. Or maybe you make good money in your day job, and you're already not spending enough time on your health, hobbies, or family. In cases like these, hire this part out.

IS THIS WHY I GOT INTO INVESTING IN REAL ESTATE IN THE FIRST PLACE?

We started investing in real estate to create passive income. "Passive" is an essential piece of this equation. While the MTR strategy is not as passive as long-term rentals and definitely not as passive as investing in other people's deals, the returns are almost always higher. Because of this, we are investing in real estate using the MTR strategy to maximize cash flow, even if it means being less passive.

However, if you have, say, a thriving law practice and want to spend more time with your three children, then maybe furnishing a unit on a weekday is not the right business or investing move for you. That's when we recommend hiring it out.

WOULD MY MONEY GO FURTHER IF I HIRED A PROFESSIONAL TO DO THIS FOR ME?

First, you should ask yourself: Are you good at finding deals? If you are looking to invest in real estate because you want to spend more time with family and less time working, then we recommend you hire a professional to do the work for you.

Sarah once had a tenant/roommate who had never been to IKEA. She also has a trust fund. (Why was she renting a room from me rather than buying her own home? This is still a mystery.) IKEA is not the right store for everyone, nor is it the right store for every unit. Suppose you are furnishing a high-end luxury mountain villa in Aspen; you should not be filling it with IKEA furniture. However, if you are a newly employed 25-year-old in Kansas looking to furnish a bedroom in a house you are renting, you should consider picking up a few items from IKEA.

When Sarah brought her friend there, she walked through it in a daze, which is not uncommon, since the store is a complete maze. After deciding she didn't want to purchase anything, she drove straight to West Elm and spent $150 on a throw pillow and $900 on a few other odds and ends.

"This was so much easier," the friend said as she swiped her credit card at the West Elm register.

"Well, duh," Sarah wanted to say.

Like many of you, this tenant would prefer the ease of a luxury store to shop for goods. If money was never an issue, we'd venture to say most people would do the same thing.

If you don't like to bargain shop or don't have a knack for finding deals, you can always hire someone who does. You could even save money in the long run by paying someone to do all of this for you. For example, let's say you hire someone for $3,000 to furnish your unit, and they have the know-how and the patience to shop at discount stores like At Home, HomeGoods, and IKEA. Maybe they also purchase used items through sites like Facebook Marketplace or Craigslist. The time they spend hunting for deals could save you more than $3,000.

How to Hire It Out

You can hire an interior designer or a company that specializes in furnishing MTRs and STRs for investors. Both will charge you for their services, plus there may be an upcharge on furniture. They will not only professionally design the space but also save you tens of hours. Possibly most importantly, your rental will go live on the market, earning money sooner.

An interior designer will carefully curate the space and choose a beautiful design that will make your unit stand out in listings, leading to higher rent and lower vacancy. This all means more money in your pockets. However, let us warn you that interior designers sometimes overspend. Your MTR unit in St. Louis does not need a $4,500 couch and a $3,000 rug. Cream-colored Moroccan poufs that your guests will put their feet on may be a good look at your primary residence or even your mountain home in Sedona, but they will not stay clean. In our opinion, there is not a good return on investment in an MTR unit in Oklahoma or Ohio on designer rugs, fine art, or delicate white throw blankets. Keep durability in mind, and it will save you money in the short term and in the long run.

Before you decide to do everything yourself, determine what your hourly rate is. For example, if you make $500/hour as an attorney, then it would make more sense to hire someone at $100/hour to furnish your unit for you. However, if you are determined to do this on your own, we can recommend a few things.

How to Do It Yourself

Hiring out the furnishing process may not be appealing for some of you. Maybe you are investing in furnished units because furnishing the units is half the fun. Or maybe you are still a new investor and a little strapped for cash, looking to save money wherever you can. If you are still willing to do the dirty work yourself, let us show you where to spend and how to save your money.

If you are investing in your own market, you can start collecting items from the moment you go under contract. However, we generally recommend waiting until you get through the inspection period. Contracts can go under for many reasons before closing, and you don't want to be stuck with a stack of furniture specially selected for a property you will now never own. Instead, we recommend waiting until you are confident you are going to close on the property.

Still, do not wait until the day of closing to begin thinking about how you will furnish the unit. Instead, start looking at decor options, drawing out your plans for the space, or even ordering before you close (if possible; we still recommend playing it safe). Often, items take longer than two days to ship, so plan ahead. Since the COVID-19 pandemic, logistics and shipping have been unpredictable. Planning is essential.

IF YOU'RE FLYING IN

It can be challenging to coordinate deliveries if you invest out of state, but it is doable.

If you are living out of state and plan on flying in to furnish a unit, we recommend taking a taxi or rideshare to the nearest U-Haul store and picking up a cargo van for your stay. A U-Haul van will often be the same price as a rental car and makes purchasing and hauling items easier, and protects them from rain, without being as cumbersome to drive as their oversized trucks. You can park in a big-box store parking lot or a residential street more easily. A van allows you to lock up the belongings, so you'll worry less about people stealing things than with an open-bed truck where items can be taken from the back on your quick trip to Target.

Last year, we flew to St. Louis, Missouri, to refresh two of Zeona's units. We recommend flying out to visit your unit or hiring someone to do this every two years. Items will not last through tens of guests, so you must have someone checking on the property at least once every two years. This person can be your cleaner or handyperson, but sometimes they miss things that you or another person with a fresh perspective might catch. Does the couch look dingy? Does the shower curtain liner need to be replaced? Stay ahead of normal wear and tear to keep your units looking fresh, homey, and appealing.

FURNISHING FROM AFAR

As you know, you can order almost anything online. Shopping online will save you so much time and allow you to copy and paste hyperlinks into your task-management software more efficiently. If you plan to purchase multiple MTR units, we recommend systematizing as much as possible. One way to do that is by purchasing from big-box stores and tracking what you buy and where you purchased it. We have a go-to set of pots, pans, kitchen knives, plates, and more for our units and clients. Anything that we can replicate, we do—as the famous adage goes, time is money.

Out with the Old; In with the New by Zeona

When I started, I was frugal and spent an incredible amount of time driving around to thrift stores and scouring through garage sales. Looking back, the end product was less than stellar. While it worked at the time, I see my style has grown and evolved with my wallet—thank goodness! In 2015, when I furnished two small (900-square-foot) two-bedroom homes, it took me about sixteen days to furnish them with the help of my two co-owners.

Flash forward to 2022, when I flew to Washington State with Amy Levine to furnish my rural blueberry cabin. We didn't have the "luxury" of secondhand items due to the small-town location, so I sucked it up and bought new. I budgeted seven days and hoped we would be able to pull it off in time, knowing I could extend my trip if I had to. To my surprise, we were essentially done by Day Three and spend the rest of the time sightseeing around the area while waiting for the last few packages to arrive.

With precise planning, buying new can save an incredible amount of time and provide you with items that will last much longer through guest wear and tear.

Staying Organized

Whether you hire the furnishing process out or do it yourself, we recommend using some type of task management software like Asana, Trello, or Monday. Some critics describe these apps as glorified to-do lists; different investors have different requirements when staying organized, but we've both found these programs do so much more than that. Task-management software will allow you to keep track of items you purchased, what's been delivered, and what you have left to find.

Sarah likes Asana because it enables her to add collaborators to a project. Thus, she can have other people on the Arya Design Services team look over what she has yet to buy for a unit. Asana also has a feature allowing you to include hyperlinks to the products you purchase, making it easier to track your purchases. You can keep receipts in Asana as well. It is a great way to keep organized.

At Arya Design Services, Sarah has a custom-made tracker sheet that monitors deliveries and estimated arrival times. Anyone who has furnished a unit can tell you that once the boxes start to arrive, the next thing you know, you cannot open your front door.

The Rent-Ready Process

Whether you are hiring it out or doing it yourself, here is the nine-step rent-ready process we follow.

Step 1: Gather information on the property and measure

Step 2: Design

Step 3: Order

Step 4: Ship

Step 5: Repairs and renovations as needed

Step 6: Clean

Step 7: Furnish, assemble, and decorate

Step 8: Photograph

Step 9: List

STEP 1: GATHER INFORMATION ON THE PROPERTY AND MEASURE

During the due diligence period, you must document as much as possible to make furnishing easier and faster. If you have access to the property, go armed with a tape measure and notebook. You will want to capture as many measurements as you can on that first visit to avoid making multiple trips to the property.

If you are an out-of-state investor, ask your agent or property manager to photograph the unit with as many angles and details as possible.

The next step is to get measurements of everything—and we mean everything.

Each Room

Unsurprisingly, you will need to measure every room. You may think a king bed fits, drive forty-five minutes to IKEA and forty-five minutes back, and put the bed frame together (for those IKEA shoppers, you know this is the most frustrating part), just to realize that it does not fit in your room; it takes up the entire room, with no more than eight inches to walk around the bed. Now you have to disassemble the bed frame, pack it into your Prius, drive forty-five minutes back to IKEA, stand in line to return it, and then navigate IKEA again to find the queen-sized bed. Not to mention you will have to cancel your mattress order, which you won't do in time, so you must make a trip to UPS to return that too. Oh, and the queen mattress you now need to order will come in nine days after your anticipated listing date.

This is a true story. Learn from our mistakes.

Each Wall

Often, investors take down room dimensions but forget to measure the property's wall space. We recommend ordering furniture pieces that properly fit instead of guessing and buying a piece of wall art that doesn't fit over the couch. The more time you spend buying the wrong decor and furnishing, the less time you spend analyzing deals and writing offers on your next deal. Build a scalable business by saving time.

Window Sizes

Your MTR unit must have blackout curtains in the bedroom. Blackout shades in the living room or other parts of the house are not a necessity (we don't recommend them, in fact), but in the bedroom, they are crucial.

Measure every window. Do not assume windows in the same room are the same size, even if they look like it. Trust us. We buy old houses, and we can tell you that it is rare that window frames or even the windows themselves are the same sizes.

We recommend putting the curtains three inches above the top window frame to create an illusion that the ceilings are higher than you think. For smaller windows, you can place curtains outside the window frame to trick the eye into thinking the window is bigger.

We also prefer the curtains to come one to two inches from the floor for the same effect. Do not let the curtains touch the floor. Tenants will never keep floors as clean as you'd like, and if the curtains are touching the floor, they will need to be cleaned or even replaced. They are also more likely to be tripped over, pulling the curtain rod off the wall and damaging it. Replacing curtains twice or even once a year takes time and money. Suppose you are investing from afar like us—who is replacing them and physically putting them back into the unit? Get ahead of those issues and keep those curtains off the ground.

Floor Space Where Rugs Will Go

One of the most common mistakes investors make is buying rugs too small for the space. Too-small rugs look tacky, but they also make the room look smaller than it really is. When an eight-foot-by-ten-foot rug fits, spend the money and make it work.

With that being said, do not splurge on rugs. If you allow pets, the rugs will not last, unfortunately. They will need to be replaced every two to three years, if not more often. We recommend low-pile rugs over anything too high to keep the rugs lasting longer. Also request that your cleaner deep cleans the rug every four to six months if you do not allow pets, and after every guest if you do allow pets.

Learn from Our Mistakes

Nothing had made Sarah laugh harder than when her friend Mary texted her a photo: It was of the kitchen table Sarah's mom had ordered for one of Sarah's MTR units in Omaha. Unfortunately, the table was twenty-four inches in diameter instead of the desired forty-two inches. The place looked ridiculous with a tiny, lonely table in the middle of the room. Unfortunately, Mary had already assembled it. This meant she had to disassemble it and make a trip to UPS to return it. Learn from our mistakes. Be sure to look over your measurements before ordering. Slow down. Ensure pieces fit before ordering to save time later in the process.

STEP 2: DESIGN

When purchasing items, two of the most important questions to ask yourself are: "Is it easy to clean?" and "Is this going to last?"

Replacing items costs money and decreases profitability. Just because something is cute or beautiful does not mean it belongs in your MTR. Personally, I do not recommend fake plants. There, I said it. I think they simply collect dust. Are they beautiful? Yes, sometimes. Are they a pain to clean? Yes! If your cleaner charges by the hour, and they spend forty-five minutes dusting each leaf—which often cannot be done with a duster but instead requires carefully wiping each leaf with a wet washcloth—it is not worth it. Find another way to make the unit stand out.

For sheets, pillows, linens, and throws, avoid materials and weaves that easily snag. Instead, focus on what washes well and will last. Rely heavily on reviews, and when in doubt, hire it out.

Design Tips from Sarah and Arya Design Services

When I am decorating a space, I think of three things:
- Drawing the eye in
- Stretching my or my clients' dollars
- Being mindful of the longevity of the pieces

Drawing the eye in means making the listing pop. You can do this by following the simple rules of interior design better than your competition.

One rule that I love to use is faking height where I can. We mentioned earlier how to place your curtains to give the illusion of a higher ceiling. If your unit has low ceilings, paint the walls, trim, and ceiling the same color to allow the eye to travel up with ease. Another trick we like to use is playing with low-profile furniture, such as low-to-the-ground coffee tables or couches. The other way I like to fake it is with a mirror. Mirrors add depth to a space and can give the illusion that an area is bigger than it is. For mirrors, bigger is always better.

Unlike the haircut I got in Italy that I regret, layers are always the answer in decor. This does not mean throwing things against the wall to see what sticks, figuratively or literally. Instead, thoughtfully layer in different textures, like with a statement rug. It's okay to opt for the plain couch; I usually do. But give it life with a textured or patterned pillow.

Hang your art correctly. Nothing irritates me more than when I ship artwork to a client's unit only to have them hang it three inches from the ceiling. The perfect height is eye level, which means the center of the art piece should be about 57 inches from the floor. There is no shame in getting out your tape measure!

The other art faux pas I see far too often is too-small art. A 3x5 postcard is cute when framed but not when hung on a seven-foot wall all by itself. If you place a piece of art on the wall and think, "Is this too small?" The answer is probably yes. Just like with mirrors, bigger is better. Are you trying to save money? Visit Hobby Lobby every week until the art is 50 percent off—they place their wall art on sale every other week (the alternating week is table decor). There you go! Oh, and furniture is always 30 percent off there, so don't get too excited.

If you want your listing to stand out from your competitors, make sure something stands out. Picture your living room right now. You likely see a lot of rectangles, right? The TV stand, the TV itself, the couch, the Wayfair side table, the West Elm pillows you got on clearance—all rectangles. I recommend throwing in some shapes. Swap your rectangle coffee table for a round one, or add an oval-shaped chair or ottoman. Another tip is to not go too big with your coffee table. You don't want it to overpower the couch and the room.

Stretching my clients' dollars is a top priority of mine because we are investors, after all. If you want to splurge on a handmade rug for your personal home, do it! But I don't advise that for a high-foot-traffic area in a property you are renting to strangers with pets. While there are things that I wish every unit had, I stay conservative in my spending when furnishing medium-term rental units. This is why I shop at budget-friendly stores like Hobby Lobby for artwork and At Home for washable rugs. Remember, this is not your chance to be featured in *Luxe Interiors + Design* magazine.

In addition to keeping an eye on the budget, I'm mindful of the longevity of pieces. For example, certain fabrics do not wash well. Pillows without washable covers will have to be thrown away when a nurse spills wine on it after a long shift at work. Durability is just as important as decor when you are furnishing an MTR.

Catering to Nurses

As we've discussed, the primary tenant pool for MTRs is traveling medical professionals. As of January 2021, there were around 1.7 million traveling nurses in the United States.[17] Plus, the U.S. is seeing an increased need for traveling nurses; as of September 2021, there were an additional 30,000 open positions.[18] The nature of the traveling nurse job means that nurses are taking twelve- to eighteen-week contracts and so need temporary housing. Many owners of these furnished rentals have the ability to switch to the medium-term model, yet this isn't happening. We believe this is mainly because the opportunity is not widely known.

Zeona first heard about renting to traveling nurses from a friend who was a nurse herself. Of those nearly 2 million traveling nurses this year, many may be ready to book your unit! Even if you aren't planning on marketing exclusively to nurses, furnish it so they book yours over any other competition in your market. Here's what nurses want.

- **Blackout curtains.** We recommend curtains that match the wall color or similar. You do not want bold colors that stand out. Also, when in doubt, order longer rather than short. It will make your ceilings look higher rather than having them end just below the windowsill.
- **An incredible mattress.** We recommend the twelve-inch Zinus Green Tea mattress.
- **A safe and secure place to park and a well-lit entrance**, as they may be coming and going at odd hours of the day.

Purchasing Furnished Homes

Instead of worrying about furnishing a home, some investors prefer to purchase pre-furnished homes. If you are using financing to buy the property, it can be nice to avoid the upfront cost of furnishing an entire unit and instead wrap some of those costs into your loan. If you purchase a furnished property, we recommend having an itemized list of everything included in the sale, such as furniture, kitchenware, linens, and towels.

Purchasing a furnished rental could save on initial setup cost, but some investors find themselves still replacing much of the furniture in the house because it hasn't lasted through the wear and tear of multiple seasons of guests. Other times, the investor does not like the aesthetic of the current decor. In these cases, they will replace some of the furnishings and decor after close.

Unless she buys a stunningly decorated unit, Sarah prefers a blank slate. It

---

17 https://www.beckershospitalreview.com/nursing/let-s-talk-about-the-nursing-shortage.html

18 https://www.beckershospitalreview.com/nursing/going-back-to-a-staff-job-is-just-not-an-option-high-travel-nurse-pay-worsens-shortages-across-us.html

can be more involved than you'd expect to decide what items will stay and g
in a pre-furnished unit. In contrast, Sarah has a plug-and-play list that she uses
that allows her to purchase and deliver items straight to the unit with a few
clicks—saving her time. Plus, she knows the quality of the items is up to her
standards, including the aesthetic she wants for the property.

STEP 3: ORDER

Now that you've measured and planned all the spaces in your unit, it's time to
order everything. If you are furnishing from afar (or even if you're in your local
market), you'll likely be buying most or all your furnishings online to expedite ·
the process and create a scalable business model for yourself. There are four items
you should be sure *not* to skimp on.

1. The mattress
2. Blackout curtains
3. Quality bedsheets
4. Something to make the listing photos pop. These can be beautifully
   curated pieces like coffee table books, a great accent chair in the living
   room, or even an accent wall in a bedroom. Whatever you decide, we
   recommend making it unique yet budget friendly.

Furnishing your rental doesn't only refer to the big-ticket items like couches
and beds. And your furnishing doesn't stop at decor and rugs either. You also
need to include the basics that will make living in this rental a pleasant and
comfortable experience. We call this the "MTR starter kit." Having these items
readily available when your tenant arrives allows them to come and enjoy the
unit comfortably without having to run to the store to buy essentials like toilet
paper or hand soap.

It is essential to note that what you would include in an STR would differ from
an MTR. Unlike a vacation-oriented Airbnb, you do not need to provide a week
or more supply of paper products or coffee. You want to give just enough that they
can get by for a few days. Keep in mind that many traveling nurses are coming
from another state and often move in just before orientation or their first day at
the hospital. Making their lives easier means you are more likely to get a five-star
review or someone who wants to extend their stay. A little extra hospitality can
translate to fewer vacancies, which means more money in your pocket.

we include in the MTR starter kit.

lls of toilet paper

box of trash bags

l of paper towels

ponge or dish brush. This is especially important if your unit does
not have a dishwasher. You will want to make it easier for your tenants to
wash their own dishes, leaving less for your cleaner to do. This also helps
with the longevity of your kitchen utensils, silverware, and pots and pans.

- Two dishwasher pods if you have a dishwasher, or a small container of dish
  soap if your tenants will be handwashing
- Two laundry pods if you have a washer and dryer either in the unit or on
  the premises

While we provide these supplies as part of the MTR starter kit, the guest is
responsible for replenishing the items. Unlike with STRs, we do not provide toilet
paper and trash bags for the entirety of their stay.

Cleaning Supplies

We recommend providing some cleaning supplies to make it easier for the tenant
to clean the unit. If a tenant is living in the unit for three months, you hope they
are cleaning the floors, kitchen, and bathroom thoroughly, at least a few times.
While some tenants will go out and buy cleaning supplies, most will find a way
to skip cleaning altogether if possible. Thus, we encourage you to offer cleaning
supplies, including:

- A multi-surface vacuum
- A mop or Swiffer
- A bucket with washcloths
- A multi-surface cleaner to wipe down countertops
- Glass cleaner
- Toilet bowl brushes

You want to make it easy for the guest to clean the unit.

Kitchen

We recommend providing everything you need to cook a meal from beginning
to end (minus the ingredients) for the kitchen. This includes plates, bowls, cups,

wineglasses, mugs or coffee cups, pots, and pans. Think of it as including everything you would need to cook a pasta dish:

- A large bowl
- A strainer
- A pot
- A pan
- Tongs
- A baking pan in case they want lasagna (or brownies)

While that is not an exhaustive list, use it as a guideline. You don't want your guests to be frustrated that they don't have what they need. A guest staying three months will cook some meals from home, but they also won't want to run out and purchase a saucepan or wine glasses. Be sure to include those. If this is a high-end home, we also recommend a blender, tea kettle, toaster, and anything else you'd like to have in your own home. Remember that the rental price point may dictate the nurses' expectations. At the same time, this is not a short-term rental, so you will not be expected to include all the same bells and whistles of a luxury short-term rental.

Often, your guests will leave some ingredients in the kitchen after they check out. Ensure you ask your cleaner to check the fridge, freezer, and kitchen cabinets for things that should (or should not) be thrown away.

Kitchen basics also include olive oil, coffee, tea, sugar, salt, and pepper. Beyond that, it is up to you. Do not go wild buying the best of the best. Instead, focus on durability and practicalities. It is easy to say, "Oh, I love having this in my kitchen!" But this is not your kitchen. This is your investment. You want happy guests, but you also want a comfortable balance on your checking account.

STEP 4: SHIP

Once you have started to order everything, this is where chaos can ensue. We recommend tracking everything, including delivery dates and prices. Carefully tracking everything takes time up front, but it will save you from finding out you missed something essential (like bedsheets).

Tracking Shipments

In the shipping phase, we set up what Sarah calls a "Furniture Tracker." It is a thoughtfully designed spreadsheet that Kendra Martin, Sarah's business partner at Arya Design Services, created. It allows us to categorize each item by room—living room, bathroom, kitchen, bedroom one, bedroom two, dining room, and so on. Each item we need is listed with a hyperlink to the purchased product. This helps us go back and match throw pillows to the rug or ensure we ordered the correct curtain color. In addition to the hyperlink, we include the date it was ordered and the estimated delivery date. We also add a drop-down menu to help us track shipments. This list indicates if the item has been ordered, is in transit, or has been delivered. The Furniture Tracker allows us to keep everything in one place and keep track of shipments, orders, and pricing. Trust us: When you have more than one unit being furnished at a time, some type of tracking system is crucial.

Sarah has been at the store on a mission to purchase artwork for a bedroom and forgotten what duvet cover she ordered. With her Furniture Tracker, Sarah can easily open the tracker on her phone and instantly see the duvet cover, throw pillows, and rugs she purchased. The Tracker allows her to match and coordinate without the frustration of buying the wrong thing. Trust us, the fewer surprises you have when installing, the better.

STEP 5: REPAIRS AND RENOVATIONS AS NEEDED

Depending on the unit, you may not have any renovations or repairs. In this case, make an itemized list of what needs to happen before furnishing the unit.

Zeona tends to buy properties that require little to no renovations. On the other hand, Sarah buys properties that need at least minor repairs or TLC. She has even purchased a property where she took the entire second floor down to the studs.

We recommend that you purchase something you are comfortable with and that fits your budget. We have seen investors take on a $50,000 renovation only to end up $25,000 over budget and three months over. Be sure you have a clear idea of what kinds of renovations you are willing to make.

If you have renovations to complete at the unit, you must plan accordingly. For example, do not have an upholstered bed frame in the bedroom when your general contractor is scraping the popcorn ceilings. Instead, plan and time everything so that furniture arrives after the renovation and after the unit has been deep cleaned. This may mean you need to hold off on ordering furniture—but trust us that it is better to delay delivery than to clean paint off a brand-new rug or accent chair.

Once your unit has repairs and renovation completed, it's time for a deep clean.

STEP 6: CLEAN

This book has an entire chapter (Chapter Ten) dedicated to finding and managing your cleaner because it is that important. We recommend having the cleaner deep clean the unit before you start furnishing. You will want kitchen cabinets and drawers cleaned out before putting in the silverware, pots, and pans. Assuming you are furnishing the unit yourself, it's better to hire a professional cleaner; let the pros do it, and spend your time getting started on the many pieces of furniture that need assembling.

STEP 7: FURNISH, ASSEMBLE, AND DECORATE

Depending on the size of your unit, plan on at least twenty hours of assembling and moving boxes. It takes more time than you think to open packages, build furniture, and clean up the mess of opening twenty to seventy cardboard boxes.

The pro of buying furniture already assembled is that you can skip the unboxing step. The issue you can run into with preassembled furniture is if you do not have a vehicle that fits the furniture or if you cannot maneuver the furniture up staircases or into the unit itself. Keep this in mind when ordering. It may save you time to order a dining room table online, even if you must assemble the pieces in the unit.

If you purchase furniture in person, you can rent a U-Haul cargo van or truck for as little as $20 per day, allowing more flexibility with furniture pickups. This is also a great option if you decide you want to scour the internet looking at places like Facebook Marketplace and Craigslist. When you walk into a house to pick up something from a seller, make sure to ask, "Is there anything else you're selling?" Sarah once walked away with an entire living room full of decor for less than $75.

The Dark Side of Facebook Marketplace by Sarah

I have spent hours on Facebook Marketplace purchasing everything from floor lamps to couches to televisions. You can waste so much time. Depending on your day job, it may not be worth it.

Sellers can:

- Flake on you and not respond to your messages.
- Tell you that you can purchase their item and then sell it to someone else before you can pick it up.
- Coordinate poorly, wasting your time, and be inflexible with their availability.

- Provide inaccurate descriptions of an item, making it seem like a better deal than it is. Then, because you drove all the way over to their house to pick it up, you purchase something that you may otherwise have passed on. This is particularly frustrating when you've rented a U-Haul to pick up an item. If you get there and the table isn't quite what you pictured, you are likely still going to buy it because you don't want your trip to be a total waste of time.

Overall, my negative experiences with Facebook Marketplace have made it a less-attractive option as time has gone on. Plus, I am furnishing more and more units these days. I need a more scalable business model, and, unfortunately, messaging strangers online to buy their used Keurig is not a good use of my time.

That being said, when I first started investing in real estate, I was short on cash and flush with time. I worked from home, and sending a few dozen messages on Facebook Marketplace was not a colossal waste of time. If anything, I enjoyed it. In between meetings, I would run out and pick up items around town as long as they fit in my handy Prius. (I can comfortably fit a queen bed frame, a queen mattress, and three eight-foot-by-ten-foot rugs with those back seats laid down. Comfortably might be a stretch, but you get the picture: A lot fits in a Prius. When Toyota is ready to sponsor me, let me know!)

As my business and portfolio grew, my time became more limited, so I am more likely to purchase everything online rather than hunt for deals like I used to. Every investor should find the option that best fits their unique needs in time, money, and convenience.

STEP 8: PHOTOGRAPH

First and foremost, your listing photos must be professional. *You must hire a real estate photographer.* You could furnish your home beautifully, but if you have amateur photos, it does not matter.

Ideally, you hire a photographer who specializes in interior design photography. Do not hire a portrait or wedding photographer for your listing photos. If you are spending the money to photograph the property, ensure the photographer has experience photographing property interiors. It is a bonus if they already have experience photographing furnished units for sites like Airbnb and Vrbo. That way, they know that sites like Airbnb favor photos shot in landscape rather than in portrait. If your photographer doesn't know this, you run the risk of paying for professional photos that hurt your listing rather than help. Airbnb can also connect you with a photographer, often for a discounted rate. In Zeona's experience, it can take up to two weeks to get the person to your home, so plan ahead. We have not used this feature, so we cannot endorse it at this time.

Here is where we recommend spending money to make your photos pop:

- **Improve the exterior.** We don't recommend overextending your budget to spruce up the exterior like you would if you were about to list a property for sale. However, we do recommend taking a moment to improve the landscaping. Also, the positive effect of a power wash should be noted.
- **Ensure the property is well lit.** Not only is this aesthetically pleasing, but it also helps guests feel safe when entering the unit. If you plan on renting to traveling nurses, remember that they are sometimes working really early in the morning or coming home after dark. Be mindful of safety to ensure they can enter the unit safely.
- **Clean the unit.** This may seem like a no-brainer, but you'd be surprised how many units photograph dirty. Take a moment to look on Furnished Finder for yourself, and you will see how cluttered and even dirty some units are in your local market. And please shut the toilet seat before photographing!
- **Ask your photographer to also take up-close shots of details like your coffee table books.** Capture the beauty of an accent wall, or any other feature that will help your listing pop. Remind your photographer that you want to use these photos to list on websites like Vrbo, Airbnb, and Furnished Finder.

STEP 9: LIST

Listing your unit for maximized profits is a detailed process. Read more on how to list your property in Chapter Thirteen.

Furnishing units can be exhausting but also really rewarding. The great news is that even though it's an intense process, it's also an iterative process—the more you do it, the better your systems will become. Learn how to do it right the first time. Then you can save money and time in the long run by understanding what pieces to invest in. As with many real estate ventures, the lion's share of the work is up front—which makes the payoff that much sweeter.

CHAPTER TWELVE

HOW TO PRICE YOUR MTR

> Challenges are what make life interesting; overcoming
> them is what makes life meaningful.
> —JOSHUA J. MARINE

ZEONA

I love Airbnb. You might think it's my ten-plus-year history with the site, but it's actually because of the opportunities it brings with its extensive marketing reach. Ultimately, Airbnb is just a marketing site, as are Vrbo, Expedia, and the like. People often think of them as techie engines with lots of functionality, but at the end of the day they are well-marketed classifieds.

When I switched to medium-term rentals, I thought I might only use Furnished Finder and retire my Airbnb profile. But I quickly learned that was not the best plan for me. While Furnished Finder can still see some changes in demand, traveling nurses get gigs year-round. The larger platforms like Airbnb attract tourists, even for extended stays, making it very seasonal. It took one large Airbnb booking of $1,000 more than my Furnished Finder rate for me to realize that I needed both. In combination with smart pricing software, Airbnb has allowed me to claim mind-boggling rates in my high-season months.

When I switched from short-term rentals, I also considered dropping the pricing software because it did not seem set up for taking longer stays into account. Ultimately, I decided it's worth keeping to capture the seasonal swings of rates. While it's not perfect, and we'll have to wait for technology to catch up to the

MTR trend, I know it's coming. Soon, there will be ways to automate and dial it in even better than we currently have it.

Here are some factors that we appreciate about pricing in the MTR space.

Name Your Own Price

You can name your price! While there is generally a range of what people are willing to pay, there is not much of a standard set or a "market rate" in the MTR world as there is with long-term rentals. When Zeona already thought she was at the top end of her rates, she updated her furnishings (with Sarah's guidance), refreshed the photos, and set the rate for her one-bedroom from $1,300 to $1,450. It was a real nail-biter to stand by and see how the new high price would be received. Yet, no one batted an eye, and it's been full ever since.

Don't concern yourself with housing stipends. Zeona heard a nurse in St. Louis mention that his monthly stipend was $1,250 and she thought the threshold for rental rates would stop there. But she continues to push the price up between guests and receives excellent tenants. If someone falls in love with your space, they will pay a premium to treat themselves to live there.

MTR allows you to make your own price rather than have it be completely dictated by the market. For example, Sarah can increase cash flow by paying attention to furnishings and decor. When you ensure that your listings pop, you will get more eyes on your unit. More eyes should mean more demand if you are making good design choices. In Omaha, her one-bedroom units rent for $1,775 while other furnished one-bedrooms in her area rent for $1,000. Why? The biggest difference is the level of furnishings.

Low Inventory

Julia Gates, an MTR host in Savannah, Georgia, loves to note that inventory is low for furnished rentals, and they are in high demand. Even with over one hundred units between those she owns and manages, she is still finding more demand. As a result, she is moving into the motel space to up her offerings. She recently told Zeona that she found a run-down motel charging just $18 per night. This place was so low-tech they were only collecting payments in cash. Julie plans to renovate, update furnishings, and list the rooms online; she knows she will "eat their lunch." This balance between supply and demand allows you to name your price and stay competitive—as long as you offer a beautiful space.

Zeona noticed this when she started using Furnished Finder in St. Louis.

Some days, ten or more requests would come in. At the time, she had four homes booked out for three to six months. Potential guests were reaching out to double-check her availability. Sarah has seven furnished rentals in the same area in Omaha, Nebraska, and often has to turn guests away because she is fully booked. In moments like this, we both think, "We wish we owned more MTRs!"

Not Many Professionals in the Space (Yet!)

At the moment, there is still room to grow in the professionalism of the MTR space. For years, individuals opened guest rooms or simple single units up to nurses, but now people from the STR world are starting to catch on. On Airbnb, many boutique hoteliers and interior designers have dominated the space, but there is still room in the MTR world to rise above the general listings. Interjecting some of what you learn here about design, furnishing, and listing creation will allow you to charge more than most of your competition.

Pricing Software

We know you are clever; otherwise, you wouldn't be here reading this book. But don't think you are so smart that you don't need pricing software. You do! Unfortunately, Airbnb's "smart pricing" is still not great. We find the prices are always too low. Remember, they are just incentivized to get you booked, no matter how cheaply. When Zeona switched to paid pricing software on her STRs, her income increased by 30 percent. This incremental pricing is also said to boost occupancy by 12 percent. Again, this is not a perfect science yet for the MTR space. Still, we know that the interest in the community is driving demand for developers to come up with better month-to-month pricing and hopefully more automated leases. (A girl can dream!)

We respect frugality, so don't worry—we won't direct you to pay for the hundreds of programs out now that have come up through the STR space. But we will recommend that you get two. One of them is dynamic pricing software, the other is software like Hospitable, which allows you to automate your process and which we will go over in Chapter Sixteen on management.

WHAT IS PRICING SOFTWARE?

Through an API connection direct to your Airbnb or Vrbo account, pricing software gathers data from over 10 million listings and gives you pricing suggestions and statistics to help you see how you are stacking up against the competition.

While we'll recommend three programs below, every investor has their own needs and preferences for technology. Shop around and go with the option that you enjoy using and helps you adjust your pricing strategy to get the most bang for your buck.

Software that we recommend:

- **PriceLabs**. PriceLabs is a dynamic pricing system for short-term rentals with property management systems integration.

  Zeona didn't use this software for a long time because its interface was clunky and difficult to navigate. But they recently had a face-lift and it's much more appealing. Some argue PriceLabs has the best functionality in terms of gap fill, which is important if you have an MTR that is rented short-term in the high season. Price Labs charges based on a price-per-listing model, which might work out cheaper if your property is over $2,000 per month, as the competition charges based on a percentage of the rental income, and if you have multiple properties.

- **Beyond**. Beyond, formerly Beyond Pricing, offers a dynamic pricing tool for short-term rentals that also forecasts revenue and connects you with support from local experts.

  Zeona has used this software for years and loves its easy-to-use and appealing interface. This software pulls the same data, yet each software has different features, so we recommend finding the one that suits your needs. She has found their gap-fill setup to be quite confusing. Their fee is based on a percentage of your bookings.

- **AirDNA**. AirDNA is an analytics and research tool for short-term rentals that many investors swear by. You can use them to create and download market reports, and they have a pricing tool, AirDNA Smart Rates, that dynamically adjusts your pricing strategy (and tells you why).

  AirDNA comes with a lot of impressive analytical tools, so it has unseated PriceLabs as the favorite among some data-oriented investors.

Additional Pricing Considerations
DISCOUNTS

If you come from the STR space, you may be used to weekly and monthly discounts. Obviously, if you are starting at a month-long stay, there is no discount. Occasionally, however, folks will ask for a multi-month discount. If someone has the gumption to ask for a discount, we usually reward them by giving something, like 10 percent, or working with them to find a good middle ground. We would rather close the deal than say no, which can turn them away.

EXTRA CHARGES

You may be surprised to see these here, but we see all the fees as your total revenue and as multiple levers of negotiation. If you list your cleaning fee too high, for example, someone might overlook your space.

- **Cleaning fee**. We set the cleaning fee a bit higher than our monthly clean rate ($10–$20 more), as this helps us cover stocking supplies and gives us a buffer if there is a rogue disaster clean that you want to give the cleaner a little extra for. It also gives a little buffer for a Christmas or "just because" bonus for your cleaner.

- **Security deposit**. In general, we don't get to keep these, and, quite frankly, we don't want the scenario when we would. We are making mention of this here because we charge less than the standard "one month's rent" you see in long-term rentals. Zeona charges $1,000 and takes the cleaning fee out of that when she refunds them. The reason for the lower deposit is to make it easier for guests. If they are finding new accommodations every three months, they are often having to come up with that extra lump sum before getting the previous deposit back. To make it easy on her tenants, Savannah host Julie Gates charges a $500 nonrefundable deposit to hold the space at the time of booking and makes all of her guests buy a $75 travel insurance policy. Instead of holding the $500 as a deposit that can be annoying to remember to reimburse, it is credited toward the first month's rent.

- **Pet fee**. If your guest has pets, you may charge an additional pet deposit or a pet fee that you get to keep no matter what. We often stay away from travelers with pets, because in our experience, they leave the homes quite dirty and the pet hair clings to the furniture and bedding. Once you host a pet, your home is no longer free of pet dander, which is important to some tenants with allergies. We have tried both a set pet fee and a price-per-pet fee. The set fee of $50 instead of $50 per pet seemed to work best. We have also heard of charging a monthly "pet rent." This could be $50–$100 per month. Sites like Airbnb and Furnished Finder only have a single slot for a pet fee, so you would have to explain the per-pet fee or monthly pet rent structure in your description.

The moral of the story is to purchase pricing software if you are using Airbnb or VRBO to book your guests. It will increase your income and occupancy, which will more than pay for itself. If you are only using Furnished Finder to find guests, pricing software may not be necessary.

CHAPTER THIRTEEN
LISTING CREATION AND ADVERTISEMENT

It is not the mountain we conquer, but ourselves.
—EDMUND HILLARY

Do you already have an Airbnb listing? Great! But that doesn't mean that it's ready to go. Even experienced Airbnb hosts have little missing pieces to tweak. While this chapter will discuss listings with the Airbnb format specifically, you can translate, cut, and paste these sections into Vrbo, Furnished Finder, and so on.

We'll go through the essential listing sections on Airbnb so you know how to set them up. This can take sixty to ninety minutes the first time you build it, so set aside adequate time. The name of the game is being thorough. You will want to check back on your listing from time to time, as Airbnb adds new settings often, and we believe that regularly updated listings are rewarded by showing up higher in the search results.

Listing Details
LISTING TITLE

In this game, you have one tiny thumbnail photo and a snappy title to compete with, so you want to make these fifty characters count. What are the biggest draws of your space? Do you have a pool or hot tub? Is it a cabin, tree house, farm, or some other unique property? Are you close to a famous landmark or hip area? Do you have a king-sized bed? Yep, that is a big draw for taller folks. Using emojis in the title can be eye-catching too.

PHOTOS

Have your photographer take photos from all four corners of rooms (corner shots look better than straight-on ones, giving depth and showing off a larger space) with some close-ups of art, pieces of interest, and amenities. Of course, you won't put all the photos up, but keep in mind that some of the best listings have forty-plus pictures. Ensure you have a photo of the outside and yard, as well as extras like the gym or pool. Take photos during the day (although we close the blinds and turn on the lights) and edit them or have the photographer edit them to make sure they are sharp, with good lighting. If you have a view, get a few photos capturing that. We've seen some higher-end homes get exterior twilight shots. Those can look really nice and set an inviting scene. Drone photography is also become more popular as of late, and one photo showcasing the surrounding mountain landscape or illustrating the privacy of your remote getaway can be the tipping point in getting someone to book.

A quick tip on arranging photos: Your first one is the most important because it is the thumbnail that gets a person to click in the first place. Make that the best photo you have, period. Once a potential guest clicks on your listing, they see your top five images. Please don't make them five angles of the bedroom. Instead, make sure those each showcase a different part of the home with the best five photos you have.

Make your home stand out to the increasing number of digital nomads. Include a desk and a comfortable office chair. If you really want to stand out, include a monitor to plug into. Airbnb has an added feature where you can include your internet speed test to show that your Wi-Fi is top-notch.

DESCRIPTION

This is broken up into four sections: Listing Description, The Space, Guest Access, and Other Things to Note.

Listing Description

In "Listing Description," we recommend going bullet-pointed, listing all amenities that make your place stand out: king-sized bed, pool, hot tub, game tables, etc.

Here is an example listing description:

> You'll fall in love with this perfect condo on your mountain escape to Boulder! Here's why...
> ✓ Mountain views from every room
> ✓ Pool right out your front door
> ✓ Wall AC unit for cooling throughout
> ✓ Desk for business travelers
> ✓ Free Wi-Fi
> ✓ Fully outfitted kitchen
> ✓ 50" Samsung TV w/ Roku—stream Netflix, Amazon, Spotify
> ✓ Off-street parking
>
> Ready to enjoy this & gorgeous views? Book with us today!

Short and sweet.

Brand-New Host/Listing?

Brand-new to Airbnb? Don't fret. If you've traveled with your Airbnb account, you may have some positive reviews as a traveler, which helps. If not, you can reach out to a few other friends who are Airbnb users to have them write a recommendation that will show up on your profile.

When we publish a new listing, we like to include a note at the top of the description: "New listing special—book now for low rates!" This statement transforms a new listing into a unique advertisement for guests to find. When a listing is published, Airbnb boosts the listing for a day or two, which helps earn the initial bookings. It is essential to get booked in this period because bookings help give the listing an SEO boost, making it show up higher in the search. This gives the listing an opportunity to be clicked on, saved on a potential guest's wish list, booked, and reviewed after a guest's stay—all events that also boost SEO, creating a healthy booking cycle.

The Space

Airbnb has a section called "The Space." We suggest two different approaches with this section. Zeona likes to describe the home room by room in a paragraph, illustrating a story using descriptive sentences like:

- "Luxuriate in the goose-down bedding."
- "Cuddle in on the cozy couch and watch a movie."
- "Let the stress melt away while soaking in the deep tub."

Others like to continue with the list approach. If you are going to go this route, you may want to keep it engaging by starting with reasons guests love your space. For example: "The things guests love the most about my home are the gorgeous mountain views, the bright light from the big south-facing windows, and the updated, open floor plan." This can work well in bullet-point form too.

Let your place shine. This is the spot to brag. The guests reading this far want information—talk up the amenities, and don't be afraid to be detailed. Airbnb gives you a lot of space for a reason, use it! Include details about TV size, bed sizes, special appliances, and anything else that might make the user click "request booking." Don't be afraid to be transparent. It can be helpful to clearly state what people may not like about the listing to attract the right guests for you, meet expectations, and get the best reviews. For example: "Guests love our proximity to all the downtown happenings. This listing may not be for you if you are a light sleeper."

The Wish List (the little heart in the top right corner of your listing)

Getting added to someone's wish list works in your favor. Your listing shows up higher in the search and therefore has a better chance of getting booked! For example, you can include this in your listing:

> "✔ To easily reaccess this listing or make sharing with your group easier, add this listing to your wish list by clicking the <3 in the upper-right corner."

We love it because it asks for what you want—to be put on their favorites list. Ask and you have a better chance of getting it!

Our main reasoning for being so descriptive is to prevent questions. But we want you to know that many guests will not read it, so we will go over auto messages in Chapter Sixteen on management.

Guest Access

This section is where you will detail how the guests will access the property. This is a little more relevant with STRs, where guests are looking at a number of properties (e.g., condos, private rooms, ADUs). If there's special information about, for example, street parking or preferred entrances, this is the place to write that.

Here is an excellent example of what you could include here:

> ✓ The whole house is yours for your stay!
> ✓ Keyless self–check-in
>
> A couple of days before your arrival, I will message you with:
> 1. Check-in details
> 2. A digital guidebook with all the house info you need and recommendations for my favorite activities and restaurants.

Other Things to Note

This is more of a miscellaneous section for anything you feel is relevant to the listing that doesn't easily fit elsewhere. It can include information about COVID-19 cleaning protocols, pet and guest policies, considerations about the area, and more.

Here is an example from one of Zeona's listings of what can go here:

> Please remember you're staying in a person's house, not a hotel. Please treat the space with respect, just as the previous guests have. If any problems arise, I will do my best to take action ASAP, but please note nobody is living on-site 24-7.
>
> For nonemergency issues, I do not send maintenance to the property during your stay, only after you depart.
> ☞ All guests must be 25+ except for children with parents.
> ☞ 4 people max. We charge per guest; please have an accurate guest count.
> ☞ There is a camera above the front door in place for your protection. If you touch or tamper with the cameras, you will be asked to leave immediately.

> ☞ No late checkout or early check-in. If you arrive early or depart late, there will be a $50 charge per event.
> ☞ No refunds for weather/natural disasters/power outages/acts of god/ other things that are beyond our control.
> ☞ We provide a start of supplies like toilet paper and paper towels. You may need to buy more if you're booking an extended stay.

None of Zeona's places have a camera, but she says it so that people do not try to sneak more guests in. The majority of issues we have had have been with young guests. Age 25 is a good cutoff. It's important to note if you usually have a pet living with you for guests with allergies.

Property Type, Rooms, and Bed Descriptions

These are self-explanatory and essential to fill out. All these details are helpful to keep guest questions to a minimum. The ad is your first line of defense. You don't want to spend time with a lot of back-and-forth conversation if you can help it.

Amenities

This section changes frequently on Airbnb. If you manage your bookings outside of Airbnb you will want to log in once a month or at least once a quarter to update this section and check all the boxes that apply.

Keeping It Light

Lately, we have seen a lot of listings with firm language that some may find off-putting. An example might be:

"Pets are NOT allowed. If you sneak in a pet of any kind, you will be charged an additional $250 plus an additional cleaning fee, and you will be asked to leave the cabin immediately."

Keep in mind that you are advertising to potential guests worldwide, and some things may not translate well. For example, some guests have gone viral on TikTok after criticizing long lists of extreme house rules set by their hosts.

We suggest striking a balance between friendly and firm. Only you will know what that proper balance is for your listing and the type of guests your area attracts. It is important to set boundaries, but you can do so in a way that doesn't put your guests on the defensive before arriving. A little hospitality goes a long way.

Pricing and Availability
BOOKING WINDOW
We only open our calendar five to six weeks out. We want to avoid having some-one book with an awkward (and expensive) three-week gap that we won't be able to fill. Instead, we want someone to inquire who is looking to start within a few days of the unit being available.

SYNC CALENDARS
If you are hosting on Vrbo and Airbnb, make sure to get the calendars synced up so they can automatically block each other when a booking comes in. This is done by importing and exporting the calendars to your calendar of choice—e.g., iCalendar, Google Calendar, Outlook Calendar. While it may sound difficult, trust us, it's as simple as copying and pasting a link. You've got this!

Furnished Finder is a lead generator for potential guests, not a booking site like VRBO and Airbnb. Thus, when guests find our listing on Furnished Finder, they contact us, and then we set them up with a lease. Then, we must manually go into Airbnb or Hospitable and block those dates to avoid someone double-booking.

Policies & Rules
CANCELLATION
Airbnb has cancellation policy settings that you can customize depending on the length of stay.

For stays *shorter* than twenty-eight days, there are several cancellation options. For new listings with no reviews, we recommend the "flexible" setting, which will enable guests to cancel up to twenty-four hours before arrival. Once your listing has four or more reviews, we recommend changing the cancelation policy to "moderate," which allows the guest a full refund up to five days before arrival. Strict cancellation policies can work on luxury and high-demand properties but can disincentivize bookings otherwise.

For stays *longer* than twenty-eight days, Airbnb now has two different cancel-lation policy options: strict and flexible. Once you have four reviews or more, we recommend you choose "strict." This allows the guest to have a full refund only if canceled within forty-eight hours of booking and at least twenty-eight days before check-in. This protects you from having a high vacancy rate if an MTR guest cancels last minute. The other option Airbnb gives you for longer stays is "flexible," which provides the guest with a full refund up to thirty days before check-in. After that, the first thirty days of the stay are nonrefundable. The choice is ultimately yours, but we recommend protecting yourself and ensuring your guests do not cancel last-minute, leaving your place vacant.

INSTANT BOOK TURNED OFF?

We can practically hear the short-term rental hosts gasping with horror. Yes, Airbnb says your listing shows up higher and is more likely to get booked when the instant-booking setting is turned on. But we need to make sure we limit vacancy as much as possible. We have found that MTR guests often have some flexibility in their dates. Maybe they are driving up or can come to settle in a few days before their contract starts. If they are required to send an inquiry, this allows you to start the conversation.

If local regulations restrict renting for under thirty days, instant book can be risky. It's only worth having instant book on if you are allowed to rent both short and medium term. Another drawback of having instant book turned on is that guests can book on any day of the month, leaving random vacancies in between guests. If this happens, you can switch your minimum night stay to one or two nights to encourage a short-term guest to stay in between guests.

If you choose to have instant book on—such as to rank higher or because you're open to short-term stays—make sure to require guests to be verified and have positive reviews. Add any rules to agree to that are essential to you. To minimize vacancy, you may be able to alter dates, and, in the worst-case scenario, Airbnb has a clause that allows you to cancel any guest penalty-free within twenty-four hours, although you wouldn't want to make a habit of it.

You can also require that instant-book guests read and respond to a message you set. One example message Sarah set for her Omaha units is:

> I hope to welcome you to this beautiful unit in the cool Benson neighborhood of Omaha. You must be 21 years or older to book. I allow pets, and there is a pet fee, so be sure to mark that you are bringing a pet. Come see why this neighborhood is top-ranked! Sarah

You can add house rules or expectations in this message, but be sure to be friendly and kind. Those who do not meet these requirements will send a reservation request.

Having instant book on can be nerve-wracking for some, and it's good practice to keep it turned off unless you are sure that your systems are adequate and that you are following all local regulations. However, if you are diligent about keeping your calendar up-to-date and setting the above rules, it can be great for your booking. It's a great feeling to wake up to the notification "Maria booked for 79 days."

CHECK-IN/CHECKOUT

For most of our homes, check-in is 3:00 p.m., and checkout is 11:00 a.m., which allows for enough time to offer same-day checkout and check-ins, further reducing vacancy. After a multi-month stay, our cleaners sometimes need more time, especially for larger units. In this case, we will leave the unit vacant for one night in between guests to give the cleaner enough time to deep clean the unit.

We set up every home with keyless entry, so the guests have twenty-four-hour access. No one wants to meet a tenant at 11:00 p.m., so having a keyless entry allows guests to do self-check-in. Most guests prefer this system. If there is an option to have self-check-in, we highly recommend it.

Info for Guests

GUIDEBOOK

The jury is out on this, and we highly doubt that any guests spend much time on the guidebook. According to Airbnb, higher quality listings tend to rank higher in search. This includes having your listing fully flushed out, so we would say it is worth the time to fill out the guidebook even if you are the only one who reads it.

GUEST MANUAL

We love this feature. Upon booking, guests receive access to the manual instantly and have everything they need at their fingertips. We suggest sending them there before check-in for a briefing. We also recommend writing in a bullet-point style instead of paragraphs so they take in the info. Most people do a quick browse. You can leave a more detailed version in a coffee table binder in the home.

SELF-CHECK-IN

Put the code and home-access details of any fancy-locking system you might have in this box. This is information that will only be shared with guests after a reservation is confirmed. We also have it detailed in a house manual section and sent to them automatically in the check-in message, three days before arrival.

Cohosts

This is where you send an invite to your co host if you want to give your cleaner access to the calendar without the addition of property-management software or if you are hiring a property manager. It is unclear how many properties co hosts are allowed to be accountable for (it used to be three). If you have more properties than the system lets you link to, you can go into the account under payout preferences and add the cohost's bank and tax information. This section also allows you to designate the percentage you are paying for hospitality management.

Superhost Status

Airbnb launched the Superhost program in 2016, and you may have seen a fellow host post their Superhost status on their social media as a badge of honor. While there isn't much research to prove that Superhost status does result in a significant increase in occupancy and revenue, it's reasonable to think it would give you a boost in bookings, even a small one. Superhost is a status that Airbnb gives to hosts who meet the following four criteria:

1. Host a minimum of ten stays in a year (or three reservations for one hundred nights)
2. Respond to guests quickly and maintain a 90 percent response rate or higher
3. Have at least a 4.8-star rating
4. Honor confirmed reservations, canceling fewer than 1 percent of bookings

With more than 4 million hosts, it's a good idea to find a way to stand out in a crowd, especially if you are in a highly competitive market. While most guests do not know the four requirements mentioned above, Superhost status gives the guest a sense of peace knowing that you meet the standards Airbnb set out.

It seems like Airbnb adds a new feature or amenity every time we log in, so if you are managing your business outside of the site (on a property management platform), make a habit of logging on once a quarter to keep it all up to date. Happy hosting!

Where to Advertise

When hosts start on Airbnb, they are often (justifiably) excited. They ask us how many sites they should be on and which ones are the best. You might be thinking the same thing. Hold your horses! While there are dozens of sites you can use, you only need one or two. We will go over the pros and cons of the most effective ones. We usually tell our consulting clients that the best practice is to start with one (Airbnb). After a couple of months once you feel like you know your way around and can manage bookings, you can add Furnished Finder. Then add one other, if you choose.

AIRBNB AND VRBO

As you may have noticed by now, we are pretty into Airbnb as a marketing platform. It has so much brand recognition in the space that it pulls in the broadest demographic and allows you to charge a lot, seasonally, for your space. Let's go over some of the pros and cons of this platform's unique features.

Pros and Cons

- **Highest price**. It should go without saying that while we love hosting, we are also doing this for a living. We want to optimize for the highest price possible. Airbnb allows us to do this. With their low fees on the host side and their incredible marketing prowess, they reach tourists with deep pockets who will pay top dollar for your high-season months. Furnished Finder's fees are lower, but they do not sync with pricing software, thereby missing out on the advantage of seasonal highs. VRBO has an 8 percent fee per booking, so you must adjust your pricing to account for that.
- **No lease, no deposit**. Not needing a lease is a time saver and is one of our favorite things about renting on Airbnb. While you could still write up a lease if you felt like you needed to, we do not, instead enjoying the simplicity of the process. The con is that no deposit is collected without a lease. Instead, Airbnb and Vrbo offer up to $1 million in coverage per incident. We have never had to rely on our homeowner's insurance policy and have gone directly through to their insurance. The main con of using their coverage is that it is a tedious process to claim and usually results in the host receiving a lesser payout than requested.
- **Professional photography program**. Marketing sites like Airbnb know that it's all about the pictures, so they offer a way to make it easy. Their machine-learning technology has a way of identifying which listings do not have professional photos. Then it sends hosts a prompted offer to send out a photographer for a fee. Airbnb gives you a quote based on the number of bedrooms, and they pair you up with a photographer in your area. Airbnb lists the benefits as a 20 percent increase in earnings, 20 percent more bookings, and recouped costs in one night.

The downside of using their program is that they don't give you copies of the photos. Instead, they upload them directly to the website "for your convenience," which makes using the images on other listing sites more challenging.

FURNISHED FINDER

Furnished Finder is the new kid on the scene. Despite their 100 million page views a year, they are still not a household name outside the traveling nurse world. They operate as a simple lead-generation site that you pay a membership fee to be part of.

Pros and Cons

- **Low annual fee**. For the low rate of only $100 per year per listing, you get access to tons of leads within a undisclosed radius of your unit. This site works better for cities than towns, even if they are second- or third-tier cities.
- **One listing for multiple properties**. Furnished Finder simply populates a list of tenants with dates, budgets, and contact info. This means that if you have a fourplex like Sarah or multiple condos in one town like Zeona, you may be able to have a single listing and use the leads for the other units as well.
- **Traveling nurses**. In our experience, 90 percent of the tenants placed through Furnished Finder are nurses or medical professionals. This means you are getting background-checked, employed tenants who spend long hours at work. They usually make excellent, respectful tenants.
- **Traveling business professionals**. We have been seeing more and more traveling business professionals on Furnished Finder, often traveling with their families. This trend helps hosts book their two- and three-bedroom spaces.
- **Graduate-level students**. We have seen many students transferring to a graduate-level program, looking for a place to land before finding a home of their own. This is a mature and respectful tenant pool.
- **No profiles or reviews**. Furnished Finder is a pretty basic site, and it doesn't have profiles like Airbnb does. They do some host verification, but we don't believe they do much vetting of tenants. Lucky for them, they have tapped into a pretty high-caliber tenant pool, so they generally don't need those profiles and reviews (even though it would be nice). While they do offer tenants a way to review a property, we've never received one. We believe

this is because tenants do not book through their site and forget about the review after their long stay.

- **Leases**. While a lease is easy to find online, we'll be honest, they are a little annoying to fill out and get over to tenants for signatures. We hope Airbnb or Furnished Finder will upgrade to a digital lease format that the tenant can sign at booking.

FACEBOOK MARKETPLACE

Facebook Marketplace has pulled out ahead of Craigslist as the leading online classifieds hub in the past few years. It has become a crowd favorite for furnishing units and finding tenants, partially because people feel more connected to the person on the other side of the transaction and can more easily avoid scammers.

Pros and Cons

- **Unvetted tenants**. We must caution you to remember that when you use Facebook Marketplace, the tenants are entirely unvetted (unless you are so fortunate as to have a friend in common). In Chapter Fourteen, we will show you how to vet tenants, keep yourself safe, and move them through the screening process. While Zeona doesn't use it, some of Sarah's best tenants have come through Facebook Marketplace. For example, Sarah rented to a couple who were in Omaha for a rotation in a lab. They found Sarah's unit on Facebook Marketplace within a day of her posting. The wife was doing a rotation for her graduate degree, so she had a three-month placement at the hospital. Her husband worked remotely, allowing him to accompany her to Omaha and work from the unit.
- **Local tenant pool**. Even though Facebook's usage as a social media platform is declining, the Marketplace feels alive and well. This is a great way to tap into an extensive array of local tenants. This is where you may find someone doing a home renovation, needing a temporary place in between a sale and purchase of a home, and so on. The primary con here is that local tenants often do not want to pay the higher price that furnished rentals warrant.
- **Completely free**. As frugal gals, we won't argue with free. However, we'll remind you that you sometimes get what you pay for. Remember to be diligent about your screening with tenants from here.

ZILLOW

For better or worse, everyone has heard of this real estate giant. They are mostly known for their for-sale property listings, but they are also in the rental space. For a weekly listing fee ($9.99 per listing), you can reach many potential tenants. Again, this is a site where you might be able to advertise one unit and get leads or tenants for similar ones in the area. The response here can be overwhelming, so prepare yourself.

One major plus of Zillow is its built-in screening and application process. If a tenant pays for a background check through Zillow, they can seamlessly send it with their application to as many landlords as they desire, saving both time and money.

Note to Real Estate Agents

If you are a real estate agent, having furnished rentals can be a gold mine. When transplants move from out of state, they generally rent a furnished home as a temporary place to land while they start their search. Keep this in mind and ask people what brings them to town. Zeona has sold at least three homes to tenants she hosted on short-term and medium-term stays.

BUILD RELATIONSHIPS WITH AGENTS

If you are not an agent, building relationships with agents may be an excellent source of referrals for your furnished units. For example, MTR host Julie Gates mentioned that she would approach agents with her business card and say pointedly that she is not an agent (so they won't be worried about her stealing their clients). Then she would let them know that if they ever have a client needing a furnished rental, she's their gal. She gets a ton of business this way.

DIRECT BOOKINGS

We'll be honest, the above strategies have worked so well that we haven't had to go through the trouble of setting up a direct-booking system. But some people swear by it, out of a desire to be autonomous and out of fear that the big sites like Airbnb could shut down their listing, leaving them out of luck.

CASE STUDY

"Creative Marketing and Direct Bookings" by Amanda Williams

In 2017, after using Airbnb for years on my travels, I listed our house on Airbnb during a month-long trip to Mexico to "see what happens." The first two weeks of rentals paid our mortgage and then some. I thought, "I think we're onto something!"

Our business was in flipping houses, and we decided to keep the flip we were currently working on and turn it into an Airbnb. Then we bought a tiny-home log cabin. And that was just the beginning!

We pivoted to the medium-term rental space in March 2020 (when COVID-19 hit). Overnight, we lost a boatload of money as hosts. We fire-sold one of our properties, which I am kicking myself about today, as it has appreciated so much. Then, one day, we had a client call from New York City who said, "I have three kids; I'm going crazy." They said, "We are fleeing New York!" and that was the lightbulb moment for me. How many people were going stir-crazy during the pandemic and needed a safe change of scenery?

I turned to Facebook and started posting about our properties. My marketing was "Come quarantine with us!" My target audience was for people who lived in apartments in cities like New York City and Chicago. Within a week, we were 100 percent occupied, and I was helping people quarantine in a three-bedroom, two-bath house on a half-acre of land; they loved it. Their kids were homeschooling, and the parents were working from home. There was no way they could continue that lifestyle locked in an apartment in the city.

Carolina Furnished Rentals now operates eighteen furnished rentals. COVID-19 forced us—*allowed* us—to pivot our business, and now we are 95 percent occupied by direct medium-term bookings. We have built up enough momentum and recognition to even have our own direct-booking site.

An action step for you to take immediately is to get the word out to your local real estate professionals that you now offer monthly furnished rentals. We post a lot in our local Facebook community groups and even privately message agents who cater to relocating clients to offer our homes. This is also a win for the agent because it gives their clients a higher level of service.

Follow Amanda's adventures on Instagram @AmandaTheTravelingRealtor.

Your Own Website

Many of the larger property-management software companies will let you create an automated direct-booking site that will pull leads straight into your software. Remember that you will no longer have the protection of Airbnb's or Vrbo's $1 million damage protection, so make sure to draft up a solid lease, take a deposit, or require that the tenant purchase a travel insurance policy. We can stay fully booked using a combination of Furnished Finder and Airbnb; thus, we do not see the need for a direct booking site. If Airbnb changes policies making it more costly to use their site, we may change our minds, but until then, we like the ease and protection Airbnb gives us.

Social Media

We also haven't needed to do much promotion on social media for our units. However, Zeona spoke with a host at a recent meetup event who said most of her bookings came through Instagram. While you could get some bookings here, as an avenue it can require more work than one would be rewarded for (unless you are a social media savant or already have a solid presence).

Relationships with Corporations

Real estate is all about relationships and seeing the value of building them. Calling the HR department within local companies, government agencies, or hospitals could allow you to get plugged in with their placement process. It can be a worthwhile pursuit, whether you are added to a preferred contact list or connected directly to the placement agencies.

Local Film Commission

You may think that your town doesn't have a film industry, and you are likely wrong. Commercials, TV shows, and even movies are shot all over the country, and they often need homes as their "set" to shoot in. Check with your local tourism office (yes, your town has one), which can direct you to the website or a contact to list with. You can also utilize websites like Peerspace, although you may see more short-booking requests there.

There are endless ways to keep your units booked, and we believe you'll only need to master two to three of them to maintain a full calendar. Let's move on to choosing your tenants safely once you have received all these inquiries.

PART 5

Responsible Landlording

CHAPTER FOURTEEN

SCREENING YOUR TENANTS

If your dream is a big dream, and if you want your life to work on the high level you say you do, there's no way around doing the work it takes to get you there.
—JOYCE CHAPMAN

Aside from appreciation, the only way we make money from our medium-term rentals is by renting out our units. Let us repeat that: The only way we make money is by renting out our units. Thus, keeping your units occupied is of the utmost importance.

Keeping occupancy rates high and vacancy rates low is the goal, and screening your tenants is a key factor in this. We showed you in Chapter Five what markets to buy in and what types of properties work for the MTR strategy in Chapter Seven. Chapter Eleven covered how to furnish the unit for the right tenant. Now, in this chapter, we will show you how to know when you have found a good tenant.

It is key that you find great tenants to occupy your unit who (1) pay rent and (2) pay rent on time.

Trusting your gut is crucial to this; yet trusting yourself is a complex concept to quantify and teach. If a tenant gives you a bad feeling or something feels like a red flag, it often is a reason for concern. Avoid feeling like you must take the next tenant, even in the face of several red flags, out of fear that another will not come. We have mentioned the scarcity mindset a few times in the book, and for good reason.

Even after more than a decade of hosting furnished rentals, Zeona still has to remind herself that there is always another guest who will check in. Even if someone does not check in right away, a few days of vacancy will not kill your profit margin, whereas moving with haste and accepting a tenant who does not meet your criteria could wipe out profits for months. Not to mention how placing the wrong tenant can be detrimental to your sanity. Trust us.

When a guest is requesting to stay in your home, ask yourself if they:

- Sent you a message to accompany their inquiry
- Tell you about the purpose of their trip
- Wrote a thoughtful inquiry

Or did they:

- **Say something odd or off-putting.** This can be aggressive comments, bad-mouthing another host, making a reference to a planned party, or nitpicking your listing or rules, just to name a few.
- **Ask an unusual number of questions.** Difficult guest often show their colors up front. If they are really picky or particular, pleasing them may be a challenge.
- **Give you the sense that they are hiding something** (a party, guests, a pet, etc.).

The best advice we can give in this matter is just to say no if ever in doubt. The extra time it takes to collect estimates, quotes, and bids for repairs, or to field a laundry list of requests or complaints, is not worth risking renting to a difficult tenant.

That being said, you must follow local laws and avoid discrimination. You can find out more by researching your local laws and reviewing the Fair Housing Act requirements set by the Department of Housing and Urban Development (HUD), but you cannot discriminate against tenants or potential tenants based on:

- Race.
- Skin color.
- National origin.
- Religion.
- Gender or sexual orientation.
- Familial Status.
- Disability.
  - You also must, as a housing provider, provide reasonable accommodations to those with disabilities to ensure your property is accessible and habitable. You can learn more from HUD.

- Service and Emotional Support Animals (ESA): Unfortunately, there has been a considerable wave of people taking advantage of the ESA designation. This allows them to bring their pets into restaurants, airplane cabins, and pet-restricted Airbnbs. That being said, there are many people who rely on service and support animals to function and live better lives; it's not your place as a housing provider to assume whether someone is deserving of a service animal, as the reason may not be obvious. Even if your listing clearly states "no pets," know that these owners are allowed to bring their animals and do not need to warn you. Service animals in all places are not subject to pet fees, but not all states and localities require the same of ESAs. Check your local policies for more.

A crucial part of ethical landlording is ensuring you are in compliance with local and federal laws set out to protect tenants and reduce housing discrimination. You are running an MTR business, and part of being a business owner is being responsible and fair in the services you provide. Always remember that you rely on your tenants for income; in return for that, you provide them with safe housing and a positive experience. Be one of the good guys!

In our experience, most medium-term rental tenants come through three channels.

1. Airbnb
2. Furnished Finder
3. Facebook Marketplace

Tenant Requests from Airbnb

We have a protocol for reviewing requests we receive from Airbnb. We review the guest's verification and read what other hosts had to say about them. If they do not have a profile picture, we do not accept them. If there are no reviews or negative reviews, we decline their request. This makes screening through Airbnb a quick and straightforward process. Keep in mind that, as you are booking through a third-party service, Airbnb will take steps to ensure you are protected in the case of tenant-liable damages (up to $1 million, as we mentioned earlier). However, by automatically saying no to guests who don't meet the simple criteria of having a picture and positive review, you should be able to filter out the most likely troublemakers. You can also do what we do and set a minimum age limit.

Pay attention as well to the types of questions they ask. A bad guest isn't always one who damages your property; they can also be impossible to please or unrealistically high maintenance. It's fair for guests to expect a clean, comfortable, quality space—that is the service you are providing. However, if a potential Airbnb guest is leading with a string of messages indicating that they are expecting a level of service that you cannot provide, don't be afraid to say no. The inevitable bad review will not be worth it in the end.

Tenant Requests from Furnished Finder

Currently, as of 2022, Furnished Finder does not have reviews on potential guests' profiles. Having profile pictures is also not common, so it is not a reason to decline a potential guest. Thus, you have a lot less to go off by viewing their profile on Furnished Finder. We recommend setting up a call with potential tenants—not just communicating via text. It can be a quick ten-minute call allowing you to gather more information on the potential tenant.

Things to pay attention to during the call:
- Are they negative? Do they complain during the first call? If so, they will likely be quick to complain about the unit or the conditions of their stay.
- What kinds of questions did they ask? We are weeding out anyone who sounds high-maintenance, unrealistic, rude, or aggressive.
- Did they hesitate when you asked about pets, their contract length, or when you asked for references?

Asking the right questions could ensure that you are protecting your unit and your time. If a potential guest is being rude before booking, imagine how they may act when they are living in your unit and something goes wrong. We suggest screening tenants before offering them your furnished rental.

Tenant Requests from Facebook Marketplace

If tenants find your listing on Facebook Marketplace, you can view their public Facebook profile. But you *must* abide by the laws put in place by the Fair Housing Act. Therefore, it is best to have the same protocol for all potential tenants and follow it, rather than judging them solely from their social media.

We ask all tenants from Furnished Finder or Facebook Marketplace for the following.
- A photo of their driver's license
- Proof of employment
- Email and phone number of a previous landlord

If they are a traveling nurse, we will ask that the previous landlord reference be from a stay they had as a traveling nurse. We skip a criminal background check because, as a nurse, they have already gone through multiple screenings. Therefore, we do not feel the need to charge the tenant for a background check. However, if the tenant is staying for another reason or is not a traveling nurse, we do require a criminal background check from a source like My Smart Move or Experian, paid for by the tenant.

When checking references, we ask the previous landlord the following questions:
- Does TENANT have any outstanding rent due?
- Did TENANT pay on time every month?
- Did TENANT leave your property in an acceptable condition?
- Would you rent to TENANT again?
- Anything else we should know about TENANT? Anything regarding noise disturbances or cleanliness that we should know?
- Would you recommend we rent to TENANT?

When asking these questions, be looking for places where you can ask follow-up questions. You want to ensure your tenants are trustworthy and pay rent on time. Keep in mind that this tenant will be living in your unit with all your furniture and decor.

For tenants you find through other means, such as tourism boards and universities, word of mouth, or social media, follow these same protocols.

If you have a bad feeling about a guest, it is best to pass (as long as you are in compliance with the Fair Housing Act).

Pets

By now, it should be clear that we love renting to traveling nurses. That's one of the reasons we wrote this book! We have to admit, however, that we do not love renting to their furry friends. Life can be lonely out on the road, and we've noticed that most traveling nurses bring a four-legged companion with them on their assignments. Other tenants, such as those displaced during renovations and remote workers, also are inclined to bring pet companions with them to their medium-term stays.

Zeona's policy is not to allow pets, except those support companions that cannot be turned away. She believes nurses work too long of hours to give pets the attention and time out of the home that they require. While Sarah would prefer not to rent units to nurses with pets, she tends to allow pets because it ensures lower vacancy. She believes it's good business. When you don't allow pets in your unit, you pass on a large portion of the tenant pool.

We are not saying you *must* allow pets in your furnished units. It is up to you to make a calculated decision on whether it's the best option for your unit and your market. We have both received unhappy calls from our cleaners after a traveling nurse with a pet moved out—it is disheartening to hear that there is pet hair everywhere or that furniture has been damaged. However, this is a cost of doing business. Ensure your cleaner is aware that the tenant had a pet during their stay, which usually indicates the unit will take more time to clean, and compensate your cleaner accordingly.

By communicating with your cleaner when a tenant has a pet on their lease, you can also have eyes and ears on the ground for tenants who are not supposed to have pets (or who have not indicated that they are bringing an animal into the property). That way, if the cleaner finds signs of a pet present, you can collect the unpaid fees. Just like many long-term rentals, Sarah charges her MTR tenants a pet fee (nonrefundable) and a pet deposit (refundable). The fee covers the additional cleaning that a unit turnover after a pet mandates. The deposit only gets used if there is additional damage.

Pet damage will occur. That is when it is important to have your lease protect you. (For more on leases, read Chapter Fifteen.) If a rug is chewed up (an incident that has happened to both of us), the cost of replacing the rug is passed on to the tenants—as long as the lease indicates that as an option.

Managing Tenant Expectations

We take pride in offering safe and secure homes for all our tenants. We make a unit beautiful, and this includes routine maintenance, deep cleaning, and carefully curated decor and furnishings. However, this does not mean our units are always perfect. Sometimes, a bathroom sink is too small, a toilet is too low, or a closet just really isn't big enough. We do our best to prepare our tenants for what they are walking into. This includes honest descriptions of the unit and no hyperbole. Telling the tenant that there is some light street noise will save you in the long run when you have a tenant wanting to break their lease. We recommend honest communication from the beginning, because that's what you also expect from the tenant. Like any good relationship, communication is key. Be sure to tell your tenant everything that is in the unit so they can prepare.

CASE STUDY

"Building Relationships Brings Bookings" by Sarah Karakaian

We moved from New York City to Columbus, Ohio, specifically for Columbus's booming real estate market. Columbus is the only city in the Midwest to gain over 100,000 new residents over the past decade. Growth in this market is exciting, and it has been short- and medium-term rental friendly since Airbnb rose in popularity. Investors here enjoy both appreciation and cash flow.

We purchased our first MTR in January 2022 for $230,000 in downtown Columbus. We used conventional financing (before rates went up, whew!) and 20 percent down. The market didn't allow short-term rentals, so we knew we'd have to have a strong medium-term rental strategy. The property is a shot gun–style condo with a flex space at the front followed by a long hallway leading to a bedroom, a living/dining space, and a kitchen. A nice-sized bathroom and stacked washer and dryer are on the other side of the kitchen. We decided to make the front flex space a dedicated office because we've seen a trend of traveling couples needing to work from anywhere. The separate workspace has made our place stand out. We spent about $10,000 furnishing the home with quality furniture that will stand the test of time. This investment should have a cash-on-cash return right around 26 percent.

Nurses aren't the only target market, and with the pandemic (hopefully) subsiding, we may not see the crazy demand we saw from nurses from 2020–2021. Government, educational, and corporate medium-term contracts are also very lucrative, with fantastic guests. Make sure your name and properties are on file with housing agencies that work with insurance claims. Once these relationships are built, they pay dividends.

Online travel agencies (OTAs), like Airbnb, are truly structured for short-term stays. We used to rely on leads from OTAs for our MTRs. However, the host fees were so high that our numbers rarely worked! Since dialing in a proper marketing strategy, complete with social media and monthly email broadcasts, all of our medium-term bookings either happen from Furnished Finder, word-of-mouth referrals, or relationships we've built from cold-calling universities, HR departments, or local government agencies.

Start building relationships with businesses that would benefit from your MTRs *before* you need them. Write a weekly or biweekly newsletter about furnished rentals in your area and include local happenings—always be on their radar! Make sure you have a way for these businesses and medium-term guests to book directly with you. And have a contract ready to go that is specific to your MTR.

Check out the *Thanks for Visiting* podcast and watch their entertaining reels on Instagram at @thanksforvisiting_.

CHAPTER FIFTEEN
LEASES

Believe you can and you're halfway there.
—THEODORE ROOSEVELT

If we could complain about anything in the wonderful world of MTRs, we would about leases. Anyone who has written up a one-month lease knows the annoyance of spending thirty minutes on a document for a tenant who will only give you one rent check.

There are a couple of ways around a "traditional" lease.

If it's a short stay—under three months—we direct them to book through Airbnb. Sure, you are losing out on 3 percent, but those are fees you can write off on your taxes. Consider it a convenience fee.

You can also hire an assistant or virtual assistant (VA) to handle the paperwork. For example, for a unit listed for $2,500 per month, you would be paying $75 to Airbnb per month to avoid writing the lease. If Airbnb can get you a higher rate than you would have expected—say $3,500 that month—it's worth a higher fee. But if you hire an assistant at $10–$25 per hour, the price could be $5–$13 per lease. That's a great deal. The caveat here is that you must have enough tasks or volume to keep an assistant engaged. You can hire a VA for much less if you look for help in Asia through Upwork, although what you save in price, you may pay for in time zone challenges and lack of English proficiency (it can be easier with tenants and maintenance calls to have someone more local fielding those assignments).

In other scenarios, you will have to draw up a lease. This is an important tool of the trade as a real estate investor. To reiterate, leases are not relevant for booking platforms like Airbnb. But tenants sourced through Furnished Finder, Facebook Marketplace, word-of-mouth referrals, tourism boards, and so on will all need leases.

Where to Get the Lease

Congratulations! You found a tenant, and they passed your thorough screening process. Now you need to lock in the contract. Let's help you find or make the right lease for you.

CITY SAMPLE

In Boulder, Colorado, where Zeona lives, the city offers a free sample lease agreement, which she has used at all her Colorado properties. The Boulder city lease is a very tenant-favorable lease, but Zeona doesn't mind. It's worth noting that a lease is a way of formalizing an agreement, having terms to refer to, and, hopefully, making the tenant feel accountable. If you intend to use it as an enforcement tool in a court of law, you are likely mistaken.

Involving lawyers and going to court—even small claims—is usually not worth it. Legal battles are such an expensive pursuit (both monetarily and energetically) that we hope you never need to do it. We have never taken a tenant to court, but even if you win the case, it doesn't mean that the tenant will pay, especially if they don't have the means to do so, which can make it a worthless pursuit. This is why Chapter Fourteen, on screening your tenants, is so essential.

BIGGERPOCKETS

BiggerPockets offers lawyer-reviewed, state-specific leases with a Pro membership and for purchase ($99 per state) with a free membership. These include a rental application, comprehensive residential lease, pet addendum, lease extension, lease guaranty, move-in/move-out form, lease amendment, and lease addendum.

ONLINE

Many online legal sites—such as Rocket Lawyer and LegalZoom—provide official contracts drafted by lawyers at a much lower fee than if you had one custom-made. Many of these have a monthly membership, although you might be able to grab a few drafts of leases, operating agreements, management contracts, etc. (depending on the type of business you plan to do) through the free trial.

MAKE YOUR OWN

Another option is to find multiple leases for your specific state that you like the wording or terms of and take preferred sections from each that you find the clearest and easiest to understand, making a new lease. Zeona has done this for her management contracts in the past and then added new sections as iterations were necessary. We recommend using an attorney who is familiar with laws in that particular county when making changes to a legal document such as a lease.

Terms to Include
HOW RENT IS TO BE PAID

We love websites like Apartments.com and Avail. Not only are they free to use, but they are also automated. Sure, their functionality is a bit limited—they can't return a deposit to the tenants or prorate the final month—but for a free service, we think they're pretty great. These sites allow you to send a sign-up link via email to your tenants so they can enter their payment information directly into their system without having to give you, some random person from the internet, their private information. We prefer automated ACH deposit over PayPal, Venmo, or—god forbid—check by mail, as the funds are deposited directly into your bank account without any other steps required by you.

PREPAYMENT/PRORATION

How much do you require up front? We prefer a deposit upon signing and requiring rent to be paid three days before moving in. Another option is to ask for a nonrefundable amount (around $500) up front, which is then credited to the first month's rent. Then you can require that they get a travel insurance policy and not have to deal with the extra responsibility of holding on to the deposit. Many tenants appreciate having to hand less money over and feel relaxed knowing that they are not being scammed for their security deposit.

DEPOSIT TERMS

To make it affordable and straightforward, we only charge $1,000 as a deposit instead of the equivalent of one month's rent. You will want to have in writing how long you have, after the guest checks out, to return the deposit. Seven to ten days is usually sufficient and fair. You will also want to clearly define how the cleaning fee is paid. We take it out of the deposit before we return it to our guests. It is essential to have the fee amount in writing, for reference and to make sure it is clear to both sides up front.

PARKING

Do you have a reserved space, a garage, or a carport? Or will they park on the street? Make this clear to meet expectations when they arrive.

UTILITIES

What utilities do you cover? We do all the basics: water, sewer, trash, Wi-Fi, electricity, gas, and lawn care. We do not include cable but provide a smart TV and Netflix. Different investors have different policies on this front—whatever you choose, be sure it's convenient to the tenant and written up in the lease.

EARLY TERMINATION

Most of your tenants will be reserving the property sight unseen. What do you do if they don't like it? Zeona requires fourteen days' notice to cancel so that she has time to find a new tenant. This allows them to pay for the prorated days or use the time to find a new place. Requiring a notice period is a fair way to ensure the tenant is not stuck in a lease at a place they hate (risking a bad review for you and a bad experience for both of you), and it protects you from extended vacancy.

SMOKING

Whether it's cigarettes or marijuana, the smell can stick to the fabrics in the home and scare off future tenants, so we add a no-smoking rule to the lease and find guests who don't smoke. Breaking rules in the lease can result in removal from the property.

PETS

If you choose to allow pets, make sure to detail out any pet fees, deposits (as discussed in the previous chapter), or rules.

EXTENDING THE LEASE

We don't want to write up a new lease if a guest extends from a three-month travel plan to six months. All of our leases continue on a month-to-month basis if extended beyond the lease term.

TRASH

Clearly outline the trash day, pickup location, and the fact that it is the tenant's responsibility to put it out and bring it back in. Trash is a major headache for any STR operator, but it is a breeze with MTRs.

MOVE-OUT INSTRUCTIONS

This is optional, but it's not a bad idea to include move-out instructions in your lease. At a minimum, you should have an automated message that goes out to guests the day before checkout. But by including instructions in the lease, the tenant knows what is expected of them from the beginning.

Filling Out the Lease

If you are managing your MTR from a distance (and even if you aren't), it's best to fill out the lease online in a platform that allows for e-signatures from both you and your tenant for ease of use. Here are a few that we like.

- **DocHub**. A Google software that allows for five free signed documents per month. If you have multiple Gmail accounts, you can get five per account per month.
- **HelloSign**. Offers a free plan option with three signed documents per month.
- **DocuSign**. Has a free edition with cloud storage, as well as a variety of plan options.

How to Handle Deposits
REFUNDABLE

As we mentioned earlier, we collect a $1,000 security deposit for our properties. After the lease is signed, we send the future tenant a link to Apartments.com to sign up for automated rent payments. This link includes the security deposit collection as well as a move-in or cleaning fee. For the security deposit, we send this back to the tenant via check.

Please look up your state's rules around holding deposits. For example, if you are a licensed real estate agent, you need to hold them in a separate trust account, so they do not commingle with your money. Some states, like Colorado, also require that you pay interest on the deposit for the time it was held. As with rent collection (and any type of banking), there are a variety of options. You can find the best option for your needs. Just be sure you are obeying local laws and *not* using the deposit for your own use. If you do use the deposit for damages, be sure to document every item.

NONREFUNDABLE

Some hosts may choose to go the nonrefundable route and require insurance instead. Travel insurance independently covers the tenant, and you can take the policy fee out of the first month's rent. For a $70 fee, for example, Generali Insurance's travel policy covers up to $3,000 worth of damages to the unit. Avail has a partnership with Lemonade, an insurance tech company that uses AI instead of insurance agents and offers low-cost insurance options for both renters and homeowners. In recent years, many Craigslist scammers have been stealing security deposits. This is why we do not list on Craigslist anymore. Having an insurance policy instead is comforting to many guests and protects both parties.

Collecting Rent

The final step is collecting rent. We like to stagger this to help out the tenant. The $1,000 deposit is due upon signing, often a month or more before moving in, and we only collect rent three days before arrival. Since nurses have flexibility and rarely arrive on the first of a given month, we usually must prorate the first month, and often the last.

As we mentioned previously, we recommend automated rent collection. Why automate? Because you don't have to remember what day rent is due. You can also automate late payment fees, although we have a great tenant payment rate. We had used Venmo and PayPal in the past, but we would never recommend them. If you give tenants the ability to pay via Venmo or PayPal, then they can deposit money into your account at any time, which makes it much more difficult to remove a tenant or end a lease if they can simply just keep giving you money. Do not allow this.

Next, we will put this all together by giving you the tricks of the trade to maximize your profits and self-manage with confidence from anywhere in (or out of) the country.

CHAPTER SIXTEEN
MANAGEMENT

Either you run the day, or the day runs you.
—JIM ROHN

When it comes to managing your rental, we are all for doing it yourself to maximize your profits. Self-management is surprisingly doable with all the software automation available these days, such as dynamic pricing software and automatic messaging.

It's totally possible to manage your own rentals, even if you have a full-time job or live out of state.

That said, many people really don't want to manage their furnished rental themselves. For some, one of the main appeals of real estate investing is its ability to be entirely passive. If that sounds like you, here are our best tips for finding a top-notch management company.

Hiring Property Management
FIND SOMEONE WHO IS HIGHLY RECOMMENDED

Like any contractor, it's always best to find someone who comes recommended by other investors or your real estate agent instead of just searching on Google and picking the first option. The BiggerPockets forum can be an excellent resource for investor-vetted recommendations. Your real estate agent may also be able to make a recommendation of property management companies.

WHAT KIND OF SYSTEMS ARE THEY USING?

For short- and medium-term rentals, you want your management company to be tech-enabled to ensure they're operating efficiently, achieving the best dynamic pricing, and making a great impression on guests. When vetting your options, ask them what software and systems they use, as well as how their cleaners report and document damage and replenish cleaning supplies. This stuff may sound boring, but if not done well, it *will* impact your return.

HOW OFTEN DO THEY VISIT THE PROPERTY?

While this isn't so essential when a good cleaning team is in place, it's reassuring to know that someone has eyes on the space regularly. Be sure to ask how often they would inspect your property—monthly, quarterly, semi-annually? We like to see that a property manager is checking on the property at least once every six months to ensure the tenant is following the lease and to change the air filter.

ASK TO SEE LINKS TO OTHER PROPERTIES THEY CURRENTLY MANAGE

Evaluate examples of other short- or medium-term rentals in your potential property manager's portfolio. Are the rentals up to your standard or representative of how you would like your property to look? Read through the reviews to spot any red flags for management issues. If they have listings on Airbnb, check whether they have earned the designation of Superhost. If they haven't, inquire why not. Sometimes managers with an extensive portfolio and high volume of rentals can have their average dragged down by one problem property or a less than stellar neighborhood.

ASK FOR REFERENCES FROM CURRENT AND PAST CLIENTS

You want to make sure from references that they are doing a good job and keeping their clients happy. Communication is the No. 1 priority.

ASK IF THEY WORK WITH OUT-OF-STATE INVESTORS

Even if you live in the same market as your MTR, it's key to have a property manager who is set up to work with investors who reside elsewhere. Working with out-of-state investors indicates an emphasis on communication; plus, who knows what the future may hold? You want to make sure you're working with someone set up for the possibility that you'll leave. And if you're paying for property management, it's key that you *can* be hands-off and they are not relying on your location. Be sure to ask how they will ensure communication is clear even from hundreds of miles away.

TRUST YOUR GUT

You need to trust your management company and believe that they can create an excellent experience for guests. At the end of the day, reviews are everything. You need to make sure you will have happy guests. If you have any doubts when interviewing the management team, just move on! There will be someone else you feel better about.

MAP OUT YOUR POTENTIAL ROI

Remember to take into account the cost of property management when you're calculating the potential return you can make on your properties. Ask for rates and determine the percentage of return your property will still earn *after* paying your expenses.

Why We Self-Manage and How You Can Too

As we've mentioned a few times, neither of us uses a property manager. Why? Because optimizing our returns is extremely important to us for the time being. Property management can come at a high cost—typically 10 percent for long-term rentals, 15 percent for MTRs, and 20–35 percent for STRs. Those percentages are coincidentally also the threshold for returns we look for in those different categories, meaning that property management, after expenses, can leave you with a small slice of the profits—if you can cash flow at all.

While self-managing your rental is a guaranteed way to maximize your return, it can seem a bit overwhelming—especially for short-term rentals, where you're dealing with multiple guests every month.

Spending all day, every day answering guest inquiries is the opposite of freedom!

Thankfully, technology is our friend here. You can automate so much of the day-to-day running of your business—from dynamic pricing to dealing with tenant inquiries to balancing your books.

Here are a few savvy tools that can save you a lot of time and boost your revenue.

- Automated pricing tools like PriceLabs and Beyond have been proven to increase your revenue by up to 40 percent (which we discussed in Chapter Twelve).
- The website Hospitable makes it a breeze to message renters and respond to their inquiries so you don't have to be tied to your phone.

While these are paid tools they are worth their weight in gold and are undoubtedly still cheaper than hiring a property manager. With those two tools, we are able to significantly reduce our time commitment to guest communication, self-manage our properties from anywhere, and rest easy knowing that our rates are optimized for the highest possible price for each location—all automatically.

Additionally, as we mentioned in Chapter Fifteen, on leases, we would encourage you to consider hiring an assistant for $10–$30 per hour who can help manage your properties, as well as handle other administrative tasks. With automated pricing and messaging, it is easy to learn and a low time commitment.

SAVED REPLIES

Guest communication can be one of the most disruptive parts of being an Airbnb or Vrbo host. If you manage more than a few properties, you may want to consider using a receptionist service. Alternatively, for those frugal full-timers who want to maximize their profits, there's an easy loophole: saved replies!

Airbnb calls these saved messages, and you can find them at the bottom of the message box in your message history with any guest. If you click on saved messages, a few will already pop up if you have filled them out in your listing, such as:

- **House rules**. This is where you want to include such basics as "No smoking," "No parties or events," "Please remove your shoes," and the like.
- **House manual**. You can cut and paste a digital house manual under the "basics" section in the "manage listing" area. This is highly recommended, as every guest will automatically be sent a link to the manual in the confirmation email upon booking.
- **Directions**. Is your driveway a little tricky to find, or are you in a large apartment complex? Detailed directions or helpful tips can be saved in the "location" section.
- **Wi-Fi**. You can enter your network name and password in the "basics" section to auto-send to guests and for quick access to the saved replies.

You can access these features from the desktop website as well as the phone app.

The way described above is the free, manual route. However, you need to subscribe to at least a basic property management software like Hospitable or Your Porter to get automated messaging. Even if you accept direct bookings through Furnished Finder or Facebook Marketplace, you can enter the guest and reservation details into the software to have automated messages sent to your guests and cleaners.

The saved replies that we suggest you add in addition to what Airbnb will supply you with are as follows. (Of course, you don't need to cut and paste these exact words; make it your own!) Note also that the information inside of the "% %" fields are dynamic variables that can be changed per guest, house, or stay. This is the way they are set up on Hospitable; they may vary on other software platforms, but the principles are the same.

Booking Confirmation

Send this the moment a client books; it cuts down on them asking a million questions. The booking confirmation should include the property's check-in time, address, and any other essential items for planning their arrival. You don't want to give them too much information and overwhelm them at this stage. You will also notice that we are already setting our guests up to give us a five-star review. Ask, and you shall receive:

Hello %guest_first_name%, thank you so much for booking with us!

We are hosts who really care about our guests and their experience in our home. We are delighted to host you and want to earn your 5-Star Review.

I wanted to confirm, right away, your reservation in %listing_city%.

Details:

Check-in is at %check_in_hour% on %check_in% and checkout is at %check_out_hour% on %check_out%.

Address:

%listing_full_address%

I will contact you before your arrival to give you all the instructions for a smooth check-in.

I look forward to hosting you!

Best regards,

%host_first_name%

Check-In Instructions

Send this message three days before check-in. These check-in instructions should cover the basics of check-in: where to park, keyless entry, and Wi-Fi. You want to be preemptively answering their questions.

Hi %guest_first_name%,

It is my pleasure to welcome you as you prepare for your trip to %listing_city% on %check_in%.

You are welcome to check in anytime after %check_in_hour%.

ADDRESS:

%listing_full_address%

PARKING:

%parking%

KEYLESS ENTRY:

24-hour access

Press the "Schlage" button to light up.

To unlock: Code %door_code%.

To lock: Press "Schlage" button (you do not need to reenter the code).

WI-FI:

Network name: %wifi_name%

Password: %wifi_password%

There is also a printed house manual in the home with everything else you need to know.

Safe travels!

Best regards,

%host_first_name%

First Morning

Zeona sets this message to go out seventeen hours after check-in. For her typical 3:00 p.m. check-in time, that puts it at 8:00 a.m. The aim is to catch the guests before breakfast, but not early enough to wake them up. Zeona used to send this a few hours after check-in and then felt awkward if the guest said that they hadn't checked in yet. Sarah sets up a message to go out at 9:00 a.m. on the guests' first morning.

We share a coffee shop or brunch spot recommendation because we want to add value since we are bothering them, and to get ahead of the question before they might ask it.

> Good morning %guest_first_name%,
>
> We hope you had a wonderful evening!
>
> If you haven't had breakfast or coffee yet, I recommend Ozo Coffee (5340 Arapahoe Ave).
>
> They serve carefully sourced, house-roasted beans. Plus, it is a wonderful place to work from.
>
> Have a great day!
>
> %host_first_name%

Trash Instructions

Send the day before trash pickup. Hospitable has settings to allow you to send it the first Wednesday of their stay (if pickup is Thursday) or every Wednesday depending on how often you want to remind your guests. If you have a condo with communal trash dumpsters, you can skip this message.

> Hope you're having a great Sunday, %guest_first_name%. Tomorrow (%trash_day%) is trash day at our place. The trash and recycling bins are located at the side of the home and need to be taken to the street for pickup.
>
> We appreciate your help, %guest_first_name%. This helps us keep the cleaning fee low.
>
> %host_first_name%

Cleaner Contact

Send this on day seven (for guests staying longer than fourteen days). We want to encourage the cleanest home possible and help our cleaner get business, so we share their contact information with guests.

> Hi %guest_first_name%,
>
> We hope you are enjoying your stay! Since you are staying for a longer period we wanted to give you our cleaner's contact so you can use her as a resource if you wish.
>
> %local_cleaner%. Our cleaner will communicate her hourly rate to you directly.
>
> Feel free to contact her directly if you are interested. We hope you have a great day!
>
> With appreciation,
>
> %host_first_name%

Checkout Instructions

Send checkout instructions on the guests' last day at the unit. You can schedule this to send at 3:00 p.m. the day before checkout, giving the guest plenty of time to prepare as needed.

> Hi %guest_first_name%,
>
> We hope you have enjoyed our space and felt at home during your stay.
>
> Just a friendly reminder that checkout is by %check_out_hour% tomorrow, unless explicitly agreed otherwise. No need to take out the trash; we will do that for you. If you used any dishes, please wash and dry them. Other than that, you are good to go!
>
> We appreciate you booking with us and look forward to your 5-star review.
>
> Let us know if you have any questions.
>
> Safe travels,
>
> %host_first_name%

Review Request

Set a message to go to the guest 24 hours after checkout. We believe you don't get what you don't ask for, so ask for a five-star review. On platforms where reviews are a possibility, message the guest thanking them for renting from you and ask for a five-star review. If you are using a software program like Hospitable, these messages can be saved, stored, and scheduled. This may seem less important when you have one MTR unit, but keeping the door open to scaling is important. It is not possible for either of us to memorize all of our door codes, Wi-Fi passwords, and more. We must have efficient systems in order to make this business scalable.

> Hi %guest_first_name%,
>
> Thank you so much for staying with us! It truly was a pleasure to host you!
>
> To help us grow our business and to find wonderful guests such as yourself, we would appreciate a 5-star review. It would really mean a lot to us, %guest_first_name%.
>
> If you have any feedback on how we can improve, we'd love to hear it!
>
> Please add us to your Airbnb wish list by selecting the heart in the upper right-hand corner of our listing. This creates an easy reference for future stays in %listing_city%. We'd gladly host you again, %guest_first_name%.
>
> We look forward to reading your review.
>
> Thank you,
>
> %host_first_name%

- **Use "home" or "space" to describe your place.** Saying "house" or "condo" would require you to change it for each listing based on the dwelling.
- **Be careful what you ask for.** Do not write "Let me know if you have any questions" in your replies. Asking this makes guests look for questions they may not ask otherwise. You are not aiming to prolong the conversation. Instead, make your ad and house manual super thorough so guests won't have questions.
- **Use exclamation points!** They read as excitement and enthusiasm, which somehow translates into friendliness. Obviously, not every sentence should end with an exclamation mark, but well-timed friendly punctuation adds a personal touch and makes the communication seem less transactional. Trust us; people love it!

Our software sends automated messages to our cleaners for scheduling, cancellations, and alterations to the schedule. You can also just forward booking notifications you receive to use for scheduling. It's nice to save time and automate as much as possible.

CALENDAR MANAGEMENT

Your listing is set. You've got those saved replies scheduled—now on to calendar management. How far in advance should you open your calendar? Zeona's opinion is five weeks. This gives guests the minimum of thirty days, plus a week of wiggle room to find their perfect start date. We include in our listing description that "we welcome longer stays but only open our calendar one month at a time." The aim of the game is to minimize vacancy. You don't want someone to be able to book three weeks out, leaving you with nearly a month that can't be rented.

Remember: Extended stay guests often have some flexibility, so once they inquire, we always ask if they can check in on the day another guest is checking out to fill any gap.

If you do use a light property management software like Hospitable, we recommend only managing your calendar and emails from there. You want to make sure that you don't block dates directly in Airbnb and forget that on Vrbo those same dates are wide open!

One of the benefits of having a few units in town or having a mix of owned and managed is that you can shuffle guests around as needed. This gives you much more flexibility and limits gaps. Zeona has found that being "in the know" about furnished units has been a form of social currency. Many folks in town think of her when needing a rental, and she wants to be able to place them when they have a request.

CLEANING WINDOW

We aim to have same-day turnovers to minimize vacancy, so we establish a cleaning window. We have found 11:00 a.m. checkout with a 3:00 or 4:00 p.m. check-in works well (depending on the size of the home). If you are doing multi-month stays with pets, we highly recommend a one-day grace period, as your cleaner never knows what they will walk into. In units with pets, the cleaner needs more time to deep clean the unit and ensure small things are replaced or fixed. We have both had things like a rug or the blinds damaged. This can also be helpful if you would like time to air out the place. Having a day of buffer is less stressful for everyone. Your cleaning window also depends on whether you have a two-person cleaning team or just one cleaner on the job. This is another reason why we like to introduce our guests to our cleaners, in the hopes that they might use them and make the final clean less intense.

MANAGING FROM AFAR

In our opinion, if your MTR property is forty-five minutes or more away, it might as well be out of state. The truth of the matter is that you are not going to jump in your car for every distress call if it's forty-five minutes away (and you may even think twice at thirty minutes). It's best to establish a solid boots-on-the-ground team, like we discussed in Chapter Nine. Earlier this year, Zeona was stalking a home in Washington State that she ended up offering on. Had she ever met her agent? Set foot in the town? Nope and nope. And yet, she's no stranger to out-of-state management, and she knows she can get all the contacts she needs for her team from her agent.

Like we have mentioned before, remote management is made easier by the fact that the MTR strategy lends itself to checks and balances with the guests and cleaners. The guest will tell you if the home is not up to an impeccable standard; likewise, the cleaner will let you know if the guest left the home in disarray.

The other beauty of self-managing is that it is more scalable than you might initially think. Adding more properties to your portfolio does not lead to exponentially more effort on your end managing. Once you build out a great system, you can drop any new property into it, and it will work like a well-oiled machine.

CHAPTER SEVENTEEN
MOVE-IN AND MOVE-OUT

If you fell down yesterday, stand up today.
—H. G. WELLS

Congratulations for making it this far. It was a long road to get here, and we are glad you are. By this point, you either have identified a market (or are ready to), zeroed in on your crystal clear deal criteria, written an offer (or several), closed on a property, furnished and listed the unit, and secured tenants. Now it is time for the tenants to move in.

This chapter will help you make the move-in and move-out processes seamless. We will show you how to handle both the move-in and the move-out processes from afar, making it possible for you never to visit the unit. In order to do this, you will need to spend ample time setting everything up properly.

Showings

One of the most common questions we get asked is how we handle showing properties that we self-manage. Short answer? We don't.

Medium-term rental tenants almost always book sight unseen. Similar to booking a short-term stay on Airbnb, guests do not have the option to tour the property first. Most traveling nurses we house come in from out of state; thus, they sign a lease before seeing the unit.

On the rare occasion a tour is necessary, Zeona will give the potential tenant a code to the keyless door lock. The tenant will do the showing on their own, and directly after they view the unit, she will change the key code using a Wi-Fi-enabled lock. Some hosts use cameras, like a nest doorbell, to know when a potential tenant has arrived and has departed after their walk-through.

This is one of the main reasons we love the MTR strategy. We can handle the move-in and move-out processes from our phones, even when we are in the jungle of Guatemala or furnishing our next unit in Iowa (both of which happened while we were writing this book).

The Move-In Process

A few things must happen every time a tenant is moving into your MTR unit. Before move-in:

- Ensure the unit is clean and rent-ready.
- Verify that the tenant has sent payment. This includes security deposits, pet deposits, and the first month's rent.
- Send a welcome email to the tenant.

Typically, we message the tenant three days before move-in.

In the welcome message, we include driving directions and parking details. We either thank them for sending the payment or remind them payment is due. We notify them that they will receive an email on the morning of check-in with directions on how to enter the unit. Often, the unit is available for check-in anytime after 3:00 p.m. The tenant can let themselves in at any time they wish after 3:00 p.m. With keyless locks on the doors, there is no need to exchange keys or for someone to be present to let them in.

As we have mentioned, automated messaging will save you time and money. Software like Hospitable allows you to automate messages not only to the guests but also to your cleaner and maintenance team. We recommend spending time to set this up properly so you do not miss a cleaning.

MESSAGING THE CLEANER

One of the worst things that can happen is having a guest show up to a unit that is not ready, or, worse, that is a disaster with dirty linens and towels. Ensure your cleaner always knows when the guest is checking in or checking out by setting them up to receive automated messages every time a guest checks in.

CASE STUDY

"A List Would Have Helped!" by Hannah McCoy

I found my property on Facebook Marketplace—of all places—and immediately reached out to the seller. The seller was an older woman who was open to the idea of seller financing. The duplex is located in a cute little town called Volant in Pennsylvania. I have had my eye on this area for a while. I am familiar with the rental market; it is within twenty minutes of my house. I know how great the demand for traveling nurse housing is in my area.

In addition to being a great long-term rental market, Volant also is within twenty miles of five hospitals and an hour north of Pittsburgh. Volant also hosts multiple festivals and events throughout the year, which I knew could also bring short-term interest.

I agreed to purchase the property for $119,000 using seller financing. (Read more on seller financing in Chapter Four.) However, the seller wanted a larger down payment ($20,000) since we did seller financing.

After purchasing the property, I put about $8,000 worth of rehab and furniture into the bottom unit. I listed it on Furnished Finder for traveling nurses, and I also listed it on Airbnb. So far, it has been occupied solely by traveling nurses who pay $1,100 each month.

The top unit of the duplex is still currently rented by the original tenants, who have signed a lease for another year. When they eventually decide to move out, I plan to convert the top unit into a medium-term rental.

I choose to use MTR strategy because it's less wear and tear than short term. I've also found that traveling nurses and other professionals are very considerate and don't have a lot of issues. However, it's a fairly untapped market in my area, and I wanted to test out the MTR strategy to see if I should convert some of my other rentals as well.

When I think about what I would have done differently, I would have tried to negotiate less down for the seller financing. That way, I could've saved more capital and spent less overall getting the unit ready. I also learned that it takes longer than I thought to prepare for every possible thing they could want. For example, I thought I had the entire property ready to go and then realized I never bought trash bags. I've since created a supplies list, similar to what's used for STRs, which has been extremely helpful.

Next, I plan on purchasing more properties that I could use as MTRs! I loved the process of furnishing the unit and the customer service side of renting medium-term leases.

The numbers:
- Purchase price: $119,000
- Down payment: $20,000
- Renovation and furnishings: $8,000
- Medium-term rental income: $1,100 per month

Find out more about Hannah on Instagram @thatscrappyinvestor.

THE HOUSE MANUAL

It is possible to minimize communication between you and the guest *and* provide concierge-level customer service. It may seem counterintuitive, but you almost never want to hear from your guests until they leave a five-star review after checkout. If the tenant did not message you during their stay, it usually means everything was easy on their end.

They knew how to:
- Pay rent on time.
- Access the unit.
- Use all appliances.
- Make coffee, watch TV, log into the Wi-Fi, and more.

The house manual is a key part of this service. We recommend including a detailed list of every appliance in the house and how to use them. This will limit the number of messages you receive from your guests, which saves you a lot of time and interruptions. The last thing you want to do is constantly field messages from tenants asking how to use the television or the Keurig. The house manual is usually an editable document created in either Google Docs or Canva.

It used to be common to have this printed, but you no longer need to print the house manual (although you can, of course). By having the house manual in a digital format, you can continually update it as new issues and questions arise during a tenant's stay. If you keep your manual in digital format, you can hyperlink restaurant menus as well as use instructions (written and video) for appliances. Take note of what common issues arise during stays and add those to the house manual for future guests. For example, if the thermostat is very old in one unit, and often guests do not know how to use it, you should add detailed instructions to the house manual, making it easy to read and operate. If a guest does have a question about the thermostat, you can send them a link to the house manual. This should solve the confusion 100 percent of the time.

Now, some of you may be thinking, "Why don't you replace the thermostat with a smart thermostat?"

While this is a great addition to any unit where you are paying the utilities, we recommend keeping a current, functioning thermostat until it breaks. Once it bites the dust, definitely upgrade to a thermostat that allows you to monitor and operate from afar. In the meantime, if you had an issue with a tenant's sky-high or out-of-line utility bill, your lease should protect you from this, and you can charge the tenant for the extra costs.

To reiterate, by having a comprehensive house manual that you can update as needed, you can nip many problems in the bud before they escalate into real issues or time wasters. As with many other elements of the MTR strategy, a bit more work up front will save you massive amounts of time and effort further down the road.

Damaged, Lost, or Stolen Property for Airbnb Guests

When your guest books through Airbnb, you can easily submit a dispute and request money with a click of a button. Sarah has done this twice with no trouble at all. On the first occasion, an Airbnb guest brought their dog. The cleaner noticed the dog had eaten chunks of the blinds, so she offered to go to Home Depot to purchase new blinds and replace them. Meanwhile, Sarah fired up the Airbnb app on her phone. After a few clicks, Sarah sent a money request to the guest, explaining that the blinds needed to be replaced. The guest accepted the request and sent the money and a detailed apology without hesitation.

A few months later, Sarah had an incident where a dog peed in the unit. The cleaner immediately notified Sarah and cleaned it up in time for the next guest to check in. The cleaner charged Sarah twice what she normally charges—as she should have!—so Sarah passed that cost on to the guest through a money request. Again, it was a flawless process.

To check for lost items, Sarah has a cleaner look at the listing photos to ensure everything is in its proper place during each clean. This is also a great way to ensure the unit looks the way the guest expects. We also recommend keeping an inventory list for each unit. That way, if something is missing, Sarah will notify the guest via Airbnb in the same way.

Damaged, Lost, or Stolen Property for Non-Airbnb Guests

Airbnb features make requesting money or reporting an issue easy. With tenants who you found on Facebook Marketplace, Furnished Finder, through referrals or companies, or anywhere else other than Airbnb, you will not have the option to click a button and request funds. This is why we recommend having a security deposit and a valid, enforceable lease with all guests you secure outside of Airbnb. You can refresh your memory on leases in Chapter Fifteen.

When damage occurs, be sure to follow local guidelines and procedures when it comes to keeping a portion of the security deposit. Sarah has had a tenant's dog vomit on a rug, and the tenant did not clean it up. She was able to charge the tenant for the cost of a new rug because it was not possible for the cleaner to salvage the rug—nor did she want to force her cleaner to do so. In this case, her pet deposit was $200, which covered the cost of the eight-foot-by-ten-foot rug. Recently, a tenant left with the kitchen hand towels. When the cleaner notified Sarah that they were missing, she simply contacted the tenant. He apologized and admitted he didn't know they were hers. With a simple click-to-order from Target, new hand towels were delivered directly to the unit for the next tenant to use, and the cost of the towels was removed from the previous tenant's security deposit. Things like this will happen. Take it in stride and protect yourself as much as possible for these eventualities.

Mindset Check-In with Sarah

One of the most frequently asked questions owners of furnished and unfurnished units get is: "What do you do when something breaks?"

The answer is simple: You fix it. Or, better said: You pay someone to fix it.

In the cases described here, you can see that the cost is passed on to the tenant whenever possible. It took a few texts with the cleaner, some purchasing or coordinating replacements, and a simple payment request to the tenant either via the Airbnb app or by taking it out of their security deposit. Is this our favorite part of running an MTR? No, of course, not. But does it bother us? No, not really. Things break. In fact, we have both broken something on an Airbnb stay! And we'd like to think we are fantastic guests.

Things happen. Things will break. How you handle it will determine your ability to keep your blood pressure regulated and if this business model is for you.

Larger items will also break. For example, when Sarah stayed at Zeona's furnished rental in Boulder for a month, she had trouble with the dishwasher.

Zeona had her plumber over at the unit within hours. Because she had built a solid on-the-ground team, it was easy to address issues as they arose.

As for the emotional stress of running an MTR, we often remind ourselves how much we cash flow each month. When I was working on Chapter Eleven, the furnishing chapter, a tenant texted me at 9:00 p.m. on a Sunday that she could not figure out how to use the thermostat. Instead of being frustrated or even stopping what I was doing, I calmly read the text, addressed the issue, and communicated that it was something I would be able to handle in the morning. In this case, it was a simple reply: "Sorry that's happening! I recommend checking the batteries. It could be that the batteries are dead. If not, there should be spare batteries in the left-hand kitchen drawer."

A few moments later, my screen lit up with: "Yup! Fixed it. Lol. Thanks."

Now, do we want to be sending messages at 9:00 p.m. on a Sunday? Of course not! But for now, we both self-manage all our units to keep costs down and profits high. That unit's rental income covers 88 percent of my PITI for the fourplex, making the other three units almost 100 percent profit. The ability to send a text message not only solves problems but it also provides top-notch service to our tenants; thus, we are happy to do so. Plus, I never forget I'm essentially being paid to do this—and the hourly rate is phenomenal.

However, it wasn't always like this. At first, I owned just two rental properties: a single-family and a duplex. When something would break, I would nearly be on the verge of tears. A tenant would contact me or submit a maintenance request for something large like the air conditioner. I would immediately go into panic mode, thinking, "Oh no! How much is this going to cost? This is going to wipe out all my cash flow." The reality was that the property brought in $2,300 a month in rental income, and my PITI was $1,478. I didn't pay any utilities for the property, and it had zero vacancies.

Once I sat down and did the math, I realized a $400 air conditioner repair would not bankrupt me; frankly, I wouldn't even feel it. Plus, I wasn't living off the cash flow. I was simply stacking the cash in a savings account to save up for the down payment on my next rental property. There was no reason to panic. The moment I realized this and started to put it into practice, running my rental property business became much smoother sailing—no panic moments or heart-stopping text messages. Now I simply consider it a part of doing business.

If you own a property that is only cash flowing $50 per month and you do not have reserves set aside for a large repair like a furnace replacement, then I would recommend reevaluating your rental strategy. However, I find that most of my consulting clients are worrying about things that are not really an issue.

A tenant may steal a towel, and a thermostat may need to be replaced. When those things occur, stay calm, address the issues, and be sure you have a solid local team to help you. And if you find that you are willing to take the hit on your return to avoid handling these issues at all, that's when you might be a good candidate for hiring property management.

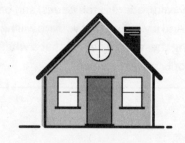

CONCLUSION

Life begins at the end of your comfort zone.
—NEALE DONALD WALSCH

We have covered many topics in this book, from writing a lease to furnishing a unit, but we hope you leave with more than those tactical pieces of information. We want our readers to see that there is more to investing than counting the number of doors you own. It's also not just about the amount of rental income you collect each month; we hope you have started to carve out space in your life for things that you love. Using the MTR strategy has allowed us to do just that.

ZEONA

It's difficult to imagine what life would be like if my mom were still here today, especially as the years tick by and my memories of her drift ever so gently away. I imagine she would be incredibly proud. She was always my cheerleader, and I can vividly picture her jumping up and down like a mother on the sidelines of a T-ball game, cheering her baby on. With her parting gift of a $250,000 life insurance check, I was able to build a real estate portfolio of more than $2 million in just eight years.

More important than the size of that portfolio is what it represents. It is about the legacy of being able to help my younger sister buy land to build a home, gift my nephews a fourplex to pay for their college, and assist my half-brother in selling his house with confidence after a divorce. It is also about getting to live through and therefore share these stories with all of you and seeing what beautiful lives you create for yourselves. That is the ultimate gift.

SARAH

So far this year, I have hosted four intimate events for real estate investors, where we spent time unpacking some of the things holding us back in life. Then we dove deep into one another's investing strategies and left the weekend feeling more empowered, with more clarity around our goals. After that, I traveled to Guatemala for a month. My business partner and a group of real estate investors joined me too. Next, I spent a week in Mérida, Mexico, with a group of people pursuing financial independence and a life full of travel. Since then, I returned to Guatemala with investors for a month-long adventure. I traveled to present at a few real estate brokerages and real estate conferences. This is not to boast about my travel schedule but rather to show you how investing in medium-term rentals has allowed me more freedom than I could have ever imagined possible.

I am a girl from Kansas who put her head down and didn't listen to people who said investing in real estate was risky or a luxury reserved only for the rich. Instead, I listened to myself when I said I wanted to travel the world and earn returns from real estate investments to fund my ideal life.

We hope you are armed and ready to use the MTR strategy after reading this book. We believe this strategy is for any investor looking to maximize cash flow. For us, it is also the strategy that aligns with our goals of traveling when we want, where we want, and with whom we wish to. We hope this allows you to do the same.

Whatever your ideal life looks like for you, we hope you choose to pursue it wholeheartedly. Maybe you only need to own one MTR to meet your real estate investing goals. However, some of you will want to own ten or more units, and we hope you reach all your investing goals.

When you do, please share with us! You can message us on Instagram at @sarahdweaver and @zeonamcintyre. If you post on social media, use the tag #MasterTheMTR and we will be sure to give it a like!

ACKNOWLEDGMENTS

We are still pinching ourselves that *30-Day Stay* is a reality, and we want to acknowledge the many souls who helped us along the way. This book was largely made possible from the urging of friends who both led the way as authors themselves and those who knew we had a book inside of us to share. Thank you for believing in us and for your persistence (ahem, Sam Gastro).

There is so much more than putting ideas down on paper that goes into making a book. We could not have done this without the incredible team at BiggerPockets—Savannah Wood, Kaylee Walterbach, and Katie Miller. Thank you first for not dismissing Zeona's wild idea, and thank you for your ongoing encouragement and heaps of editorial guidance. We also would like to thank the marketing and design teams for making the book a piece of art and helping us share it with the world.

Finally, a huge thank-you to you, the reader! We felt so inspired throughout this process, knowing that you would be taking in all our lessons and hard knocks and then marching out into the world to create beautiful spaces to share with guests. We hope this strategy will help you build a cash-flowing portfolio faster so that you can live the life of your dreams.

ZEONA

I would like to extend deep gratitude to my partner, Benjamin Caillat, who gave endless amounts of pep talks and kept me fed and nourished when I was running up against big deadlines. You're the best.

This book is the culmination of over ten years of experience in creatively renting units and testing things out along the way. Many of these lessons came through brainstorming sessions with friends and family, some of which I like to think of as my investing board of directors—Adam Palmer, Cecilia Taddiken, and Joshua Barad.

SARAH

I want to acknowledge with gratitude the support and love of my parents, Leslie and Craig Weaver, who trust my decision-making even when it means galivanting around the world and buying houses in places I've never visited.

I am incredibly grateful to Jim and Betty Johnston, Ruth and Dennis Hemphill, and Judy Weaver. Thank you, Betty, for my love of reading and learning. This book is written for so many brilliant women who support me—always.

To the women of Super7, you inspire me to be a better version of myself every single day. Thank you for pushing me in more ways than one. May our competitive spirits keep us growing, and our compassionate hearts keep us humble. And to my friends Bridget Bowles, Diana Ossa, Haley McLaughlin, Sylvia Santelli, Sarah King, and Maria Koch, I am forever grateful for the encouragement, tough love, and grace you have given me over many months, and for sending words of encouragement. Those efforts helped make this book possible. And thank you to the countless travelers and investors who have endured me speaking about my love of both travel and investing. May my stories live on beyond the pages of this book. Life is a grand adventure.

More from
BiggerPockets Publishing

Short-Term Rental, Long-Term Wealth:
Your Guide to Analyzing, Buying, and
Managing Vacation Properties
From analyzing potential properties to effectively
managing your listings, this book is your one-stop
resource for making a profit with short-term rentals! Airbnb, Vrbo, and other listing services have
become massively popular in recent years—why not
tap into the gold mine? Avery Carl will show you
how to choose, acquire, and manage a short-term
rental from anywhere in the country, plus how to
avoid common pitfalls and overcome obstacles that
keep many would-be investors from ever getting
started.

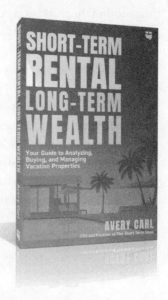

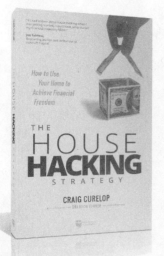

The House Hacking Strategy
Don't pay for your home. Hack it and live for free!
When mastered, house hacking can save you thousands of dollars in monthly expenses, build tens of
thousands of dollars in equity each year, and provide the financial means to retire early. Discover
why so many successful investors support their
investment careers with house hacking—and learn
from a frugality expert who has "hacked" his way
toward financial freedom.

If you enjoyed this book, we hope you'll take a moment to check out some of the other great material BiggerPockets offers. Whether you crave freedom or stability, a backup plan, or passive income, BiggerPockets empowers you to live life on your own terms through real estate investing. Find the information, inspiration, and tools you need to dive right into the world of real estate investing with confidence.

Sign up today—it's free! Visit www.BiggerPockets.com
Find our books at www.BiggerPockets.com/store

Buy, Rehab, Rent, Refinance, Repeat

Invest in real estate and never run out of money! In *Buy, Rehab, Rent, Refinance, Repeat*, you'll discover the incredible strategy known as BRRRR—a long-hidden secret of the ultra-rich and those with decades of experience. Author and investor David Greene holds nothing back, sharing the exact systems and processes he used to scale his business from buying two houses per year to buying two houses per month using the BRRRR strategy.

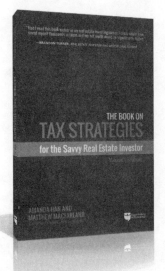

The Book on Tax Strategies for the Savvy Real Estate Investor

Taxes! Boring and irritating, right? Perhaps. But if you want to succeed in real estate, your tax strategy will play a huge role in how fast you grow. A great tax strategy can save you thousands of dollars a year. A bad strategy could land you in legal trouble. With *The Book on Tax Strategies for the Savvy Real Estate Investor*, you'll find ways to deduct more, invest smarter, and pay far less to the IRS!

CONNECT WITH BIGGERPOCKETS

Live Life on Your Terms Through Real Estate Investing!

Facebook
/BiggerPockets

Instagram
@BiggerPockets

Twitter
@BiggerPockets

LinkedIn
/company/Bigger
Pockets

Website
BiggerPockets.com